Soap Opera Mania

Love, Lust and Lies from Your Favorite Daytime Dramas

Tom Biracree

PRENTICE HALL GENERAL REFERENCE
NEW YORK • LONDON • TORONTO • SYDNEY • TOKYO • SINGAPORE

DEDICATION

As always, for Nancy and Ryan

ACKNOWLEDGMENTS

This book is the brilliant conception of Traci Cothran, who is also a kind and talented editor. Heartfelt thanks also go to Gerry Helferich, Tony Seidl and Jane Checkett. I am also grateful for the world's best production and design team at Pink Coyote, including Pat Reshen, Joel Ponzan, Bob Quintana and Eduardo Andino.

PRENTICE HALL GENERAL REFERENCE
15 Columbus Circle
New York, New York 10023

Library of Congress Cataloging-in-Publication Data
Biracree, Tom, 1947-
    Soap Opera Mania: Love, Lust and Lies from your favorite
    daytime dramas / Tom Biracree.

        p.   cm.
    Includes index.
    ISBN 0-671-88120-5
    1. Soap operas—United States—Miscellanea. 2. Soap operas—
    United States—History and criticism. 3. Television actors and
    actresses—United States—Biography.   I. Title.
PN1992.8.S4B57   1994
791.45'8—dc20 93-21064

Designed by Joel Ponzan
Art Direction Eduardo Andino,
Pink Coyote Designs, Inc.

Manufactured in the United States of America

10 9 8 7 6 5 4 3 2 1

First Edition

Contents

III. THE CHARACTERS AND PLOTS

IV. BIOS OF YOUR FAVORITE SOAP STARS   156

Appendix

Introduction

A dultery. Amnesia. Long-lost husbands. Rebellious daughters. Bedroom frolics. Boardroom fights. Cozy dinners. Exotic locales. Erica's husbands. Sheila's victims.

From this short list almost anyone who's ever turned on a television set could deduce that the subject of this book is the world of soap operas. For of all types of programming that fill the forty or more channels received in the average household, only daytime dramas deliberately encompass every conceivable form of human emotion and human relationship. In other words, soap operas are about life, the fascination of which draws tens of millions of viewers everyday.

That doesn't mean, of course, that the shows exactly mirror real life. Every soap viewer has to put up with non-viewers who scoff that daytime dramas are not based on "real life." My response—neither are James Bond films, *Star Trek*, "Sesame Street," or the novels of Stephen King. But like these classics, soaps are an enduring source of great entertainment that has lasted for more than six decades.

If the fans of soap operas are more passionate than most other fans, it's undoubtedly due to the very special type of story telling that's only possible on daytime television. That type of storytelling is called a serial, and it dates back to ancient times. From Homer's magnificent *Iliad* to the rich novels of Charles Dickens, history's greatest minds have captivated generations by spinning episodic stories that involve the detailed goings-on of dozens of major characters. Today, soap operas carry on this tradition by drawing viewers, every weekday, into the lives of men, women, and children that become as familiar as neighbors or coworkers. Daily storytelling involves a lot of airtime—for an hour show, 260 hours per year, 2,600 hours in a decade. In the history of television, total soap programming has exceeded more than 100,000 hours.

No book, even a multi-volume encyclopedia, could present a *comprehensive* look at this massive volume of work—indeed, soap opera staffs are so preoccupied with the monumental task of producing a show every weekday of the year that there is often no time for detailed record keeping. But *Soap Opera Mania* does delve into this treasure trove to dig up some favorite stars, favorite moments, and favorite memories for your enjoyment. Along with this historical perspective comes heaping doses of information about today's shows and performers, including biographies of more than 75 of daytime's brightest stars. The package adds of up to many hours of fascinating and fun browsing guaranteed to enhance your enjoyment of the wonderful world of soap operas.

I

The History of Soap Operas

A Brief History

The first radio stations began broadcasting near the end of World War I, but it was almost a decade before companies were formed to provide programming to a large number of radio stations. These companies, called networks, created a number of nighttime serial comedies that became extremely popular ("Amos and Andy," "The Goldbergs," "Myrt and Marge"). However, most radio executives didn't feel that daytime audiences were large enough to justify the expense of producing network daytime shows.

That left local stations to produce their own programming, and anyone who was willing to work for almost nothing had an excellent opportunity to get on the air. One person who took this advantage was a young Dayton, Ohio, schoolteacher named Irna Phillips, who traveled to Chicago and persuaded WGN to give her fifteen minutes a day for a family drama she called "Painted Dreams." That's how Phillips, who would later become the most prominent television soap creator, conceived the very first soap opera.

The very next year, the NBC Blue network originated four daytime serials, one of which ("Betty and Bob," starring Don Ameche) was the first true network soap. The real explosion of popularity, however, came in 1933 when a husband-and-wife advertising team, Frank and Anne Hummert, created "Just Plain Bill," "The Romance of Helen Trent," and "Ma Perkins." These shows proved to have an immense appeal to the housewives who were struggling to survive the hardships of day-to-day life during the Depression. By the late 1930s, more than thirty radio serials reached a daily audience of forty million—twice the audience reached by television soaps today!

This vast audience was a bonanza for program sponsors. "Ma Perkins" sent the sales of Oxydol, a laundry detergent, through the roof. Soap companies plunged into the business of producing serials that featured their products, and they so dominated daytime that the serials became known as "soap operas."

Although all soaps fancied themselves "true to life," they

really presented a fantasy world typified by the epigraph of the "Romance of Helen Trent."

> And now "The Romance of Helen Trent": the real-life drama of Helen Trent, who, when life mocks her, breaks her hopes, dashes her against the rocks of despair, fights back bravely, successfully, to prove what so many women long to prove—that because a woman is thirty-five or more, romance in life need not be over, that romance can begin at thirty-five.

This uplifting message had enormous appeal during some of the darkest days of American history.

When times improved later in the 1930s, Irna Phillips created "Guiding Light," "The Road of Life," and "Woman in White," soaps that focused on the lives of professionals such as ministers, doctors and nurses. The genre remained immensely popular throughout World War II and the happy, prosperous years that followed.

In the late 1940s, the fledgling entertainment medium called television was experimenting with various forms of programming. The first local attempt to bring soap operas to television was "A Woman to Remember," which was telecast from New York's Dumont Studios for a brief time in 1947. In 1950, CBS created "The First Hundred Years," a daytime comedic serial which was canceled a little over a year later. But in 1951, radio soap veteran Roy Winsor created two daytime serials, "Search for Tomorrow" and "Love of Life." These shows concentrated almost exclusively on the problems encountered in marriage, child rearing and family life, and captured the attention of 1950s housewives just as the fantasy-based radio serials had engaged Depression-era women.

Over the next five years, the networks aired 25 additional soap operas—some original, some based on popular radio series. Only a handful lasted more than a few months. Among them were Winsor's "The Secret Storm" and Irna Phillips's "Guiding Light." In 1956, Phillips astonished most industry observers when she created a successful half-hour soap, "As the World Turns," which was soon joined at the top of the ratings by her crime-oriented half hour "The Edge of Night."

In the early 1960s, doctor shows such as "Dr. Kildare" dominated nighttime programming. Daytime programmers responded in 1963 with "General Hospital" and "The Doctors," both of which proved popular. Of the many more traditional soap efforts, only "Another World" (1964) and "Days of Our Lives" (1965) still survive.

The next soap revolutionary was Agnes Nixon, a protege of Irna Phillips. Nixon translated the turmoil of the 1960s into two soap operas that were based on real social concerns of the time, covering the Vietnam war to abortion. These shows, "One Life to Live" (1968) and "All My Children" (1970), attracted a new, younger audience to daytime television.

Soap operas had traditionally been low-budget productions, and it showed in their quality. Then in 1973, William Bell brought prime time superior production values to daytime with the premiere of his immediate hit, "The Young and the Restless." In turn, the producers of the other daytime soaps were faced with the challenge of making their shows more relevant by increasing quality and targeting younger audiences. Over the next decade, a number of old favorites failed to make the transition, including "Search for Tomorrow," "Love of Life" and "The Secret Storm."

With harder economic times upon us once again, soaps—as a form of escapism—have increasingly been populated with wealthy, glamorous characters who live the lives many people can only fantasize about. At the core of all shows, however, are strong family values. Many soap opera characters, like their viewers, seek the stability of a traditional marriage and family life. Of course, to make the plots interesting, these dreams are often shattered by the complex problems of real life—from corporate greed to drug abuse to AIDS. But modern dramas seldom become melodramatic; modern soap writers inject enough humor to make the experience of watching a soap opera more fun than wrenching.

Despite competition from dozens of cable networks, the genre remains strong with millions of faithful viewers. The ten existing network soaps have an average daily audience of twenty million and a yearly audience of fifty million Americans.

Soap Firsts

First radio soap-First true radio soap opera was NBC's "Betty and Bob," which first aired in 1932 and starred Betty Churchill and Don Ameche.

First hit radio soap-"Just Plain Bill," which aired night-times in 1932 and moved to daytime in 1933, centered on the problem-solving barber in a small town. It ran until 1955.

First television soap-"A Woman to Remember" was produced by New York's Dumont Studios from February to July, 1947.

First network soap-"The First Hundred Years" debuted on CBS in 1950, but its run fell 98.5 years short of its title's premise.

First hit soap-"Search for Tomorrow" debuted on CBS on September 3, 1951 and ran for 31 years.

First half-hour soaps-"As the World Turns" and "The Edge of Night" both premiered on April 2, 1956.

First soap to expand to one hour-"Another World," on January 6, 1975.

First soap to switch networks-"Edge of Night" moved from CBS to ABC on December 1, 1975.

First soap to expand to ninety minutes-"Another World," from March 5, 1979 to August 1, 1980.

First soap opera taped on location-"All My Children" was taped in St. Croix in 1978.

First spin-off from a soap-"Somerset," a spin-off of "Another World," premiered on March 30, 1970.

First prime time spin-off from a daytime soap-"Our Private World," a spin-off of "As the World Turns," was a short-lived prime time serial in 1965.

First daytime soap to premiere in prime time-"Capitol" debuted as a one-hour prime time special on March 26, 1982, three days before its daytime start.

First daytime serial to win an Emmy-"The Doctors" won in 1972.

First case of amnesia on a soap-Creator Irna Phillips first used this time-honored plot device when Joe Marlin developed amnesia on the radio soap, "The Story of Mary Marlin."

First sudden death on a soap-Keith Barron died in an automobile accident six weeks after the premiere of "Search for Tomorrow" on September 3, 1951.

First murder on a soap-Gangster Miles Pardee was gunned down on "Love of Life."

First major soap character to be jailed-Meg Dale was falsely accused of murdering Miles Pardee and jailed on "Love of Life."

First soap character to come back from the dead-Bruce Edwards, the long-dead husband of Jane Edwards, appeared in time to prevent Jane from marrying widower Peter Ames on "The Secret Storm."

First pregnancy deception on a soap-On "Guiding Light," Kathy Roberts, pregnant by her secret marriage to Bob Lang (who died in an auto accident), told her second husband, Dr. Dick Grant, that the baby was his.

First alcoholic on a soap-Bill Bauer, Bert's husband, hit the bottle and caused untold hardships on "Guiding Light."

First marriage interrupted at the altar-Joanne Barron was about to marry Arthur Tate on "Search for Tomorrow" when a woman showed up claiming to be Hazel, the wife Arthur thought was dead. She turned out to be Sue, twin sister of the deceased Hazel.

First marital infidelity on a soap-Unhappily married Jim Lowell had an affair with Edith on "As the World Turns" in 1956.

The first major female black character on a soap was Nurse Martha Frazier, who was portrayed by Cicely Tyson on "Guiding Light."

First suicide on a soap-Julie Conrad killed herself in a mental institution on "Guiding Light."

First controversial character death on a soap-"Guiding Light" received thousands of angry letters and phone calls after Kathy Roberts was killed in an auto accident in 1958.

First legal abortion on a soap-Erica Kane aborted Jeff Martin's baby on "All My Children."

First male prostitute-Sandy Cory, the illegitimate son of Mac, admitted that he had once been a "call boy" in Las Vegas, on "Another World."

First major black characters on a daytime serial-Nurse Martha Frazier and her husband Dr. Jim Frazier on "Guiding Light."

The first major male black character on a soap was Dr. Jim Frazier, who was portrayed by Billy Dee Williams on "Guiding Light."

First real-life medical procedure on a soap-"All My Children" aired the real-life face lift of actress Eileen Letchworth as part of a storyline featuring the face lift of her character, Margo, in 1974.

First major openly gay character on a soap-Hank Eliot on "As the World Turns."

First major lesbian character on a soap-Child psychologist Lynn Carson on "All My Children."

First mastectomy on a soap-Jennifer Brooks underwent a mastectomy and then sought counseling to regain her self-esteem on "The Young and the Restless."

First marital rape on a soap-"As the World Turns" saw Dr. John Dixon brutally rape his wife Dee.

First interracial romance on a soap-David Banning and Valerie Grant fell in love on "Days of Our Lives," 1976.

First Vietnam P.O.W. on a soap-Phil Brent disappeared in Southeast Asia in 1970, only to return later with a brand new face.

First mid-life pregnancy-Clarice Ewing on "Another World" became pregnant in 1982 and became the first character to undergo amniocentesis.

First incest storyline on a soap-On "As the World Turns," Angel Snyder arrived in Oakdale with a terrible secret— she'd been sexually molested as a young child by her father, Henry Lange.

First character with bulimia on a soap-Tracy Abbott went to extreme lengths to lose weight on "The Young and the Restless" in order to win the attention of singer Danny Romalotti.

Do You Remember?

*T*he ten daytime serials currently airing on the major networks are the handful of survivors in a brutal competition for the affections of TV viewers. In the TV graveyard are three times as many shows that fell by the wayside. Some of those shows had long, glorious runs and still live in the hearts of many fans—like "Search for Tomorrow," "The Edge of Night," "Love of Life" and "The Secret Storm." However, the majority of them disappeared in a few months. See how many of these efforts you remember.

ALL THAT GLITTERS-The success of his "Mary Hartman, Mary Hartman" led Norman Lear to create this tongue-in-cheek soap centered on the Globatron Corporation, in which all the executives were women and all the secretaries were men. So few people appreciated the role reversal humor that the show lasted just three months, April to July, 1977.

Jack Lemmon was a star of the short-lived soap "A Brighter Day."

ANOTHER LIFE-This 1981-1984 soap opera, produced by the Christian Broadcasting Network, was based on the philosophy that all problems of life could be solved "through the application of Judeo-Christian principles." Set in the fictional town of Kingsley, "Another Life's" production team included Roy Winsor, creator of "Search for Tomorrow" and "The Secret Storm."

BEN JERROD-One of TV's shortest-lived soaps (April 1 to June 28, 1963), this NBC daytime serial focused on the lives of two small town attorneys. "General Hospital," which premiered the same day, just celebrated its 30th anniversary on the air.

THE BEST OF EVERYTHING-"Best" was only evident in the title of this ABC daytime serial (based on the 1959 movie of the same name), which centered on three women making their careers in publishing. Its brief run: March 30 to September 25, 1970.

BRIGHT PROMISE-NBC tried to attract younger viewers with this daytime serial, set at small midwestern Bancroft College. Running from September, 1969 to March, 1972, the cast included Dana Andrews as the college president and Dabney Coleman as a professor.

A BRIGHTER DAY-"A Brighter Day" premiered on radio in 1948 and on television January 4, 1954. The central character in the show was the Reverend Richard Dennis, a widower with five children. It was canceled in late 1962, three months after its time slot was changed from late afternoon to late morning.

CAPITOL-This daytime half-hour soap opera was set in Washington, D.C., and centered on the feud between two powerful families, the McCandlesses and the Cleggs. The show premiered on March 29, 1982, and was canceled almost exactly five years later.

THE CLEAR HORIZON-The first daytime serial to originate in Hollywood, this show attempted to capitalize on the public's interest in the space program by focusing on the lives of astronauts and their families. It had two brief runs: July, 1960 to March, 1961 and February to June, 1962.

CONCERNING MISS MARLOWE-This daytime serial ran for exactly one year (July, 1954 to July, 1955) and concentrated on the forgettable adventures of a forty-year-old New York actress. Its only notable contribution to TV history was that it marked the first television roles for Efrem Zimbalist, Jr., and Jane Seymour.

CONFIDENTIAL FOR WOMEN-Jane Wyatt (of "Father Knows Best" fame) narrated this daytime series that presented a new five-part story each week. It aired from March to July, 1966.

DARK SHADOWS-With its cast of vampires, ghosts, werewolves and other peculiar beings, "Dark Shadows" easily wins the nod as most distinctive of all soap operas. The central character of this show, which ran from June, 1966 to April, 1971, was 200-year-old vampire Barnabas Collins (Jonathan Frid). NBC revived the show as a prime time series in 1991.

A DATE WITH LIFE-This was the first soap set in a fictional town, "Bay City." "A Date With Life" lasted just nine

Larry Hagmann played Ed Gibson on the mystery-based "The Edge of Night" before becoming involved in the intrigues on the hit night-time soap "Dallas."

months (October, 1955 to June, 1956). The central character was a newspaper editor.

THE DOCTORS-This popular medical drama ran for nearly twenty years, from April, 1963 to December, 1982. The show began as a daily anthology of half-hour stories revolving around one of four characters (three doctors and a chaplain) who worked at Hope Memorial Hospital. Within a year, the show evolved into a conventional soap, and became the first daytime serial to win an Emmy.

THE EDGE OF NIGHT-"The Edge of Night" premiered on April 2, 1956, sharing the honor of being the first half-hour daytime soap with "As the World Turns." This show, whose storylines emphasized mystery, crime, and courtroom drama, got its name from its early evening time slot. It aired on CBS for nearly 20 years, then became the first soap to switch networks when it was picked up by ABC in 1975. By the time the series ended on December 28, 1984, 7,420 episodes had aired over a time span of more than twenty-eight years.

THE EGG AND I-It isn't difficult to figure out that this early daytime serial had a comic intent once you hear that the story involved a young woman from New York City who married an upstate chicken farmer named MacDonald. This series, based on a 1947 Claudette Colbert movie of the same name, ran from September, 1951 to August, 1952.

FAIRMEADOWS, U.S.A.-This show began in November, 1951 as a Sunday afternoon serial focused on a general store in a small town. It was moved to weekdays as a fifteen-minute segment of "The Kate Smith Hour" until it was canceled in April, 1952.

FLAME IN THE WIND-This ABC half-hour daytime drama premiered in December, 1964. In June, 1965, it was renamed "A Time for Us." A youth-oriented soap, it was canceled in December, 1966.

FOLLOW YOUR HEART-The continuing saga of a Philadelphia society girl who didn't want to marry the man

Dixie Carter was a daytime star as Olivia "Brandy" Henderson on "The Edge of Night."

her family had selected for her, this NBC soap lasted just five months—August, 1953 to January, 1954.

FOR BETTER OR WORSE-A combination of soap and anthology, "For Better or Worse" featured stories about marriage problems told from the point of view of a professional marriage counselor. It lasted one year, from June, 1959 to June, 1960.

FOR RICHER, FOR POORER-Originally titled "Lovers and Friends," this show went back into the shop to be retooled and emerged largely intact under its new title. Set in suburban Chicago, "For Richer, For Poorer" had a longer run the second time around—December, 1977 to September, 1978.

FULL CIRCLE-This short-lived (June, 1960 to March, 1961) daytime serial is memorable only because it starred a very young Dyan Cannon as Lisa Crowder, a young widow who fell in love with a romantic drifter.

GENERATIONS-"Generations," which aired on NBC from March, 1959 to January, 1961, was the first daytime serial in which one of the two central families was black. Set in Chicago, the show never attracted enough viewers to hold its time slot.

GOLDEN WINDOWS-A young woman who left Maine to pursue a show business career in New York was the central character in this fifteen-minute NBC daytime serial which aired from July, 1954 to April, 1955.

HAWKINS FALLS-After a very brief run as a prime time show, "Hawkins Falls" debuted on daytime TV in April, 1951. This soap focused on life in a fictional small town in Illinois, with exterior footage filmed in Woodstock, Illinois. It was canceled on July 1, 1955.

HIDDEN FACES-NBC tried to equal the success of "As the World Turns" by introducing this soap in December, 1968, but due to poor scheduling, it was cancelled in June, 1969.

HOTEL COSMOPOLITAN-This serial was set at a New York hotel called—you guessed it—The Cosmopolitan. CBS broadcast this show from August, 1957 to April, 1958.

Christopher Reeve portrayed Benno Harper on the longtime favorite soap "Love of Life."

THE HOUSE ON HIGH STREET-This serial focused on dramatizations of problems faced by real-life families. Social worker John Collier, played by Philip Abbot, provided the continuity that kept viewers coming back. It aired from September, 1959 to February, 1960.

KITTY FOYLE-"Kitty Foyle" was a radio serial for sixteen years before coming to life on the small screen in January, 1958. Its brief run—it was canceled in June, 1958—was notable primarily for its casting of eleven-year-old Patty Duke.

LOVE IS A MANY SPLENDORED THING-This show debuted in September, 1967 as a continuation of the 1957 movie of the same name that starred William Holden and Jennifer Jones. CBS squashed the Asian-Caucasian interracial romance, so the show veered toward more mainstream romance and intrigue. The show lasted until March, 1973.

LOVE OF LIFE-"Love of Life" aired its first show on September 24, 1951, just three weeks after "Search for

Tomorrow" debuted. For the next twenty-eight years, viewers were treated to a serial that often centered around the conflict between two sisters: noble, good-hearted Vanessa Dale and her villainous sister, Meg Dale. The rather stern moralistic tone of the show was deemed "old-fashioned" in the late 1960s, but attempts to remodel the show along the lines of the more hip "The Young and the Restless" alienated many longtime viewers. The show's return to more traditional storylines in the mid-1970s prolonged its life until February 1, 1980.

LOVERS AND FRIENDS-"Lovers and Friends" (a title which could just about sum up any soap) had a brief run on NBC from January to May, 1977. The most unusual aspect of this serial, which focused on two families (one wealthy, one not so wealthy) in a Chicago suburb, was that it popped up seven months after its cancelation under the title, "For Richer, For Poorer."

MARY HARTMAN, MARY HARTMAN-This syndicated parody of soap operas, created by Norman Lear of "All In the Family" fame, generated enormous publicity when it appeared in 1976. The show starred Louise Lasser as Mary, a heroine who, in more than 300 episodes, suffered an avalanche of tragedy and embarrassment. The show spawned a spin-off, "Fernwood 2-Night," which enjoyed a short run under the name "Fernwood Forever" before ending in late 1977.

MISS SUSAN-Created in 1951, "Miss Susan" was a unique soap opera in that its star, Susan Peters, was a paraplegic. She played a wheelchair-bound attorney who practiced in a small town in Ohio.

MOMENT OF TRUTH-Produced in Toronto, "Moment of Truth" ran from January to November, 1965. It was then replaced by another show that had more staying power— "Days of Our Lives."

MORNING STAR-This NBC daytime serial focused on a young woman who moved from England to New York City after the death of her fiancé. It ran from September, 1965 to July, 1966.

NEVER TOO YOUNG-An ABC effort that featured teenagers frolicking on Malibu Beach aired from September, 1965 to June, 1966. The cast featured Tony Dow of "Leave It to Beaver" fame.

THE NURSES-This half-hour ABC daytime soap was based on the CBS prime time serial "The Nurses" (later "The Doctors and the Nurses") that had a four-year run in the early 1960s. The soap aired from September, 1965 to March, 1967.

ONE MAN'S FAMILY-This long-running radio serial (1932-1959) came to TV twice: first as a prime time show (November, 1949 to June, 1952) and then as a daytime serial (March, 1954 to April, 1955). Ironically, in the TV versions, the plots started where the radio show had begun in 1932, so TV viewers were twenty years behind the radio listeners!

OUR FIVE DAUGHTERS-Guess what? This daytime serial focused on the lives of the five daughters of the Lee family. Few people cared, and the soap ran only from January to September, 1962.

PARADISE BAY-"Paradise Bay" was the title of the show and the name of the California town in which this half-hour NBC soap took place. The manager of a radio station and his family were the central characters. Its brief run: September, 1965 to July, 1966.

PORTIA FACES LIFE-"Portia" was born as a radio serial in 1940 and came to TV fourteen years later with Frances Reid (who later portrayed Alice Horton on "Days of Our Lives") as attorney Portia Blake Manning. The show lasted a little more than a year—April, 1954 to July, 1955.

RETURN TO PEYTON PLACE-"Peyton Place" was an enormously successful prime time serial that aired from 1964 to 1969 on ABC. NBC tried to achieve similar daytime success with a half-hour daytime soap that picked up where the prime time show left off—but without the all-star cast that had distinguished the nighttime version. The soap had a short life, April, 1972 to January, 1974.

RITUALS-This half-hour syndicated soap, set in a college town outside Washington, D.C., was produced in 1984-1985.

The cast included George Lazemby (a one-time James Bond), Patti Davis (daughter of President Reagan) and Kin Shriner (who later won an Emmy for his role as Scott Baldwin on "General Hospital").

ROAD OF LIFE-"Road of Life," an enormously popular radio serial from 1937 to 1959, never quite captured the attention of TV viewers during its December, 1954 to July, 1955 run. The main character was a surgeon named Dr. Jim Brent.

ROAD TO REALITY-This show, which followed the lives of a therapy group conducted by a psychoanalyst, is notable as the first daytime serial aired by ABC. It lasted from October, 1960 to March, 1961.

RYAN'S HOPE-During its fourteen-year run (July, 1975 to January, 1989), this high-quality, half-hour soap won two Emmys for Outstanding Daytime Drama Series. The focus of the show was Ryan's Hope, a Manhattan tavern located near Riverside Hospital, and the central characters were tavern owner Johnny Ryan, his wife Maeve and their five children. When the show was moved to a late morning time slot, it had a crippling effect, and many network affiliates chose to air local news or other programs in that slot instead.

SANTA BARBARA-This one-hour NBC soap, which premiered on July 30, 1984, garnered much acclaim during its nine-year run. The show centered on two wealthy Santa Barbara families, the Capwells and the Lockridges, as well as the lower class Castillos, Di Napolis and Donnellys. Despite two Emmy awards for Outstanding Daytime Drama Series, it was canceled in 1993.

THE SEEKING HEART-This fifteen-minute medical soap aired briefly on CBS (July to December, 1954).

SOMERSET-"Somerset" was the first daytime serial spin-off of another daytime serial and was titled "Another World—Somerset" when it first aired on March 30, 1970. Its major characters and storylines, however, were developed independently of its parent soap. The first head writer had worked on "The Edge of Night," which explained its early emphasis on crime and intrigue. The show was canceled on New Year's Eve, 1976.

Long before "Cheers," Ted Danson appeared on "Somerset" as Tim Conway.

STRANGE PARADISE-"Dark Shadows" spawned a syndicated, Canadian-produced replica that took place on a haunted, voodoo-dominated Caribbean island. The half-hour show was produced for only one season in 1969.

TEXAS-NBC hoped to capitalize on the popularity of the prime time serial "Dallas" when it premiered the daytime serial "Texas" on August 4, 1980. Unfortunately, this glamorized portrayal of Houston oil barons was aired at the same time as "General Hospital," which was peaking in popularity. The show never attracted a large audience and was canceled in December, 1982.

THESE ARE MY CHILDREN-One of the first daytime serials, this fifteen-minute show centered around a Chicago boardinghouse and ran just four weeks, January 21 to March 4, 1949.

THREE STEPS TO HEAVEN-You know it must have been the early 1950s when moving from a small town to New York City was considered a step closer to heaven! This daytime serial centered on model Poco Thurmond. It ran from August, 1953 to December, 1954.

A TIME FOR US-See "Flame in the Wind."

A TIME TO LIVE-This Chicago-based fifteen-minute daytime serial focused on the world of journalism. It aired from July to December, 1954, on NBC.

TODAY IS OURS-This half-hour daytime serial about a divorced female high school principal ran from June to December, 1958.

VALIANT LADY-After 14 years on the radio, this daytime serial moved to CBS TV in October, 1953 and ran until August, 1957. The main characters on the show—broadcast live from New York—were Helen and Frank Emerson.

WHERE THE HEART IS-Set in a New York suburb called Northcross, "Where the Heart Is" focused on the romantic liaisons of the Hathaway and Prescott families. The show spent three-and-one-half years on CBS before giving way to the future soap blockbuster "The Young and the Restless."

A WOMAN TO REMEMBER-This very early serial, which featured the cast of a fictional radio serial, aired on daytime in February, 1949, then moved to nighttime before ending in July, 1949.

WOMAN WITH A PAST-This daytime serial about a dress designer began the same day as "The Secret Storm," but lasted only five months (February to July, 1954).

A WORLD APART-Written by the sister of famed soap opera writer and creator Agnes Nixon, this show centered on a television writer and her two adopted children. It aired from March, 1970 to June, 1971 on ABC.

YOUNG DOCTOR MALONE-This serial that featured the chief of staff at Valley Hospital in the fictional town of Three Oaks had a 21-year run on radio (1939-1960), but a much more modest four-and-one-half year stint on NBC TV.

THE YOUNG MARRIEDS-This soap attempted to attract an after-school audience by focusing on young marrieds in suburbia. It aired from October, 1964 to March, 1966.

When Did The Current Daytime Serials Debut?

*J*ust two of the first generation of TV soaps have survived—"Guiding Light" and "As the World Turns." Both managed to survive the "modernization" of soaps that began with the 1973 debut of "The Young and the Restless." But survival isn't easy even for a modern soap; despite some great writers and great actors, award-winning shows such as "Ryan's Hope" and "Santa Barbara" didn't make it.

Following are the debut years of today's soaps.

1952	"Guiding Light"
1956	"As the World Turns"
1963	"General Hospital"
1964	"Another World"
1965	"Days of Our Lives"
1968	"One Life to Live"
1970	"All My Children"
1973	"The Young and the Restless"
1983	"Loving"
1987	"The Bold and the Beautiful"

Who Created Today's Soaps?

oday's ten daytime serials are the survivors of a brutal competition for viewers that has seen more than sixty competitors bite the dust. It seems only a handful of talented people mastered the winning formula that makes a soap long-lived. The following are the creators of current soaps.

ALL MY CHILDREN (ABC)
Agnes Nixon served her apprenticeship under Irna Phillips. Nixon was a headwriter of "Guiding Light," a co-creator of "As the World Turns," and creator of "One Life to Live."

ANOTHER WORLD (NBC)
Irna Phillips originally conceived this show as a companion to her "As the World Turns," but it ended up on another network.

AS THE WORLD TURNS (CBS)
Irna Phillips created this soap in 1956.

THE BOLD AND THE BEAUTIFUL (CBS)
William Bell, creator of "The Young and the Restless," originated the youngest current soap.

DAYS OF OUR LIVES (NBC)
Ted Corday, Irna Phillips' director and partner on "As the World Turns," created this show.

GENERAL HOSPITAL (ABC)
Frank and Doris Hursley, former head writers of "Search for Tomorrow," were hired to create this medical soap.

GUIDING LIGHT (CBS)
Irna Phillips created this radio serial in 1937 and orchestrated its move to television in 1952.

LOVING (ABC)
Agnes Nixon created this show with Douglas Marland, for-

mer head writer for "The Doctors," "General Hospital" and "Guiding Light."

ONE LIFE TO LIVE (ABC)
Agnes Nixon created this show in 1967, three years before she created "All My Children."

THE YOUNG AND THE RESTLESS (CBS)
William Bell, who had been head writer on "Days of Our Lives," created this groundbreaking soap opera.

Soap's Hometowns

O ne of the easiest questions we all have to answer is "Where do you live?" But you can watch a soap opera for a long time and not know where its characters actually are. The goal of most soap opera writers is to create an "Anytown, U.S.A.," a place with which almost all viewers can identify. But, inevitably, they drop some clues that allow us to get a general idea of where the action takes place. Following are the locales—fictitious and real—for today's soaps.

ALL MY CHILDREN
Pine Valley is an affluent Philadelphia suburb that's within easy driving distance of New York.

ANOTHER WORLD
Bay City was originally conceived as a midwestern city near Oakdale, the locale of "As the World Turns." Because NBC aired the soap instead of CBS, the two soaps never mentioned each other, but Bay City remains somewhere in America's heartland.

AS THE WORLD TURNS
Oakdale is a typical mid-size, middle class, midwestern city.

THE BOLD AND THE BEAUTIFUL
Los Angeles, the only real-life setting for a soap opera.

Demi Moore portrayed Jackie Templeton on "General Hospital."

DAYS OF OUR LIVES
Salem is a heartland city much like Oakdale and Bay City, largely because the show came from the same creators.

GENERAL HOSPITAL
Port Charles is identified as a city in New York.

GUIDING LIGHT
Springfield, the TV location of the soap, is probably somewhere in Illinois. The radio soap was transplanted from a fictional Los Angeles suburb to Springfield, which is why the show now features Cedars Hospital, modeled on L.A.'s Cedars of Lebanon Hospital.

LOVING
Corinth, home of Alden University, is located in Pennsylvania.

ONE LIFE TO LIVE
Llanview is a Philadelphia suburb close to Pine Valley—and characters sometimes move from one town to the other.

THE YOUNG AND THE RESTLESS
Genoa City is yet another midwestern place that may be modeled on a Minnesota town near the boyhood home of creator William Bell.

Who's Who On The Soaps

W hen you walk into a baseball park, vendors shout, "You can't tell the players without a program." Even faithful viewers sometimes get confused about who's who on shows. The following is a "program" for each daytime serial.

ALL MY CHILDREN

Laurel Banning (Felicity LaFortune)-A woman with a mysterious past
Lucas Barnes (Richard Lawson)-Terrence's father
Detective Berniker (Michael Guido)-Pine Valley detective
An Li Bodine (Lindsay Price)-Student; Brian's ex-wife
Brian Bodine (Brian Green)-Trask's brother; married to Dixie
Charlie Brent (Christopher Lawford)-A private investigator
Adam Chandler (David Canary)-Skye and Adam, Jr.'s father; married to Gloria
Adam Chandler, Jr. (Kevin Alexander)-Dixie and Adam's son
Gloria Chandler (Teresa Blake)-Nurse; married to Adam
Stuart Chandler (David Canary)-Adam's twin brother; lost his wife Cindy to AIDS
Dixie Cooney (Cady McClain)-Palmer's niece; Adam Jr.'s mother; married to Brian
Opal Cortlandt (Jill Larson)-Tad's mother; Palmer's wife
Palmer Cortlandt (James Mitchell)-Dixie's uncle; Opal's husband; Peter's father
Livia Cudahy (Tonya Pinkins)-Terrence's mother; Derek's sister; Tom's wife
Tom Cudahy (Richard Shoberg)-Brooke's ex-husband; Livia's husband; owns a health club
Trevor Dillon (James Kiberd)-Pine Valley policeman; husband of Natalie
Brooke English (Julia Barr)-Phoebe's niece; ex-wife of Adam and Tom; mother of Tad's child; married to Tad; editor of *Tempo Magazine*
Myrtle Fargate (Eileen Herlie)-Owns a boutique
Derek Frye (William Christian)-Livia's brother; Terrence's uncle

Terrence Frye (Dondre Whitfield)-Student; Livia's son

Edmund Grey (John Callahan)-Newspaper reporter; half-brother of Dimitri

Dr. Stephen Hamill (Andrew Jackson)-Doctor

Kendall Hart (Sarah Michelle Gellar)-Erica's daughter

Galen Henderson (Karen Person)-Lawyer

Jeremy Hunter (Jean LeClerc)-Natalie's ex-husband; David's father; Ceara's husband

Timmy Hunter (Tommy Michaels)-Son of Natalie and Alex Hunter

Erica Kane (Susan Lucci)-Daughter of Monica; mother of Bianca and Kendall; CEO of Enchantment

Lucy (Kelly Clark)-Dimitri's maid at Wildwind

Dimitri Marick (Michael Nader)-Half-brother of Edmund; owner of Wildwind

Joe Martin (Ray MacDonnell)-Chief of staff of Pine Valley Hospital; Tad's adopted father

Ruth Martin (Mary Fickett)-Joe's wife; Joey's mother; Tad's adopted mother

Tad Martin (Michael E. Knight)-Ruth and Joe's adopted son; Opal's natural son; Jamie's father; Brooke's husband

Bianca Montgomery (Lacey Chabert)-Daughter of Erica and Travis

Jackson Montgomery (Walt Willey)-Travis' brother

Peggy Moody (Anne Meara)-Former maid; current nursing home resident

Mimi Reed (Shari Headley)-Police officer

Taylor Roxbury Canon (Ingrid Rogers)-Step-daughter of Lucas

Maria Santos (Eva LaRue)-Neurologist

Casper Sloane (Ronald Drake)-Palmer's butler; Myra's husband

Olga Svenson (Peg Murray)-Palmer's housekeeper

Mona Tyler (Frances Heflin)-Erica's mother; widow of Dr. Charles Tyler

Hayley Vaughn (Kelly Ripa)-Trevor's niece; Will's ex-wife; Adam's daughter

Langley Wallingford (Louis Edmonds)-Phoebe's husband

Phoebe Wallingford (Ruth Warrick)-Langley's wife

Winifred (Cheryl Multeen)-Adam's maid

ANOTHER WORLD

Kevin Anderson (Jamie Goodwin)-Lawyer; Jake's half-brother

Darryl Becket (Eric LaRay Harvey)-Doctor

Bridget Connell (Barbara Berjer)-Hudson's housekeeper

Amanda Cory (Christine Tucci)-Mac and Rachel's daughter

Matthew Cory (Matt Crane)-Rachel's son

Paulina Cory (Judi Evans)-Mac's illegitimate daughter; half-sister to Matt, Amanda and Jamie

Rachel Cory (Victoria Wyndham)-Mac's widow; Matt, Amanda and Jamie's mother

Lorna Devon (Alicia Coppola)-Daughter of Felicia and Lucas; Jenna's half-sister

Dean Frame (Ricky Paull Goldin)-Musician; Frankie's cousin; father of Jenna's baby

Steven Frame (John Nash)-Son of Vicky and Jamie

Felicia Gallant (Linda Dano)-TV talk show host; mother of Lorna; adoptive mother of Jenna; widow of Lucas

Brett Gardner (Colleen Dion)-Architect

Grant Harrison (Mark Pinter)-Congressman; Ryan's brother; Vicky's husband; Spencer's son

Kelsey Harrison (Kaitlin Hopkins)-Doctor

Ryan Harrison (Paul Michael Valley)-Detective; Grant's younger brother; Carl's son

Spencer Harrison (David Hedison)-Grant's father

Vicky Harrison (Jensen Buchanan)-Marley's twin sister; mother of Stephen; married to Grant

Donna Hudson (Anna Stuart)-Mother of Vicky and Marley

John Hudson (David Forsyth)-Father of Gregory; ex-husband of Sharlene

Carl Hutchins (Charles Keating)-A businessman

Hank Kent (Steve Fletcher)-Blue-collar worker

Tommy Kent (Cory Lee Rogers)-Hank's son

Marley Love (Jensen Buchanan)-Vicky's twin sister; ex-wife of Jake

Liz Matthews (Irene Dailey)-Employee of Cory Publishing

Jake McKinnon (Tom Eplin)-Video expert

Stefanie Preston (Sarah Malin)-Grant's assistant

Sloan Wallace (Orlagh Cassidy)-Television producer

Iris Wheeler (Carmen Duncan)-Mother of Dennis

Cass Winthrop (Stephen Schnetzer)-Lawyer

Frankie Winthrop (Alice Barrett)-Detective; Dean's cousin

AS THE WORLD TURNS

Kirk Anderson (Tom Wiggin)-Head of Walsh Enterprises
Courtney Baxter (Hayley Barr)-Andy's wife
Andy Dixon (Scott De Freitas)-John and Kim's son;
Courtney's husband
John Dixon (Larry Bryggman)-Chief of staff of Oakdale
Hospital; father of Margo, Andy and Duke
Lucinda Dixon (Elizabeth Hubbard)-Business tycoon;
raised Lily
Scott Eldridge (Joe Breen)-Lisa's son
Lamar Griffin (Michael Genet)-Jessica's brother
Bob Hughes (Don Hastings)-Kim's husband; father of
Frannie, Sabrina, Tom and Chris
Chris Hughes (Christian Seifert)-Bob and Kim's son
Kim Hughes (Kathryn Hays)-Bob's wife; mother of Andy,
Sabrina and Chris
Margo Hughes (Glynnis O'Connor)-Tom's wife; Adam and
Casey's mother
Tom Hughes (Scott Holmes)-Margo's husband; Bob's son;
Casey's father
Hutch Hutchinson (Judson Mills)-College student; Linc's
brother
Connor Jamison (Allyson Rice-Taylor)-Evan's sister
Evan Jamison (Greg Watkins)-Connor's brother
Royce Keller (Terry Lester)-Architect
Linc Lafferty (Lonnie McCullough)-Loves Connor
Dan McCloskey (Dan Frazer)-Police lieutenant; Nancy's
husband
Nancy McCloskey (Helen Wagner)-Dan's wife; Bob's mother
Larry McDermott (Ed Fry)-Susan's husband
Duncan McKechnie (Michael Swan)-Co-owner of Argus;
married to Jessica
Jessica Griffin McKechnie (Tamara Tunie)-Attorney;
married to Duncan
Lynn Michaels (Courtney Sherman)-Doctor
Lisa Mitchell (Eileen Fulton)-Mother of Tom and Scott
Barbara Munson (Colleen Zenk-Pinter)-Ex-wife of Hal;
mother of Paul and Jennifer-Louise
Hal Munson (Ben Hendrickson)-Police detective; Barbara's
ex-husband; Adam's father
Lyla Peretti (Anne Sward)-Mother of Margo, Craig, Cricket
and Katie
Rosanna (Yvonne Perry)-Works on Hutchinson farm

Audrey Samuels (Maggie Burke)-Doctor
Debbie Simon (Sharon Case)-Ned's daughter
Ned Simon (Frank Converse)-Debbie's father
Aaron Snyder (Mason Boccardo)-Son of Holden and Julie; adopted by Iva
Emma Snyder (Kathleen Widdoes)-Matriarch of Snyder family
Holden Snyder (Jon Hensley)-Amnesia victim; Aaron's father; ex-husband of Emily, Angel and Lily
Iva Snyder (Lisa Brown)-Natural mother of Lily; adopted Aaron
Julie Snyder (Susan Marie Snyder)-Model; mother of Aaron
Lily Snyder (Martha Byrne)-Ex-wife of Holden; raised by Lucinda
Ellen Stewart (Patricia Bruder)-Stewart family grand-mother
Emily Stewart (Kelley Menighan)-Susan's daughter
Susan Stewart (Marie Masters)-Emily's mother; Larry's wife
Cal Stricklyn (Patrick Tovatt)-Oil man

THE BOLD AND THE BEAUTIFUL

Sheila Carter (Kimberlin Brown)-Eric's wife
Steven Crown (Perry Stephens)-Attorney for Forrester Creations
Connor Davis (Scott Thompson Baker)-Businessman
Darla Dinkle (Schae Harrison)-Sally's secretary
Sly Donovan (Brent Jasmer)-Bartender
Brooke Forrester (Katherine Kelly Lang)-Ex-wife of Eric; mother of Eric, Jr.; mother of Ridge's baby
Eric Forrester (John McCook)-Head of Forrester Creations; husband of Sheila; ex-husband of Stephanie and Brooke; father of Eric, Jr.
Macy Forrester (Bobbie Eakes)-Separated from Thorne; Sally's daughter
Ridge Forrester (Ronn Moss)-Married to Taylor; father of Brooke's baby
Stephanie Forrester (Susan Flannery)-Eric's ex-wife
Thorne Forrester (Jeff Trachta)-Separated from Macy
Jack Hamilton (Chris Robinson)-Taylor's father; employee of Spectra
Taylor Hayes (Hunter Tylo)-Doctor; Blake's ex-wife; Ridge's wife

Pierre (Robert Clary)-Restaurant owner
Karen Roberts (Joanna Johnson)-Caroline's sister
Saul (Michael Fox)-Sally's right-hand man
Sally Spectra (Darlene Conley)-Head of Spectra Fashions; mother of Clarke, Jr. and Macy
Bill Spencer (Jim Storm)-Businessman

DAYS OF OUR LIVES

Nicholas Alamain (Erik von Detten)-Son of Carly and Lawrence
Vivian Alamain (Louise Sorel)-Lawrence and John's aunt
John Black (Drake Hogestyn)-Brady's father
Kristen Blake (Eileen Davidson)-Social worker
Bo Brady (Robert Kelker-Kelly)-Caroline and Victor's son; Shawn's father
Caroline Brady (Peggy McCay)-Mother of Brady family
Carrie Brady (Christie Clark)-Roman's daughter
Kimberly Brady (Ariana Chase)-Daughter of Caroline and Shawn; recovering from split personality
Marlena Brady (Deidre Hall)-Roman's wife; mother of Samantha and Eric
Roman Brady (Wayne Northrop)-Son of Caroline and Shawn; Marlena's husband; father of Carrie, Samantha and Eric
Samantha Brady (Alison Sweeney)-Roman and Marlena's daughter; Carrie's sister
Shawn Douglas Brady (Scott Groff)-Son of Bo and Hope
Jennifer Deveraux (Melissa Reeves)-Bill and Laura's daughter; Jack's wife; Abby's mother
Alice Horton (Frances Reid)-Tom's wife; matriarch of Horton family
Bill Horton (Ed Mallory)-Tom and Alice's son; father of Jennifer
Maggie Horton (Suzanne Rogers)-Mickey's wife
Mickey Horton (John Clarke)-Tom and Alice's son; Maggie's husband
Tom Horton (Macdonald Carey)-Chief of staff at University Hospital; husband of Alice
Victor Kiriakis (John Aniston)-Bo and Isabella's father
Carly Manning (Crystal Chappell)-Doctor; Nicholas' mother
Wendy Reardon (Lark Voorhies)-Runaway; unwed teenage mother

Austin Reed (Patrick Muldoon)-Billie's brother; boxer
Billie Reed (Lisa Rinna)-Austin's sister; recovering drug addict
Kate Roberts (Deborah Adair)-Mystery woman
Lucas Roberts (Bryan Dattilo)-Kate's prep school son
Vern Scofield (Wayne Heffley)-Journalist

GENERAL HOSPITAL

Ruby Anderson (Norma Connolly)-Bobbie's aunt
Jenny Ashton (Cheryl Richardson)-Bill's sister; separated from Ned
Ned Ashton (Wallace Kurth)-Tracy's son
Gail Baldwin (Susan Brown)-Lee's wife; Psychiatrist
Lee Baldwin (Peter Hanson)-Gail's husband; Scott's father
Scott Baldwin (Kin Shriner)-Widower of Dominique
Julia Barrett (Crystal Carson)-Brenda's sister
Sheila Cantillon (Stacey Cortez)-Nurse
Jagger Cates (Antonio Sabato, Jr.)-Works for Ruby
Ryan Chamberlain (Jon Lindstrom)-Dangerous man
Lucy Coe (Lynn Herring)-Carried Scott and Dominique's baby
Marco Dane (Gerald Anthony)-Con man
Sean Donely (John Reilly)-Tiffany's husband; police commissioner
Tiffany Donely (Sharon Wyatt)-Sean's wife; TV reporter
Bill Eckert (Anthony Geary)-Sly's father; Jenny's brother
Sly Eckert (Glenn Walker Harris, Jr.)-Bill's son
Audrey Hardy (Rachel Ames)-Steve's wife
Dr. Steve Hardy (John Beradino)-Chief of staff at General Hospital; Audrey's husband
Paul Hornsby (Paul Satterfield, Jr.)-Dylan's father
Reginald Jennings (Stephen Kay)-Quartermaine butler
B.J. Jones (Brighton Hertford)-Tony and Tania's daughter; Bobbie's stepdaughter
Bobbie Jones (Jackie Zeman)-Tony's wife; Ruby's niece; Bill's cousin; B.J. and Lucas's stepmother
Felicia Jones (Kristina Malandro)-Divorced from Frisco; mother of Max
Tony Jones (Brad Maule)-Bobbie's husband; B.J.'s father
Jack Kensington (Stan Ivar)-U.S. Senator
Meg Lawson (Alexia Robinson)-Nurse
Chief Lewis (Don Dolan)-Police chief
Victoria Parker (Terri Garber)-Ex-lover of Bill
A.J. Quartermaine (Sean Kanan)-Alan and Monica's son; recovering alcoholic

Emma Samms plays Holly Scorpio on "General Hospital."

Alan Quartermaine (Stuart Damon)-Monica's husband; A.J. and Jason's father

Edward Quartermaine (John Ingle)-Lila's husband; father of Alan and Tracy

Jason Quartermaine (Steve Burton)-Alan's son

Lila Quartermaine (Anna Lee)-Edward's wife; Alan and Tracy's mother

Monica Quartermaine (Leslie Charleson)-Alan's wife; A.J.'s mother; Jason's stepmother

Mac Scorpio (John J. York)-Robin's uncle

Robin Scorpio (Kimberly McCullough)-Robert and Anna's daughter

Lucas Stansbury (Chuckie and Kenny Gravino)-Robert and Cheryl's son; raised by Bobbie and Tony

Amy Vining (Shell Kepler)-Nurse

Karen Wexler (Cari Shayne)-Rhonda's daughter

Rhonda Wexler (Denise Galik-Furey)-Karen's mother

GUIDING LIGHT

Ed Bauer (Peter Simon)-Doctor; widower of Maureen; Michelle's father

Michelle Bauer (Rachel Miner)-Ed's daughter

Jenna Bradshaw (Fiona Hutchison)-Head of Spaulding Enterprises

Julie Camaletti (Jocelyn Seagrave)-A.C.'s sister

Henry Chamberlain (William Roerick)-Vanessa's father

Frank (Buzz) Cooper (Justin Deas)-Frank and Harley's father; ex-husband of Nadine

Frank Cooper (Frank Dicopoulos)-Detective; Nadine and Buzz's son; Harley's brother

Harley Cooper (Beth Ehlers)-Nadine and Buzz's daughter; Frank's sister; a policewoman

David (Monti Sharp)-A young man who has been convicted of murder and who has a relationship with Kat

Grady (Eddie Mecca)-Businessman

Eve Guthrie (Hilary Edson)-Nick's girlfriend

Hart Jessup (Leonard Stabb)-Roger's son; father of Bridget's baby

Billy Lewis (Jordan Clarke)-Nadine's husband; Dylan, Mindy and Bill's father

Bill Lewis, Jr. (Bryan Buffinton)-Billy and Vanessa's son

Dylan Shane Lewis (Morgan Englund)-Billy and Reva's son; Mindy's brother

H.B. Lewis (Larry Gates)-Billy's father
Mindy Lewis (Barbara Crampton)-Billy's daughter; Dylan's sister
Nadine Lewis (Jean Carol)-Billy's wife; Buzz's ex-wife
Vanessa Lewis (Maeve Kinkead)-Henry's daughter; Bill's mother
A.C. Mallet (Mark Derwin)-Policeman
Ross Marler (Larry verDorn)-Attorney
Nick McHenry (Vincent Irizarry)-Alan-Michael's brother; Alexandra's son
Lillian Raines (Tina Sloan)-Nurse
Fletcher Reade (Charles Jay Hammer)-Part-owner of nightclub
Alan-Michael Spaulding (Rick Hearst)-Businessman; Eleni's ex-husband
Blake Spaulding (Elizabeth Keifer)-Holly and Roger's daughter
Eleni Spaulding (Melina Kanakaredes)-Alan-Michael's ex-wife; mother of Frank's baby
Gilly Speakes (Amelia Marshall)-Hampton's wife; TV anchor person
Hampton Speakes (Vince Williams)-Gilly's husband; Kat's father
Kat Speakes (Nia Long)-Hampton's daughter
Holly Thorpe (Maureen Garrett)-Roger's ex-wife; Blake's mother; head of local TV station
Roger Thorpe (Michael Zaslow)-Blake and Hart's father

LOVING

Clay Alden (Dennis Parlato)-Curtis' father; Isabelle's son
Cooper Alden (Michael Weatherly)-Father of Ally's baby; student
Curtis Alden (Michael Lord)-Clay's son; Dinah Lee's husband
Gwyneth Alden (Christine Tudor-Newman)-Clay's ex-wife; Curtis' mother
Isabelle Alden (Patricia Barry)-Cabot's widow; Clay's mother
Casey Bowman (Paul Anthony Stewart)-Student at Alden University
Stephanie Brewster (Amelia Heinle)-Student at Alden University
Buck (Philip Brown)-Man with a mysterious past

Leo Burnell (James Carroll)-Owner of Burnell's

Arthur Davis (Keith Brumet)-Student at Alden University

J.J. Forbes (Matthew Porac)-Stacey's son

Stacey Forbes (Lauren-Marie Taylor)-Jack's widow; J.J.'s mother

Lisa Helman (Alice Hirson)-Genetics counselor

Jeremy Hunter (Jean LeClerc)-Dean of Humanities at Alden University

Chris McKenzie (Alexander and Britton Steele)-Trucker's son

Trucker McKenzie (Robert Tyler)-Trisha's husband

Dinah Lee Mayberry (Jessica Collins)-Curtis' wife; Hannah's sister

Hannah Mayberry (Rebecca Gayheart)-Concert pianist; Dinah Lee's sister

Allison Rescott (Laura Sisk)-Kate's granddaughter; mother of Cooper's child

Ava Rescott (Lisa Peluso)-Businesswoman

Armond Rosario (Michael Galardi)-Businessman

Kate Slavinsky (Nada Rowand)-Ava's mother; Louie's wife

Louis Slavinsky (Bernie Barrow)-Kate's husband

Shana Vochek (Susan Keith)-Daughter of Cabot

ONE LIFE TO LIVE

Asa Buchanan (Phil Carey)-Rich businessman; Bo and Clint's father

Bo Buchanan (Robert S. Woods)-Asa's son; Clint's brother

Clint Buchanan (Clint Ritchie)-Asa's son; Bo's brother; Viki's ex-husband; Jessica's father

Jessica Buchanan (Erin Torpey)-Viki and Clint's daughter

Joey Buchanan (Chris McKenna)-Viki's son

Kevin Buchanan (Kirk Geiger)-Viki's son

Renee Buchanan (Patricia Elliott)-Asa's ex-wife; owner of Palace Hotel

Viki Lord Buchanan (Erika Slezak)-Clint's ex-wife; Kevin, Joey and Jessica's mother

Andrew Carpenter (Wortham Krimmer)-Cassie's husband; minister

Cassie Carpenter (Laura Bonarrigo)-Andrew's wife; Dorian's daughter

Sloan Carpenter (Roy Thinnes)-Andrew's father; former General

Billy Douglas (Ryan Phillippe)-Young man who's learning to accept his homosexuality

Hank Gannon (Nathan Purdee)-Nora's ex-husband; Rachel's father; District Attorney

Nora Gannon (Hillary B. Smith)-Hank's ex-wife; Rachel's mother

Rachel Gannon (Ellen Bethea)-Hank and Nora's daughter

Alex Hesser (Tonja Walker)-Carlo's widow; a dangerous woman

Al Holden (Michael Roman)-Max's son

Max Holden (James DePaiva)-Father of Al

Angela Holliday (Susan Diol)-Evangelist

Kim (Wai Ching Ho)-Servant at Llanfair

Clayton Powell Lord III (Sean Moynihan)-Kevin's cousin

Dorian Lord (Robin Strasser)-Cassie's mother; owner of the *Intruder*

Todd Manning (Roger Howarth)-Kevin's fraternity brother

Luna Moody (Susan Batten)-Eccentric woman

Nigel (Peter Bartlett)-Buchanan's butler

Sheila Price (Valarie Pettiford)-Young woman

Rebecca (Reiko Aylesworth)-Follower of Angela

C.J. Roberts (Tyler Noyes)-Tina and Cord's son

Cord Roberts (John Loprieno)-Tina's ex-husband; C.J. and Sarah's father

Tina Roberts (Karen Witter)-Viki's half-sister; Cord's ex-wife; C.J. and Sarah's mother

Cain Rogan (Christopher Cousins)-Former con man

Zach Rosen (Josh Philip Weinstein)-Kevin's fraternity brother

Marty Saybrooke (Susan Haskell)-Young woman who has lupus

Suede (David Ledingham)-Former con man

Jason Webb (Mark Brettschneider)-Wanda's nephew

Wanda Wolek (Marilyn Chris)-Jason's aunt; owner of restaurant

THE YOUNG AND THE RESTLESS

Jill Abbott (Jess Walton)-John's wife

Jack Abbott (Peter Bergman)-John's son; Nikki's husband; Vicky and Nicholas' stepfather

John Abbott (Jerry Douglas)-Founder of Jabot Cosmetics; Jill's husband; Jack, Ashley and Traci's father

Nikki Abbott (Melody Thomas Scott)-Ex-wife of Victor; Jack's wife; Vicky and Nicholas' mother

April (Cynthia Jordan)-Mother of Paul's child

Douglas Austin (Michael Evans)-Victor's best friend
Michael Baldwin (Christian LeBlanc)-Demented lawyer
Lynne Bassett (Laura Bryan Birn)-Paul's secretary
Blade (Michael Tylo)-Fashion photographer
Brad Carlton (Don Diamont)-Traci's ex-husband; Colleen's father
Phillip Chancellor (Scott/Shawn Markley)-Nina's son; Katherine's grandson
Cole (J. Eddie Peck)-Victor's illegitimate son
Brandon Collins (Paul Walker)-Victoria's friend
Lauren Fenmore (Tracey Bregman-Recht)-Head of Fenmore department stores; Paul and Scott's ex-wife; Scotty's mother
Scott Grainger (Peter Barton)-Doctor; Lauren's ex-husband; Scotty's father
Nathan Hastings (Randy Brooke)-Detective; Olivia's husband; Nate's father
Olivia Hastings (Tonya Lee Williams)-Nathan's wife; Nate's mother
Eve Howard (Margaret Mason)-Mother of Victor's son Cole
Mamie Johnson (Veronica Redd-Forrest)-Abbott's housekeeper; Drucilla and Olivia's aunt
Nina Kimble (Tricia Cast)-Philip's mother; Flo's daughter
Hillary Lancaster (Kelly Garrison)-Attorney; Michael's ex-wife
Ryan McNeil (Scott Reeves)-Victoria's husband
Ashley Newman (Brenda Epperson)-John's daughter; ex-wife of Victor
Victor Newman (Eric Braeden)-Businessman; ex-husband of Nikki and Ashley
Victoria Newman (Heather Tom)-Victor and Nikki's daughter; Ryan's wife
Miguel Rodriguez (Anthony Pena)-Nikki and Jack's housekeeper
Gina Roma (Patty Weaver)-Owner of Gina's nightclub; Rex's daughter; Danny's sister
Cricket Romalotti (Lauralee Bell)-Lawyer; Danny's wife
Danny Romalotti (Michael Damian)-Rock singer; Cricket's husband; Rex's son; Gina's brother
John Silva (John Castellanos)-Attorney
Katherine Sterling (Jeanne Cooper)-Rex's wife
Rex Sterling (Quinn Redeker)-Katherine's husband; Danny and Gina's father
Esther Valentine (Kate Linder)-Katherine's housekeeper; Kate's mother

Flo Webster (Sharon Farrell)-Nina's mother
Mary Williams (Carolyn Conwell)-Paul's mother
Paul Williams (Doug Davidson)-Mary's son
Drucilla Winters (Victoria Rowell)-Model; Neil's wife;
Olivia's sister
Neil Winters (Kristoff St. John)-Drucilla's husband

Most And Least Common Soap Occupations

Soap operas may present a slice of life—but it's a very curiously cut slice. The collective minds who plot and write these serials seem to concentrate on a small handful of professions, while totally ignoring others. It's interesting to take a look at the pairs of popular/unpopular occupations.

Doctor/Dentist
If the population of America mirrored the populations of soap lands, paying all those doctors would consume 50% of the per capita income! Yet, despite their perfect, gleaming white teeth, soap characters never seem to go to the dentist. Perhaps crises like impacted wisdom teeth and the trauma of needing dentures don't excite the imaginations of writers!

Lawyers/Insurance Salesmen
All the murders, rapes, swindles, accidents and other catastrophes that always seem to affect soap characters necessitate a posse of lawyers for each cast. But even though the more affluent characters must surely be well insured, nary an insurance agent appears on screen. Maybe insurance salesmen would take up too much time calling during dinner!

Police Officers/Firemen
Police officers, especially dapper male and sexy female detectives, are plentiful on soap operas. Even though firefighters are equally important to public safety, this occupation has been almost completely unrepresented.

Drug Dealers/Pharmacists
It seems that there's a drug dealer lurking around every corner on soap operas—in the case of Brooke on "All My Children," her own mother turned out to be a drug dealer who was plotting to murder her. But it also appears to be nearly impossible to fill a legal prescription, due to an almost total lack of pharmacists.

Hookers/Tupperware or Avon Ladies
Most children are taught that the way to get ahead in life is to sell oneself, and an astounding number of female soap characters seem to have taken that advice literally sometime in their past. On the other hand, the Tupperware and Avon ladies—and other salespeople who are ubiquitous in real life communities—are totally missing on daytime television.

Business Tycoons/Bankers
Ruthless business tycoons, male and female, are stock soap characters, and their avarice fuels plot lines on every show. But almost nowhere to be seen are the bankers who supply the cash for corporate takeovers.

Musicians/Actors
Musicians, from nightclub crooners like the former "Days of Our Lives" character Doug Williams to rockers like Danny Romalotti of "The Young and the Restless" are staples of daytime serials. But actors portraying actors on the soaps are as rare as hen's teeth.

Con Artists/Stock Brokers
Almost every soap features a storyline in which one character is trying to scam another. Maybe soap characters are especially vulnerable because their casts include no legitimate stock brokers (or bankers) to help them invest prudently!

TV Personalities/Radio Personalities
TV news anchors, reporters, even talk show hosts are well represented on soaps. Perhaps because we don't see soap characters driving to work, radio doesn't seem to exist—nor do radio personalities.

Nurses/Veterinarians
Nurses, be they sympathetic, sexy or sadistic, are as plentiful on soaps as are perfect hair styles. (After all, what's a hospi-

tal without nurses?) But the few pets that appear on soaps apparently must fend for themselves, because veterinarians are nearly impossible to find.

In The Beginning...

ew soaps are successful, and the key may lie in their starts. Here are the backgrounds of the current daytime dramas.

ALL MY CHILDREN

First television broadcast: January 5, 1970
Expanded from 30 to 60 minutes: 1977

In 1965, soap opera writer and creator Agnes Nixon was commissioned to create a new soap opera for Proctor & Gamble. She wrote a proposal and five complete scripts, and Proctor & Gamble optioned the idea. However, they later turned it down due to a shortage of airtime on daytime, and the disappointed Nixon put the proposal away.

After a very successful stint as headwriter on "Another World," Nixon was asked to create a new soap opera for ABC in 1968. Believing that the proposal she had written for Proctor & Gamble wasn't good enough, she developed "One Life to Live." When that show became a success, ABC asked Nixon to create another new series. Her husband reminded her about her shelved "All My Children" scripts, and she skeptically submitted the material.

ABC loved the idea for a soap that would concentrate on socially-relevant storylines, and which featured a cast that included more young actors than were usually seen on daytime serials. To give the fledgling show a greater chance at success, Nixon persuaded actress Rosemary Prinz, a retired daytime favorite who had vowed never to do another soap, to sign a six-month contract. As Amy Tyler, Prinz attracted enough viewers

Glamorous location shoots, such as this fox-hunting scene, have been trademarks of the hit soap "All My Children."

to keep the show going, and it gradually began to pick up momentum, especially with the younger viewers. By August, 1974, "All My Children" was the top-rated soap opera.

The central families in the original cast were the wealthy and socially-prominent Tyler family, headed by Dr. Charles Tyler (Hugh Franklin) and his wife Phoebe (Ruth Warrick); and the working class Martins, headed by Joe Martin (Ray MacDonnell), who eventually married Ruth Brent (Mary Fickett). Susan Lucci, one of the show's original cast members, has gone down in soap history as the married many-times-over Erica Kane.

A key to the lasting appeal of "All My Children" has been plotlines based on topics from current headlines. The soap was the first to feature a character to have a legal abortion, the first to concentrate on the problems of Vietnam veterans, one of the first to touch on the subject of a battered woman and the first to sensitively portray a woman dying of AIDS.

ANOTHER WORLD

First television broadcast: May 4, 1964
Expanded from 30 to 60 minutes: January 6, 1975
Expanded to 90 minutes: March 5, 1979
Went back to 60 minutes: August 1, 1980

Irna Phillips was writing for "As the World Turns" when she came up with the idea for a spin-off soap that would take place in Bay City, which would be located so near Oakdale that it would be possible for characters from one soap to visit the other. Proctor & Gamble liked the idea, but CBS had no spot available on its afternoon schedule. NBC, in desperate need of a daytime hit, embraced the idea.

Since Phillips couldn't have characters from soaps on two different networks visit one another, the only way she could link the already successful "As the World Turns" with the new show was to call it "Another World." She had both shows begin with the announcement, "We do not live in this world alone but in a thousand other worlds" in order to help viewers make the connection.

The central families of "Another World" were the Matthews and the Baxters. To get the show off to a rousing start, Phillips began the first show with the death of the Matthews family patriarch, soon followed by an out-of-wedlock pregnancy, a septic abortion, and a murder and subsequent trial. Unfortunately, the show's initial ratings were dismal. The Baxters soon disappeared. In 1966, new head writer James Lipton did away with the Matthews as well, but to no avail. Then, in 1967, Agnes Nixon took over as head writer. She killed off a bunch of Lipton's characters in a plane crash, brought back the Matthews and cooked up plots that sent "Another World" to the top of the ratings. With the addition of the Cory family, the show was near the top of the ratings during the 1970s, but has gradually slipped to the back of the pack over the last two decades.

In 1970, "Another World" became the first soap to spin-off another soap, "Another World—Somerset." "Somerset" was canceled in 1976 to make way for a second spin-off, "Lovers and Friends." This lasted only a few months, then came back for another short run under the title "For Richer, For Poorer." Finally, "Another World" spun-off the first original hour-length soap, "Texas," in 1980. That show was canceled in 1983.

AS THE WORLD TURNS

First television broadcast: April 2, 1956
Expanded to 60 minutes: 1975

"As the World Turns," which debuted as television's first half-hour soap, was created by Irna Phillips. When the show

Meg Ryan's first step toward stardom was her role as Betsy Stewart Montgomery on "As the World Turns."

was commissioned by Proctor & Gamble, Phillips insisted on a contract that prevented the show from being canceled during its first year. The reason: Phillips created a show that concentrated on the routines of everyday life. The center of each household was the kitchen, and viewers were treated to long conversations that recapped both recent and long-past events. The pace of the show was slow, and the plot complications were minimal.

As Phillips had anticipated, the initial ratings were poor. But ratings began to climb after six months, and by the end of its second year, "As the World Turns" was the most watched soap. The central families were the wealthy Lowells and the middle-class Hughes. Viewers especially warmed to the Hughes family, which was headed by Chris (Don MacLaughlin) and Nancy (Helen Wagner). This couple provided the emotional stability of the show for decades. The Lowells gradually disappeared, and were replaced by the Stewarts.

The show's popularity was solidified in 1960 when Eileen Fulton joined the cast as Lisa Miller, who became the most famous villain in all of daytime television. Viewers loved to hate Lisa as she destroyed marriages and broke men's hearts. In 1969, the show added another magnificent villain, Dr. John Dixon.

"As the World Turns" lost ratings in the 1970s, and the writers struggled to make the show faster paced and more current. In one memorable plotline, Dr. John Dixon was tried for the rape of his wife, the first such incident on daytime television. But the show still remains less youth-oriented than many of its competitors.

"As the World Turns" spun-off the prime time serial "Our Private World" in 1965, but it was canceled five months later.

THE BOLD AND THE BEAUTIFUL

First television broadcast: March 23, 1987

This youngest of all current soaps was created by William Bell and his wife, Lee Phillip Bell, the couple also responsible for the success of "The Young and the Restless." Although "The Bold and the Beautiful" is the only soap set in a real city (Los Angeles), its characters and settings are those of a glamourous, romantic fantasy.

The central families, the Forresters and the Logans, are involved in the fashion business. And almost every character looks like a model and lives amid the kind of luxury most viewers can only imagine. Characters do move back and forth between "The Bold and the Beautiful" and the almost equally glamourous "The Young and the Restless."

Following the formula of its older cousin has led to solid ratings for "The Bold and the Beautiful."

DAYS OF OUR LIVES

First television broadcast: November 8, 1965
Expanded to 60 minutes: April, 1975

"Days of Our Lives" was created by Ted Corday, the producer of "As the World Turns," with some assistance from Irna Phillips. Like the older show, "Days of Our Lives" began with a solemn bit of philosophy—in this case, "Like sands through the hourglass, so are the days of our lives."

Before becoming a prime time innkeeper on "Newhart," Mary Frann starred as Amanda Peters on "Days of Our Lives."

And like the older show, this new effort was focused around a couple heading an extended central family.

Corday recruited movie star Macdonald Carey to play the patriarch of the family, Dr. Tom Horton; Frances Reid was hired to play his wife Alice. Like "As the World Turns," the show got off to a bleak start—it ranked 32nd out of 34 network daytime shows in 1965. In 1967, a young man named William Bell took over as head writer. He brought to the sagging show a new sexual awareness and fast moving plots that complimented the stability of the Hortons.

By mid-1970s, "Days of Our Lives" was a ratings hit. The show's most glamorous stars were Bill Hayes and Susan Seaforth, who portrayed Doug Williams and Julie Olson. Hayes and Seaforth married in real life, two years before their characters delighted millions of fans by marrying on television. In 1979, Deidre Hall joined the cast as Dr. Marlena Evans, and she soon became one of daytime's leading stars. Her tempestuous romance with Roman Brady continues into the 1990s. Another popular character in the 1980s was Steve "Patch" Johnson (Stephen Nichols), who had a long romance with Kayla Brady before leaving the show.

"Days of Our Lives" had slipped to ninth place among

twelve soaps by 1989, but it was revived with the return of Deidre Hall and the addition of an array of younger performers such as Robert Kelker-Kelly, Matthew Ashford, Melissa Reeves and Crystall Chappell.

GENERAL HOSPITAL

First television broadcast: April 1, 1963
Expanded to 45 minutes: July 26, 1976
Expanded to 60 minutes: January 16, 1978

"General Hospital" premiered on the same day as "The Doctors." The medical shows "Doctor Kildare" and "Ben Casey" were prime time hits at the time, and ABC decided it would try to bring that successful theme to daytime. It commissioned a writer to create a daytime medical anthology that was to be called "Emergency Hospital." However, when the network learned that NBC was also planning a medical anthology, called "The Doctors," that idea was scrapped. Doris and Frank Hursley, who had been headwriters for

Two of soap's most beloved and longest-lasting characters were "General Hospital's" Dr. Steve Hardy (John Beradino) and nurse Jessie Brewer (Emily McLaughlin).

As Robert Scorpio on "General Hospital," Tristan Rogers was one of daytime's most popular leading men.

"Search for Tomorrow," were hired to create a regular soap which they called "General Hospital."

The show was first produced in black and white on a minuscule budget, but it became ABC's first hit soap opera. The show's central "family" was not a biological one, but the staff of General Hospital. A physician was hired as a medical consultant to make the scripts credible. The setting made the show seem different from the other serials, even though the romantic problems of the main characters mirrored those on other shows.

In the 1970s, however, the ratings began to plummet as the show's poor production value and stiff characters gave it an "old fashioned" feel. Just when "General Hospital" was close to being canceled, Gloria Monty took over as producer. Instead of being aired exactly as it was taped, scenes were filmed and edited together, as is done with a movie. Monty changed the focus to younger characters, like teenage lovers Scott Baldwin and Laura Vining.

In 1979, the show hired 34-year-old character actor Tony Geary to play mobster Luke Spencer, who did the dirty work for his sister, nurse Bobbie Spencer. The love affair of Luke and Laura (Genie Francis) made "General Hospital" not only the top-rated soap, but a cultural phenomenon.

But the show's ratings began to sag again when Geary and Francis left the show in 1984. It revived again in the late 1980s and aimed for the top again by reuniting Luke and Laura in the fall of 1993.

GUIDING LIGHT

First radio broadcast: January 25, 1937
First television broadcast: June 30, 1952
(as 15-minute show)
Last radio broadcast: August, 1956
Expanded to 30 minutes: September 9, 1968
Expanded to 60 minutes: November 7, 1977

The Radio Show

"Guiding Light," the longest-running program in broadcasting history, has spun tales for more than 56 years of ordinary people grappling with the problems of everyday

Soap's longest-lasting family is the Hortons of "Days of Our Lives."

Robert Kelker-Kelly plays Bo on "Days of Our Lives."

life. The program was one of the first radio serials created by the dynamic Irna Phillips, one of the founders of the soap opera genre. When she was 19 years old, the unmarried Phillips became pregnant, was abandoned by the baby's father, then gave birth to a still-born child. After this tragedy, she gained comfort from the sermons of Dr. Preston Bradley, pastor of a non-denominational Chicago church whose approach to religion stressed the brotherhood of man. Twenty-seven years later, she created "Guiding Light" with this minister and this theme in mind.

The focus of this radio serial, which was broadcast live from Chicago and owned by soap manufacturer Procter & Gamble, was the Reverend Dr. John Rutledge, the "guiding light" (symbolized by his reading light shining through the front window of his home) of his community, a fictional ethnically-mixed Chicago neighborhood called "Five Points." In contrast to the fantasy-based serials popular at the time, "Guiding Light" focused on real-life problems such as unwed mothers and alcoholism.

In the summer of 1948, Irna Phillips introduced a new family, the Baums, who after a few shows became the Bauers. This working-class German-American family featured Papa Bauer, his daughters Meta and Trudy and his son Bill. The Bauers became the anchor of "Guiding Light" for the next 35 years. Theo Goetz, who took over the role of Papa Bauer in 1949, and Charita Bauer, who took over the role of Bill Bauer's wife Bert in 1950, became two of the most beloved and enduring soap stars of all time.

The Television Show

Irna Phillips was determined to bring "Guiding Light" to television, and it happened on June 30, 1952. Procter & Gamble replaced "The First Hundred Years" (which fell 98 years short of its promise) with the first 15-minute episode of "Guiding Light."

"Guiding Light" television show was a big hit. The cast did both the radio and television broadcasts live every weekday until the radio show (still number one, but among a diminishing audience) was canceled in 1956. Charita Bauer, Ellen Demmings (Meta Bauer) and Susan Douglas (Meta's step-daughter Kathy Roberts Holden) were among the leading female soap stars of the decade. But the ratings suffered when the storyline dictated death of Kathy Holden in 1958 (her wheelchair was pushed in front of a speeding car by kids on bicycles) produced a national outrage and a flood of angry mail. Irna Phillips, who had ordered the unpopular story line, promptly left the show, turning the mess over to Agnes Nixon.

Nixon began the next decade by injecting her trademark—story lines on socially-relevent issues and events—into the show. In 1961, Bert Bauer contracted uterine cancer; the same year, nurse Martha Frazier became the first major black soap opera character. In the early 1970s, a series of off-stage tragedies culminated in the death of Theo Goetz, who had played Papa Bauer for 25 years. At the same time, the success of Agnes Nixon's new shows, "One Life to Live" "All My Children" and Bill Bell's sexy "The Young and the Restless," made older shows like "Guiding Light" seem slow-moving and bland. Procter & Gamble went through six headwriting teams in three years until they hired Brigitte Dobson (daughter of "General Hospital" creators Frank and Doris Hursley) and her husband Jerome Dobson in 1975. They created a wealth of new romantic triangles involving the new Spaulding and Marler families. And in the character of Roger Thorpe, played by Michael Zaslow, the show found one of the greatest soap villains.

The trials of young lovers Steve Sowolsky (Jorn R. Johnston) and Trisha Alden (Noelle Beck) was one of the most popular all-time storylines on "Loving."

In 1980, famous soap writer Douglas Marland moved from "General Hospital" to "Guiding Light," and the show became the most admired soap on television, receiving the Emmy for Outstanding Daytime Drama Series in both 1980 and 1981. Then Marland left the show, and it began to founder as the Bauer family—the anchors of "Guiding Light" for 35 years—were devastated. Hope and Mike Bauer were written out, Hillary Bauer was suddenly killed and the actor playing Ed Bauer was replaced. Then in 1985, Charita Bauer died, robbing the show of its Bert Bauer. The emphasis was increasingly placed on such talented younger performers as Beth Ehlens, Frank Dicopoulos, Fiona Hutchison, Mark Derwin, Rick Hearst and Melina Kanakaredes.

LOVING

First television broadcast: June 27, 1983

"Loving" was created by Agnes Nixon and Douglas Marland as a half-hour show designed to appeal to the same young audience that made "All My Children" and "General Hospital" so popular. The show was set in the town of Corinth, home of Alden University. The soap debuted as a two-hour prime time TV movie starring Lloyd Bridges and Geraldine Paige. Bridges played millionaire Johnny Forbes, whose murder shifted the focus to his son Roger Forbes, president of Alden University.

The central families were the wealthy Forbes and Aldens and the middle-class Vorcheks and Donovans. The show emphasized the proven young love storylines, but competition in its time slot from the number one rated "The Young and the Restless" has contributed to its low ratings.

The show has had numerous cast changes over the last decade, with increasing emphasis placed on the Alden family. It has consistently ranked last among the ten current soap operas. But a new production team has pledged to provide a stability that has generated enthusiasm among the show's cast and fans.

ONE LIFE TO LIVE

First television broadcast: July 15, 1968
Expanded to 45 minutes: July 26, 1976
Expanded to 60 minutes: January 16, 1978

In late 1967, ABC commissioned Agnes Nixon to create a new soap opera. Her daring (for the time) conception was a serial that focused on the intermarriages and romances between people of different economic, ethnic and racial groups. The central families were the Lords, the wealthy owners of the town newspaper; the middle class Irish-American Reillys; the struggling Polish-American Woleks, and the Jewish Siegels.

As the soap began, Victoria Lord fell in love with reporter Joe Reilly, while Joe's sister Eileen married Jewish lawyer Dave Siegel. Shortly afterwards, Nixon created the character of Carla Grey, a light-skinned black character who passed for white before the other characters (or the viewers) learned the truth. She was eventually rejected by the black doctor she loved because of her light skin.

The show was successful from the start. But in the late 1970s, when it was lengthened to an hour, it began to evolve into a more traditional soap opera. The Woleks and the Reillys gave way to the Texas oil rich Buchanan family, which consisted of father Asa and sons Bo and Clint. One measure of continuity was a decades-long rivalry between Victoria Lord (played by Erika Slezak) and Doriaan Creamer (most notably portrayed by Robin Strasser), who

Before she moved on to "Who's the Boss," Judith Light was a day-time Emmy Award winner for her role as Karen Martin on "One Life to Live."

had married her father, Victor Lord, just before his mysterious death.

THE YOUNG AND THE RESTLESS

First television broadcast: March 26, 1973
Expanded to 60 minutes: 1979

"The Young and the Restless," created by William Bell, revolutionized daytime drama. The structure of the show—which centered on two families, one rich (the Brooks), one struggling (the Fosters)—was traditional; the way in which it was executed was strikingly different. First, Bell hired suntanned and beautiful Californian actors. Second, he focused on the love affairs of the young people in the central families rather than on those of older characters. Third, he introduced a more frank atmosphere of sex and sexuality than existed on any other soap. And finally, he and producer John Conboy used movie-quality production values and artistic photography to tell stories that were romantic fairy tales.

The show was a huge and immediate hit. Gradually, the

Jess Walton stars on "The Young and the Restless."

initial central families were replaced by the wealthy Abbotts and the upwardly mobile Williams. In 1980, Bell introduced the powerful character Victor Newman, played by Eric Braeden, who would subsequently dominate the show. "The Young and the Restless" ranked second to "General Hospital" through much of the 1980s before grabbing the number one spot near the end of the decade.

One hallmark of "The Young and the Restless" has been the concentration on fewer major characters than other hour-long soaps with less cast turnover. This formula, although hard to sustain, has maintained a high level of viewer loyalty.

Rugged, handsome Tom Selleck was one of the hunks that made "The Young and the Restless" such a smash hit.

II
The Stars

$\mathscr{A}$ $\mathscr{S}tar$ $\mathscr{I}s$ $\mathscr{B}orn$

lthough it's difficult to find out what *year* some soap stars were born, their birth dates are readily available. See who shares a birthday with you!

JANUARY

1 **Alexia Robinson** (Meg, "General Hospital")
2 **Anna Lee** (Lila, "General Hospital")
3 **Frank Dicopoulos** (Frank, "Guiding Light")
   Shannon Sturges (Molly, "Days of Our Lives")
4 **Rick Hearst** (Alan-Michael, "Guiding Light")
5 **Ricky Paull Goldin** (Dean, "Another World")
19 **Richard Van Vleet** (Chuck, "All My Children")
20 **Colleen Zenk-Pinter** (Barbara, "As the World Turns")
22 **Robert Mailhouse** (Brian, "Days of Our Lives")
26 **Allison Hossack** (Olivia, "Another World")
   Walt Willey (Jackson, "All My Children")
29 **Matthew Ashford** (Jack, "Days of Our Lives")

FEBRUARY

1 **Tina Sloan** (Lillian, "Guiding Light")
4 **Marie Masters** (Susan, "As the World Turns")
   Gil Rogers (Hawk, "Guiding Light")
   Stephanie Williams (Simone, "General Hospital")
5 **Stuart Damon** (Alan, "General Hospital")
8 **Julia Barr** (Brooke, "All My Children")
9 **Charles Shaughnessy** (Shane, "Days of Our Lives")
13 **Sharon Wyatt** (Tiffany, "General Hospital")
15 **Michael Easton** (Tanner, "Days of Our Lives")
   Renee Props (Ellie, "As the World Turns")
18 **Anthony Pena** (Miguel, "The Young and the Restless")
   Jess Walton (Jill, "The Young and the Restless")
22 **Leslie Charleson** (Monica, "General Hospital")
26 **Christopher Templeton** (Carol, "The Young and the Restless")

27 **Michael Fox** (Saul, "The Bold and the Beautiful")
29 **James Mitchell** (Palmer, "All My Children")
   Antonio Sabato, Jr. (Jagger, "General Hospital")

MARCH

1 **Richard Shoberg** (Tom, "All My Children")
2 **Joy Garrett** (Jo, "Days of Our Lives")
3 **Larry Pine** (Roger, "One Life to Live")
4 **John Aprea** (Lucas, "Another World")
   Ronn Moss (Ridge, "The Bold and the Beautiful")
5 **Ray MacDonnell** (Joe, "All My Children")
   Kimberly McCullough (Robin, "General Hospital")
6 **Jackie Zeman** (Bobbie, "General Hospital")
7 **Mark Pinter** (Grant, "Another World")
9 **Joe Gallison** (Neil, "Days of Our Lives")
   Lauren Koslow (Margo, "The Bold and the Beautiful")
13 **Robert S. Woods** (Bo, "One Life to Live")
14 **Tamara Tunie** (Jessica, "As the World Turns")
   Melissa Reeves (Jennifer, "Days of Our Lives")
   Russell Todd (Jamie, "Another World")
15 **Macdonald Carey** (Tom, "Days of Our Lives")
17 **Amelia Heinle** (Steffi, "Loving")
18 **Richard Biggs** (Marcus, "Days of Our Lives")
21 **Kathleen Widdoes** (Emma, "As the World Turns")
23 **Terry Alexander** (Troy, "One Life to Live")
   Sandi Reinhardt (Amanda, "Another World")
28 **Todd Curtis** (Skip, "The Young and the Restless")
31 **Ken Meeker** (Rafe, "One Life to Live")

APRIL

1 **Bryan Buffinton** (Billy, "Guiding Light")
   Don Hastings (Bob, "As the World Turns")
2 **Amelia Marshall** (Gilly, "Guiding Light")
3 **Laura Bryan Birn** (Lynn, "The Young and the Restless")
   Eric Braeden (Victor, "The Young and the Restless")
11 **John Castellanos** (John, "The Young and the Restless")
13 **Jean Carol** (Nadine, "Guiding Light")
14 **Patricia Bruder** (Ellen, "As the World Turns")
   John Clarke (Mickey, "Days of Our Lives")
18 **Melody Thomas Scott** (Nikki, "The Young and the Restless")

19 **Robert Tyler** (Trucker, "Loving")
23 **Melina Kanakaredes** (Eleni, "Guiding Light")
26 **Michael Damian** (Danny, "The Young and the Restless")
   Heather Rattray (Lily, "As the World Turns")
27 **Hayley Barr** (Courtney, "As the World Turns")
   Chae Harrison (Darla, "The Bold and the Beautiful")
   Ingrid Rogers (Taylor, "All My Children")

MAY

1 **John Beradino** (Steve, "General Hospital")
2 **Quinn Redeker** (Rex, "The Young and the Restless")
4 **Matt Crane** (Matt, "Another World")
8 **Cheryl Richardson** (Jenny, "General Hospital")
10 **Judson Mills** (Hutch, "As the World Turns")
   Juliet Pritner (Suzanne, "Guiding Light")
12 **Linda Dano** (Felicia, "Another World")
   Beth Maitland (Traci, "The Young and the Restless")
16 **Carolyn Conwell** (Mary, "The Young and the Restless")
   Scott Reeves (Ryan, "The Young and the Restless")
17 **Don Dolan** (Chief Lewis, "General Hospital")
19 **Marilyn Chris** (Wanda, "One Life to Live")
20 **Paolo Seganti** (Damian, "As the World Turns")
22 **Ed Fry** (Larry, "As the World Turns")
   Victoria Wyndham (Rachel, "Another World")
23 **Mary Fickett** (Ruth, "All My Children")
   Staci Greason (Isabella, "Days of Our Lives")
25 **Brandon Hooper** (Eric, "General Hospital")
27 **Beau Kazer** (Brock, "The Young and the Restless")
   Dondre Whitfield (Terrence, "All My Children")
29 **Anthony Geary** (Bill, "General Hospital")
   Tracey Bregman Recht (Lauren, "The Young and
   the Restless")
30 **Scott Holmes** (Tom, "As the World Turns")
31 **Maeve Kinkead** (Vanessa, "Guiding Light")

JUNE

3 **Susan Haskell** (Marty, "One Life to Live")
11 **Peter Bergman** (Jack, "The Young and the Restless")
   Stephen Schnetzer (Cass, "Another World")
   Michael Swan (Duncan, "As the World Turns")
17 **Daniel McVicar** (Clarke, "The Bold and the Beautiful")

Ed Fry (Larry, "As the World Turns") celebrates his birthday on May 22.

18 **Linda Thorson** (Julia, "One Life to Live")
20 **Michael Corbett** (David, "The Young and the Restless")
   John McCook (Eric, "The Bold and the Beautiful")
22 **Christine Tudor-Newman** (Gywneth, "Loving")
24 **Crystal Carson** (Julia, "General Hospital")
25 **Michael Sabatino** (Lawrence, "Days of Our Lives")
28 **Steve Burton** (Jason, "General Hospital")
29 **Kimberlin Brown** (Sheila, "The Bold and the Beautiful")
   Ruth Warrick (Phoebe, "All My Children")

JULY

 1 **Constance Ford** (Ada, "Another World")
   Frank Parker (Shawn, "Days of Our Lives")
 3 **Hunter Tylo** (Taylor, "The Bold and the Beautiful")
 4 **Ellen Bethea** (Rachel, "One Life to Live")
 5 **Joseph Breen** (Scott, "As the World Turns")
   Valerie Pettiford (Sheila, "One Life to Live")
 6 **James Kiberd** (Trevor, "All My Children")
   Tom Wiggin (Kirk, "As the World Turns")
 7 **Jean LeClerc** (Jeremy, "All My Children")
 9 **Suzanne Rogers** (Maggie, "Days of Our Lives")
11 **Susan Seaforth Hayes** (Julie, "Days of Our Lives")
   Vince Williams (Hampton, "Guiding Light")
12 **Judi Evans** (Paulina, "Another World")
   Tonya Lee Williams (Olivia, "The Young and
   the Restless")
15 **Phil Carey** (Asa, "One Life to Live")
   Wayne Heffley (Vern, "Days of Our Lives")
   Kristoff St. John (Neil, "The Young and the Restless")
18 **Jensen Buchanan** (Vicky/Marley, "Another World")
   Darlene Conley (Sally, "As the World Turns")
19 **Peter Barton** (Scott, "The Young and the Restless")
21 **Jordan Clarke** (Billy, "Guiding Light")
   Patricia Elliott (Renee, "One Life to Live")
23 **Beth Ehlers** (Harley, "Guiding Light")
24 **John Aniston** (Victor, "Days of Our Lives")
25 **Bobbie Eakes** (Macy, "The Bold and the Beautiful")
   Katherine Kelly Lang (Brooke, "The Bold and
   the Beautiful")
26 **Kathryn Hays** (Kim, "As the World Turns")
27 **Michael Evans** (Douglas, "The Young and the Restless")
   Julian McMahon (Ian, "Another World")
29 **Bryan Dattilo** (Lucas, "Days of Our Lives")

30 **Lisa Peluso** (Ava, "Loving")
31 **Susan Flannery** (Stephanie, "The Bold and the Beautiful")

AUGUST

2 **Lisa Brown** (Iva, "As the World Turns")
4 **Crystal Chappell** (Carly, "Days of Our Lives")
5 **Erika Slezak** (Viki, "One Life to Live")
6 **Nathan Purdee** (Hank, "One Life to Live")
  Louise Sorel (Vivian, "Days of Our Lives")
8 **Veronica Redd-Forrest** (Mamie, "The Young and the Restless")
9 **Clint Ritchie** (Clint, "One Life to Live")
  Michael Storm (Larry, "One Life to Live")
10 **James Reynolds** (Abe, "Days of Our Lives")
12 **Jim Storm** (William, "The Bold and the Beautiful")
18 **Candice Earley** (Donna, "All My Children")
  Maureen Garrett (Holly, "Guiding Light")
19 **Paul Satterfield** (Paul, "General Hospital")
20 **Norma Connolly** (Ruby, "General Hospital")
25 **David Canary** (Adam/Stuart, "All My Children")
  Morgan Englund (Dylan, "Guiding Light")
  Christian LeBlanc (Michael, "The Young and the Restless")
26 **Benjamin Hendrickson** (Hal, "As the World Turns")
  Jon Hensley (Holden, "As the World Turns")
31 **Anthony Call** (Herb, "One Life to Live")

SEPTEMBER

3 **Helen Wagner** (Nancy, "As the World Turns")
5 **Carol Lawrence** (Angela, "General Hospital")
8 **Cari Shayne** (Karen, "General Hospital")
9 **Scott DeFreitas** (Andy, "As the World Turns")
  Brenda Epperson (Ashley, "The Young and the Restless")
  Jocelyn Seagrave (Julie, "Guiding Light")
12 **Irene Dailey** (Liz, "Another World")
  Paul Walker (Brandon, "The Young and the Restless")
13 **Eileen Fulton** (Lisa, "As the World Turns")
15 **Scott Thompson Baker** (Connor, "The Bold and the Beautiful")

17 **Suzy Cote** (Samantha, "Guiding Light")
18 **David Forsyth** (John, "Another World")
19 **Frances Heflin** (Mona, "All My Children")
   Rex Smith (Darryl, "As the World Turns")
   Alison Sweeney (Sami, "Days of Our Lives")
22 **Mark Brettschneider** (Jason, "One Life to Live")
   Lynn Herring (Lucy, "General Hospital")
23 **Shell Danielson** (ex-Dominique, "General Hospital")
   Andrew Jackson (Stephen, "All My Children")
   Patty Weaver (Gina, "The Young and the Restless")
24 **Louis Edmonds** (Langley, "All My Children")
   Larry Gates (H.B., "Guiding Light")
   Paul Michael Valley (Ryan, "Another World")
   Greg Watkins (Evan, "As the World Turns")
25 **Brett Hadley** (Carl, "The Young and the Restless")
27 **Christopher Cousins** (Cain, "One Life to Live")
   Peter Simon (Ed, "Guiding Light")
29 **Drake Hogestyn** (Roman, "Days of Our Lives")
30 **Susan Keith** (Shana, "Loving")
   Ellen Parker (Maureen, "Guiding Light")

OCTOBER

4 **Mary Ellen Stuart** (Frannie, "As the World Turns")
5 **Shell Kepler** (Amy, "General Hospital")
6 **James DePaiva** (Max, "One Life to Live")
   Jeff Trachta (Thorn, "The Bold and the Beautiful")
7 **Jill Larson** (Opal, "All My Children")
11 **Brad Maule** (Tony, "General Hospital")
13 **Cady McClain** (Dixie, "All My Children")
14 **Chris McKenna** (Joey, "One Life to Live")
16 **Ellen Dolan** (ex-Margo, "As the World Turns")
24 **Doug Davidson** (Paul, "The Young and the Restless")
25 **Jeanne Cooper** (Kay, "The Young and the Restless")
   Tom Eplin (Jake, "Another World")
26 **Allyson Rice-Taylor** (Connor, "As the World Turns")
27 **Laura Bonarrigo** (Cassie, "One Life to Live")
28 **Mark Derwin** (A.C., "Guiding Light")
30 **Nia Long** (Kat, "Guiding Light")
   Kristina Malandro (Felicia, "General Hospital")
31 **Deidre Hall** (Marlena, "Days of Our Lives")

James DePaiva (Max, "One Life to Live") is a Libra.

NOVEMBER

1 **Anna Stuart** (Donna, "Another World")
  Lauren-Marie Taylor (Stacey, "Loving")
  Michael Zaslow (Roger, "Guiding Light")
2 **Rachel Ames** (Audrey, "General Hospital")
  Kate Linder (Esther, "The Young and the Restless")
3 **Peggy McCay** (Caroline, "Days of Our Lives")
4 **Heather Tom** (Victoria, "The Young and the Restless")
5 **Chris Robinson** (Jack, "The Bold and the Beautiful")
7 **Todd McKee** (Jake, "The Bold and the Beautiful")
8 **Parker Posey** (Tess, "As the World Turns")
11 **John Reilly** (Sean, "General Hospital")
12 **Jerry Douglas** (John, "The Young and the Restless")
  Vincent Irizarry (Nick, "Guiding Light")
13 **Melissa Hayden** (Bridget, "Guiding Light")
16 **Patricia Barry** (Isabelle, "Loving")
  Tricia Cast (Nina, "The Young and the Restless")
  Jay Hammer (Fletcher, "Guiding Light")
20 **Dan Frazer** (Lt. McCloskey, "As the World Turns")
22 **Elizabeth Hubbard** (Lucinda, "As the World Turns")
23 **Jerry verDorn** (Ross, "Guiding Light")
  David Wallace (Tom, "General Hospital")
28 **Kelly Garrison** (Hilary, "The Young and the Restless")
30 **Nada Rowand** (Kate, "Loving")

DECEMBER

6 **Lindsay Price** (An Li, "All My Children")
  Kin Shriner (Scotty, "General Hospital")
9 **Frances Reid** (Alice, "Days of Our Lives")
  Anne Sward (Lyla, "As the World Turns")
10 **Wayne Northrop** (Roman, "Days of Our Lives")
  John J. York (Mac, "General Hospital")
11 **Patrick Tovatt** (Cal, "As the World Turns")
13 **Karen Witter** (Tina, "One Life to Live")
14 **Noelle Beck** (Trisha, "Loving")
17 **William Roerick** (Henry, "Guiding Light")
19 **Alice Barrett** (Frankie, "Another World")
21 **Larry Bryggman** (John, "As the World Turns")
22 **Lauralee Bell** (Cricket, "The Young and the Restless")
23 **John Callahan** (Edmund, "All My Children")
  Don Frabotta (Dave, "Days of Our Lives")
  Susan Lucci (Erica, "All My Children")

Chris Robinson (Jack, "The Bold and the Beautiful") was born on November 5.

24 **Sharon Farrell** (Flo, "The Young and the Restless")
26 **Colleen Dion** (Brett, "Another World")
27 **Barbara Crampton** (Leanna, "The Young and the Restless")
28 **Fay Hauser** (Salena, "The Young and the Restless")
30 **Bernard Barrow** (Louie, "Loving")
31 **Don Diamont** (Brad, "The Young and the Restless")
   Joanna Johnson (Karen, "The Bold and the Beautiful")

Our Town

*I*t's no surprise that far more current soap stars were born in New York City than anywhere else in the country. But it also wouldn't be surprising to find a soap star born near where you live. The following is a list of the birthplaces of some of your favorite actors and actresses.

ALABAMA
Tuscaloosa   **Teresa Blake** (Gloria, "All My Children")

ARIZONA
Phoenix   **Joanna Johnson** (Faith, "The Bold and the Beautiful")

ARKANSAS
Little Rock   **Mary Ellen Stuart** (Frannie, "As the World Turns")

CALIFORNIA
Alamo   **Cheryl Richardson** (Jenny, "General Hospital")
Arcadia   **Lindsay Price** (An Li, "All My Children")
Concord   **Larry Bryggman** (John, "As the World Turns")
Hayward   **Tom Eplin** (Jake, "Another World")
                          Kimberlin Brown (Sheila, "The Bold and the Beautiful")
Hollywood   **Katherine Kelly Lang** (Brooke, "The Bold and the Beautiful")

	Louise Sorel (Vivian, "Days of Our Lives")
	Erika Slezak (Viki, "One Life to Live")
	Brenda Epperson (Ashley, "The Young and the Restless")
Inglewood	**Michael Zaslow** (Roger, "Guiding Light")
Lake Tahoe	**Brandon Hooper** (Eric, "General Hospital")
Livermore	**James DePaiva** (Max, "One Life to Live")
Loma Linda	**Richard Lawson** (Lucas, "All My Children")
Long Beach	**David Forsyth** (John, "Another World")
	Karen Witter (Tina, "One Life to Live")
Los Angeles	**Genie Francis** (Laura, "General Hospital")
	Linda Dano (Felicia, "Another World")
	Judi Evans (Paulina, "Another World")
	Ronn Moss (Ridge, "The Bold and the Beautiful")
	Susan Hayes (Julie, "Days of Our Lives")
	John Beradino (Steve, "General Hospital")
	Morgan Englund (Dylan, "Guiding Light")
	Melody Thomas Scott (Nikki, "The Young and the Restless")
Maywood	**Robert S. Woods** (Bo, "One Life to Live")
Oakland	**Peter Hansen** (Lee, "General Hospital")
Pasadena	**Kate Linder** (Esther, "The Young and the Restless")
San Diego	**John Castellanos** (John, "The Young and the Restless")
	Michael Damian (Danny, "The Young and the Restless")

San Francisco	**Ricky Paull Goldin** (Dean, "Another World")
	Jay Hammer (Fletcher, "Guiding Light")
San Jose	**Michael Swan** (Duncan, "As the World Turns")
Santa Monica	**Michael Sabatino** (Lawrence, "Days of Our Lives")
	Melissa Hayden (Bridget, "Guiding Light")
	Scott Reeves (Ryan, "The Young and the Restless")
Stockton	**Robert Tyler** (Trucker, "Loving")
Taft	**Jeanne Cooper** (Katherine, "The Young and the Restless")
Ventura	**John McCook** (Eric, "The Bold and the Beautiful")
Unknown	**Schae Harrison** (Darla, "The Bold and the Beautiful")
	Camille Cooper (Nikki, "General Hospital")
	Shell Danielson (ex-Dominique, "General Hospital")

COLORADO

Garrett Ridge	**Patrick Tovatt** (Cal, "As the World Turns")
Gunnison	**Patricia Elliott** (Renee, "One Life to Live")

CONNECTICUT

New Haven	**Mia Korf** (Blair, "One Life to Live")
Unknown	**Chris Bruno** (Dennis, "Another World")
	Paul Michael Valley (Ryan, "Another World")

DELAWARE

Wilmington	**Kathleen Widdoes** (Emma, "As the World Turns")

FLORIDA

Fort Lauderdale	**Chris Robinson** (Jack, "The Bold and the Beautiful")

Lake Worth	**Deidre Hall** (Marlena, "Days of Our Lives")
Miami	**Traci Mittendorf** (Carrie, "Days of Our Lives")
	David Wallace (Tom, "General Hospital")
	Fiona Hutchison (Lily, "Guiding Light")
Tampa	**Nathan Purdee** (Hank, "One Life to Live")

GEORGIA

Albany	**Amelia Marshall** (Gilly, "Guiding Light")
Atlanta	**Bobbie Eakes** (Macy, "The Bold and the Beautiful")
	William Wintersole (Mitchell, "The Young and the Restless")

ILLINOIS

Chicago	**Tonya Pinkins** (Livia, "All My Children")
	Victoria Wyndham (Rachel, "Another World")
	Ed Fry (Larry, "As the World Turns")
	Darlene Conley (Sally, "The Bold and the Beautiful")
	John Reilly (Sean, "General Hospital")
	John J. York (Mac, "General Hospital")
	Lauralee Bell (Cricket, "The Young and the Restless")
	Laura Bryan Birn (Lynne, "The Young and the Restless")
	Carolyn Conwell (Mary, "The Young and the Restless")
Highland Park	**Jim Storm** (Bill, "The Bold and the Beautiful")
Hinsdale	**Heather Tom** (Victoria, "The Young and the Restless")
Melvin	**Nada Rowand** (Kate, "Loving")
Moline	**Heather Rattray** (Lily, "As the World Turns")

Park Forest	**Mark Derwin** (A.C., "Guiding Light")
Woodstock	**Quinn Redeker** (Rex, "The Young and the Restless")
Unknown	**Colleen Zenk-Pinter** (Barbara, "As the World Turns")

INDIANA
Columbus	**Brian Green** (Brian, "All My Children")
Elwood	**David Canary** (Adam/Stuart, "All My Children")
Ft. Wayne	**Julia Barr** (Brooke, "All My Children")
	Drake Hogestyn (John, "Days of Our Lives")
Indianapolis	**Steve Burton** (Jason, "General Hospital")
South Bend	**John Clarke** (Mickey, "Days of Our Lives")

IOWA
Dakorah	**Mark Pinter** (Grant, "Another World")
Davenport	**Matt Ashford** (Jack, "Days of Our Lives")
Monticello	**Ellen Dolan** (ex-Margo, "As the World Turns")
Sioux City	**Macdonald Carey** (Tom, "Days of Our Lives")
	Sharon Farrell (Flo, "The Young and the Restless")
Waterloo	**Kelly Garrison** (Hillary, "The Young and the Restless")

KANSAS
| Wichita | **Robert Kelker-Kelly** (Bo, "Days of Our Lives") |

KENTUCKY
| Hazard | **Rebecca Gayheart** (Hannah, "Loving") |

LOUISIANA
| Baton Rouge | **Louis Edmunds** (Langley, "All My Children") |
| Natchitoches | **Vince Williams** (Hampton, |

"Guiding Light")

West Monroe   **Monti Sharp** (David, "Guiding Light")

Unknown   **Kimberly McCullough** (Robin, "General Hospital")

MAINE
Portland   **Victoria Rowell** (Drucilla, "The Young and the Restless")

MARYLAND
Baltimore   **Noelle Beck** (Trisha, "Loving")
Christine Tudor-Newman (Gwyneth, "Loving")

Silver Springs   **Crystal Chappell** (Carly, "Days of Our Lives")

Unknown   **Laura Sisk** (Allison, "Loving")
Tonja Walker (Alex, "One Life to Live")

MASSACHUSETTS
Boston   **Stephen Schnetzer** (Cass, "Another World")
Scott Defreitas (Andy, "As the World Turns")
Norma Connolly (Ruby, "General Hospital")

Brookline   **Laura Bonarrigo** (Cassie, "One Life to Live")

Chelsea   **Jerry Douglas** (John, "The Young and the Restless")

Lawrence   **Ray MacDonnell** (Dr. Joe, "All My Children")

Revere   **Cady McLain** (Dixie, "All My Children")

Unknown   **Don Frabotta** (Dave, "Days of Our Lives")

MICHIGAN
Detroit   **Michael Tylo** (Blade, "The Young and the Restless")

Grand Rapids   **Richard Shoberg** (Tom, "All My Children")
Jess Walton (Jill, "The Young and the Restless")

MINNESOTA

St. Paul	**Larry Gates** (H.B., "Guiding Light")
Unknown	**Jill Larson** (Opal, "All My Children")

MISSOURI

Independence	**Daniel McVicar** (Clarke, "The Bold and the Beautiful")
Kansas City	**Lisa Brown** (Iva, "As the World Turns")
	Leslie Charleson (Monica, "General Hospital")
St. Joseph	**Ruth Warrick** (Phoebe, "All My Children")
St. Louis	**Michael Nader** (Dimitri, "All My Children")
	Stephanie Williams (Simone, "General Hospital")

MONTANA

Billings	**Wallace Kurth** (Ned, "General Hospital")

NEBRASKA

Unknown	**Crystal Carson** (Julia, "General Hospital")

NEW JERSEY

Browns Mills	**Jon Hensley** (Holden, "As the World Turns")
Cape May	**Kelly Ripa** (Hayley, "All My Children")
Eatontown	**Melissa Reeves** (Jennifer, "Days of Our Lives")
Englewood	**Jacklyn Zeman** (Bobbie, "General Hospital")
Hillside	**Jean Carol** (Nadine, "Guiding Light")
Hoboken	**William Roerick** (Henry, "Guiding Light")
New Brunswick	**Phyllis Lyons** (Arlene, "All My Children")
Princeton	**Kathryn Hays** (Kim, "As the World Turns")
Ridgewood	**Bryan Buffinton** (Billy, "Guiding Light")

NEW YORK

Albany	**Yvonne Perry** (Rosanna, "As the World Turns")
Amsterdam	**Jessica Collins** (Dinah Lee, "Loving")
Bronxville	**Mary Fickett** (Ruth, "All My Children")
	Anne Sward (Lyla, "As the World Turns")
	Tina Sloan (Lillian, "Guiding Light")
Cross River	**Joseph Breen** (Scott, "As the World Turns")
Long Island	**Phil Carey** (Asa, "One Life to Live")
	Tricia Cast (Nina, "The Young and the Restless")
New York City	**John Callahan** (Edmund, "All My Children")
	Season Hubley (Angelique, "All My Children")
	Susan Lucci (Erica, "All My Children")
	Dondre Whitfield (Terrence, "All My Children")
	Constance Ford (Ada, "Another World")
	Kaitlin Hopkins (Kelsey, "Another World")
	Patricia Bruder (Ellen, "As the World Turns")
	Don Hastings (Bob, "As the World Turns")
	Elizabeth Hubbard (Lucinda, "As the World Turns")
	Tom Wiggin (Kirk, "As the World Turns")
	Colleen Dion (Felicia, "The Bold and the Beautiful")
	Michael Fox (Saul, "The Bold and the Beautiful")
	Jeff Trachta (Thorne, "The Bold and the Beautiful")
	Peggy McCay (Caroline, "Days of Our Lives")
	Stuart Damon (Alan, "General Hospital")

Michael Lynch (Connor, "General Hospital")
Kin Shriner (Scott, "General Hospital")
Beth Ehlers (Harley, "Guiding Light")
Rick Hearst (Alan-Michael, "Guiding Light")
Vincent Irizarry (Nick, "Guiding Light")
Maeve Kinkead (Vanessa, "Guiding Light")
Peter Simon (Ed, "Guiding Light")
Nia Long (Kat, "Guiding Light")
Bernie Barrow (Louie, "Loving")
Richard Cox (Gifford, "Loving")
Larkin Malloy (Clay, "Loving")
Lauren-Marie Taylor (Stacey, "Loving")
Chris Cousins (Cain, "One Life to Live")
Chris McKenna (Joey, "One Life to Live")
Randy Brooks (Nathan, "The Young and the Restless")
Don Diamont (Brad, "The Young and the Restless")
Kristoff St. John (Neil, "The Young and the Restless")

Rochester   **Jordan Clarke** (Billy, "Guiding Light")

Troy   **Russell Todd** (Jamie, "Another World")

Valley Stream   **Peter Barton** (Scott, "The Young and the Restless")

NORTH CAROLINA

Ashville   **Eileen Fulton** (Lisa, "As the World Turns")

Fort Bragg   **Christian LeBlanc** (Michael, "The Young and the Restless")

Rocky Point   **Maureen Garrett** (Holly, "Guiding Light")

NORTH DAKOTA
Grafton   **Clint Ritchie** (Clint, "One Life to Live")

OHIO
Akron   **Frank Dicopoulos** (Frank, "Guiding Light")

Melina Kanakaredes (Eleni, "Guiding Light")

Cincinnati   **Marie Masters** (Susan, "As the World Turns")

Mark Brettschneider (Jason, "One Life to Live")

Columbus   **Richard Biggs** (Marcus, "Days of Our Lives")

Plainesville   **Shell Kepler** (Amy, "General Hospital")

OKLAHOMA
Oklahoma City   **Frances Heflin** (Mona, "All My Children")

Unknown   **Renee Props** (Ellie, "As the World Turns")

OREGON
Portland   **Rachel Ames** (Audrey, "General Hospital")

PENNSYLVANIA
Philadelphia   **Lisa Peluso** (Ava, "Loving")

Pittsburgh   **Tamara Tunie** (Jessica, "As the World Turns")

Sewickly   **Hillary Edson** (Eve, "Guiding Light")

West Grove   **Scott Holmes** (Tom, "As the World Turns")

Unknown   **Matt Crane** (Matthew, "Another World")

Sandi Reinhardt (Amanda, "Another World")

Frank Runyan (Simon, "General Hospital")

RHODE ISLAND
Providence   **James Kiberd** (Trevor, "All My Children")

David Hedison (Spencer, "Another World")

SOUTH CAROLINA

Lynn Herring (Lury, "General Hospital")

SOUTH DAKOTA
Rapid City   **Beth Maitland** (Traci, "The Young and the Restless")

Sioux Falls   **Jerry verDorn** (Ross, "Guiding Light")

TENNESSEE
Lebanon   **Sharon Wyatt** (Tiffany, "General Hospital")

TEXAS
Camp Springs   **Brad Maule** (Tony, "General Hospital")

Fort Worth   **Hunter Tylo** (Taylor, "The Bold and the Beautiful")

Lubbock   **Helen Wagner** (Nancy, "As the World Turns")

Waco   **Greg Watkins** (Evan, "As the World Turns")

Wichita Falls   **Frances Reid** (Alice, "Days of Our Lives")

UTAH
Coalville   **Tony Geary** (Bill, "General Hospital")

VIRGINIA
Col. Heights   **Suzanne Rogers** (Maggie, "Days of Our Lives")

WASHINGTON, D.C.

Judson Mills (Hutch, "As the World Turns")

Veronica Redd Forrest (Mamie, "The Young and the Restless")

WEST VIRGINIA

Allyson Rice Taylor (Connor, "As the World Turns")

Patty Weaver (Gina, "The Young and the Restless")

WISCONSIN
Milwaukee

Susan Keith (Shana, "Loving")

Foreign-Born Soap Stars

*W*hile most of our soap stars are domestic products, the following were born in foreign lands.

AUSTRALIA
Carmen Duncan (Iris, "Another World")
Julian McMahon (Ian, "Another World")

AUSTRIA
Hayley Barr (Courtney, "As the World Turns")

CANADA
Andrew Jackson (Stephen, "All My Children")
Jean LeClerc (Jeremy, "Loving")
Linda Thorson (Julia, "One Life to Live")
Beau Kazer (Brock, "The Young and the Restless")
Susan Haskell (Marty, "One Life to Live")
Ingrid Rogers (Taylor, "All My Children")
Daniel Pilon (ex-Gavin, "Days of Our Lives")

CRETE
John Aniston (Victor, "Days of Our Lives")

CUBA
Peter Bergman (Jack, "The Young and the Restless")

ENGLAND
Charles Shaughnessy (Shane, "Days of Our Lives")
Anna Lee (Lila, "General Hospital")
Tonya Lee Williams (Olivia, "The Young and the Restless")
Michael Evans (Douglas, "The Young and the Restless")

FRANCE
Ellen Parker (Maureen, "Guiding Light")
Robert Clary (Pierre, "The Bold and the Beautiful")

GERMANY
Eric Braeden (Victor, "The Young and the Restless")
Tracey Bregman-Recht (Lauren, "The Young and the Restless")

ICELAND
Maria Ellingsen (ex-Katrina, "Santa Barbara")

ISRAEL
Steve Bond (ex-Jimmy Lee, "General Hospital," ex-Mack, "Santa Barbara")

ITALY
Antonio Sabato, Jr. (Jagger, "General Hospital")
Paolo Seganti (Damian Grimaldi, "As the World Turns")

MEXICO
Margarita Cordova (ex-Rosa, "Santa Barbara")

RUSSIA
Alla Korot (Jenna, "Another World")

SCOTLAND
Eileen Herlie (Myrtle, "All My Children")

THAILAND
Jocelyn Seagrave (Julie, "Guiding Light")

Beauty Queens

*G*iven the importance of beauty and glamour on day-time serials, it's no wonder that many soap opera stars hold crowns won in beauty competitions. Here are some of those "queens."

Teresa Blake (Gloria, "All My Children")-Hawaiian Tropic Bikini/Modelling Contest winner

Laura Bonarrigo (Cassie, "One Life to Live")-Miss Teenage Maine

Kimberlin Brown (Sheila, "The Bold and the Beautiful" & "The Young and the Restless")-Miss La Mesa; Miss California

Jessica Collins (Dinah Lee, "Loving")-Miss Teen New York; First runner-up, Miss Teen U.S.A.

Bobbie Eakes (Macy, "The Bold and the Beautiful")-Miss Georgia Teen; Miss Georgia

Deidre Hall (Marlena, "Days of Our Lives")-Miss Junior Orange Bowl

Laura Herring (ex-Carla, "General Hospital")-Miss U.S.A., 1985

Lynn Herring (Lucy, "General Hospital")-Miss Virginia, 1977; Miss U.S.A. runner-up, 1978

Melina Kanakaredes (Eleni, "Guiding Light")-First runner-up, Miss Ohio, 1977

Alla Korot (Jenna, "Another World")-Miss California Teen

Teri Ann Linn (ex-Kristen, "The Bold and the Beautiful")-Miss Hawaii U.S.A.

Devon Pierce (ex-Diane, "The Young and the Restless")-Miss Teen USA

Sandra Reinhardt (ex-Amanda, "Another World")-Second runner-up, Miss Teen All American; Miss Pennsylvania in Miss U.S.A. Pageant

Tonja Walker (Alex, "One Life to Live")-Miss Maryland in Miss U.S.A. Pageant; Miss Teen All American

Star Athletes

*I*t takes a lot of stamina to be a soap star—especially to survive some of those love scenes! Here are some prominent daytime performers who are or were top athletes.

The athletic Jack Wagner was one of soap's most romantic leading men as Frisco Jones on "General Hospital."

John Beradino (Dr. Steve Hardy, "General Hospital")- Former major league baseball player who won 1948 World Series as a member of the Cleveland Indians

Steve Bond (ex-Matt, "Santa Barbara")-Professional rodeo cowboy

Philip Brown (Buck, "Loving")-Semi-pro soccer player

David Canary (Adam/Stuart, "All My Children")-Played college football on scholarship at the University of Cincinnati

Macdonald Carey (Tom, "Days of Our Lives")-Brown belt in karate for over 40 years and winner of the U.S. Karate Association Longevity Award

Phil Carey (Asa, "One Life to Live")-Accomplished equestrian who has performed in many rodeos

Frank Dicopoulos (Frank, "Guiding Light")-NCAA Division III high hurdles record holder

Drake Hogestyn (John, "Days of Our Lives")-Won baseball scholarship to the University of South Florida

Teri Ann Linn (ex-Kristen, "The Bold and the Beautiful")-Nationally ranked junior tennis player; won mother-daughter division of U.S. Open

Quinn Redeker (Rex, "The Young and the Restless")-All-American high school football player

Clint Ritchie (Clint, "One Life to Live")-Competes in long-distance endurance horse races

Michael Sabatino (Lawrence, "Days of Our Lives") Three-time NCAA pole vault champion

Richard Shoberg (Tom, "All My Children")-Football player at Albion College

Lauren-Marie Taylor (Stacey, "Loving")-Top female runner who won the Media Challenge race in Central Park

Jack Wagner (ex-Frisco, "General Hospital")-Scratch golfer and winner of the AT&T Pro-Am at Pebble Beach

Vince Williams (Hamp, "Guiding Light")-All-American quarter-miler in college track and field

Musicians

*M*any soap stars are multi-talented performers. The following have had distinguished musical careers in addition to their daytime television work.

Randy Brooks (Nathan, "The Young and the Restless")-Spent 5 years singing with the Honolulu Symphony Orchestra

Michael Damian (Danny, "The Young and the Restless")-Rock star who recently starred in a touring production of Andrew Lloyd Webber's "Joseph and the Amazing Technicolor Dreamcoat"

Morgan Englund (Dylan, "Guiding Light")-Formed rock band called 2C with Rick Hearst

Eileen Fulton (Lisa, "As the World Turns")-Singer whose most recent album is *The First Kiss*

Rick Hearst (Alan-Michael, "Guiding Light")-Plays in rock band 2C with Morgan Englund

Scott Holmes (Tom, "As the World Turns")-Piano player who performs in nightclubs with his band

Thyme Lewis (Jonah, "Days of Our Lives")-Plays sax; opened for New Kids on the Block in London

Ronn Moss (Ridge, "The Bold and the Beautiful")-His band, Player, had the No. 1 single, "Baby Come Back"

Valarie Pettiford (Sheila, "One Life to Live")-Has sung with rock groups "Raw Silk" and "Stingers"

Tonya Pinkins (Livia, "All My Children")-Recording artist and cabaret singer

Michael Sabatino (ex-Lawrence, "Days of Our Lives")-Two-time winner, Western State Accordion Festival

Rex Smith (Darryl, "As the World Turns")-Singer who has recorded six albums, including the platinum hit "Sooner or Later." He's also starred in several Broadway musicals

Jim Storm (Bill, "The Bold and the Beautiful")-Recorded country-western album *Dust Bowl*

Anne Sward (Lyla, "As the World Turns")-Singer who performs her own nightclub act

Tonya Walker (Alex, "One Life to Live")-Toured as a singer with "The Hoyt Axton Show"

Michael Weatherly (Cooper, "Loving")-Cabaret singer who played New York City clubs under the name Michael Mannion (Mannion's his middle name)

Patty Weaver (Gina, "The Young and the Restless")-Singer who toured with several bands and recorded four albums, including *Patty Weaver*

Vince Williams (Hampton, "Guiding Light")-His band, The Company of One, plays a unique blend of Latin, Haitian and African rhythms they call "Afrazz"

Hobbies

*M*any of us find our avocations more interesting than our vocations. Here are the unusual personal pastimes of some soap stars.

Wesley Addy (ex-Cabot, "Loving")-Bee-keeping

Christopher Cousins (Cain, "One Life to Live")-Accomplished painter and wood carver

Matt Crane (Matthew, "Another World")-Sculpture

Patricia Elliott (Renee, "One Life to Live")-Swimming with dolphins

Tom Eplin (Jake, "Another World")-Licensed pilot

Susan Flannery (Stephanie, "The Bold and the Beautiful")-Licensed pilot

Wortham Krimmer (Andrew, "One Life to Live")-Runs "Intellimation," a company that develops videos, video disks, and CD-ROMs for educational use

Nathan Purdee (Hank, "One Life to Live")-Accomplished artist who has sold work professionally

Chris Robinson (Jack, "The Bold and the Beautiful")-Owns several art galleries

Peter Simon (Ed, "Guiding Light")-Playwright whose works include the off-Broadway play, "In Case of Accident"

Jim Storm (Bill, "The Bold and the Beautiful")-Publishes his own newspaper, *The Garment Trader*

Michael Storm (Larry, "One Life to Live")-Raises almost 200 varieties of orchids

Christopher Templeton (Carol, "The Young and the Restless")-With her brother, owns a t-shirt business called "The T's"

Stephanie Williams (Simone, "General Hospital")-Choreographer; has her own production company

Karen Witter (Tina, "One Life to Live")-Trapeze artist

Victoria Wyndham (Rachel, "Another World")-Has managed several rock bands

Jacklyn Zeman (Bobbie, "General Hospital")-Author of the book *Beauty on the Go*

Odd Jobs

hen starting out, most actors are unable to support themselves on the wages they earn from their craft. Many future stars had to take other jobs to keep the wolf from the door. Working in a restaurant or driving a cab are two of the most common jobs found on actors' resumes. The following are some of the more unusual lines of work soap stars have taken.

Eric Braeden (Victor, "The Young and the Restless")- German-English translator

Mark Brettschneider (Jason, "One Life to Life")-Doorman at New York's Morgan Hotel

John Callahan (Edmund, "All My Children")-Nightclub manager

Frank Dicopoulos (Frank, "Guiding Light")-Tire store manager

Ed Fry (Larry, "Another World")-Butcher

Eileen Fulton (Lisa, "As the World Turns")-Selling hats at Macy's

Wortham Krimmer (Andrew, "One Life to Live")-Worked at the Environmental Protection Agency

Joe Lando (ex-Jake, "One Life to Live")-Chef

Kate Linder (Esther, "The Young and the Restless")- Stewardess for Transamerica Airlines

Amelia Marshall (Gilly, "Guiding Light")-Telephone repair supervisor

Marie Masters (Susan, "As the World Turns")-Worked on city desk of *Women's Wear Daily*

Nathan Purdee (Hank, "One Life to Live")-Mental health counselor

Quinn Redeker (Rex, "The Young and the Restless")-Commercial fisherman; paint mixer; auxiliary police officer

John Reilly (Sean, "General Hospital")-Account executive for packaging firm

Suzanne Rogers (Maggie, "Days of Our Lives")-Radio City Music Hall Rockette

Laura Sisk (Allison, "Loving")-Pumped gas at her father's station

Robert Tyler (Trucker, "Loving")-Operating backstage elevator at Radio City Music Hall

Walt Willey (Jackson, "All My Children")-Director of sales for a men's clothing company

Karen Witter (Tina, "One Life to Live")-Stewardess on a hot air balloon

The Most Durable Stars

*C*haracters on soap operas come and go with dazzling speed these days as writers attempt to engage viewers with new plots and story twists. The turnover rate is accentuated by the proliferation of opportunities created by television and film. Nevertheless, a few core performers have survived more than ten years in their current roles. Taking first place as soap's most durable star is Helen Wagner of "As the World Turns," who spoke the very first line ("Good morning, dear") on the very first telecast of that soap on April 2, 1956. The following is a compilation of soap's most durable actors, including the years in which they debuted on their shows.

1956- **Helen Wagner** (Nancy McClosky, "As the World Turns")

As Alice Horton, Francis Reid is a soap veteran.

1960- **Patricia Bruder** (Ellen Lowell Stewart, "As the World Turns")
      Eileen Fulton (Lisa McColl, "As the World Turns")
      Don Hastings (Bob Hughes, "As the World Turns")

1963- **John Beradino** (Dr. Steve Hardy, "General Hospital")

1964- **Rachel Ames** (Audrey Hardy, "General Hospital")

1965- **Macdonald Carey** (Dr. Tom Horton, "Days of Our Lives")
      Peter Hansen (Lee Baldwin, "General Hospital")

1968- **Marie Masters** (Dr. Susan Steward McDermott, "As the World Turns")

1969- **Larry Bryggman** (Dr. John Dixon, "As the World Turns")

1970- **Susan Lucci** (Erica Kane, "All My Children")
      Ruth Warrick (Phoebe Wallingford, "All My Children")
      Ray MacDonnell (Dr. Joe Martin, "All My Children")
      Mary Fickett (Ruth Martin, "All My Children")
      Frances Heflin (Mona Tyler, "All My Children")

1971- **Erika Slezak** (Viki Lord Buchanan, "One Life to Live")
      Michael Zaslow (Roger Thorpe, "Guiding Light")

1972- **Kathryn Hays** (Kim Hughes, "As the World Turns")
      Victoria Wyndham (Rachel Cory, "Another World")

1973- **Jeanne Cooper** (Katherine Chancellor Sterling, "The Young and the Restless")

1974- **Irene Dailey** (Liz Matthews, "Another World")

Don Frabotta (Dave, "Days of Our Lives")

1976- **Julia Barr** (Brooke English, "All My Children")

Deidre Hall (Dr. Marlena Evans Brady, "Days of Our Lives")

1977- **Leslie Charleson** (Monica Quartermaine, "General Hospital")

Stuart Damon (Dr. Alan Quartermaine, "General Hospital")

Richard Shoberg (Tom Cudahy, "All My Children")

Kin Shriner (Scott Baldwin, "General Hospital")

Jacklyn Zeman (Bobbie Spencer, "General Hospital")

1978- **Anna Lee** (Lila Quartermaine, "General Hospital")

1979- **Phil Carey** (Asa Buchanan, "One Life to Live")

Norma Connolly (Ruby Anderson, "General Hospital")

Doug Davidson (Paul Williams, "The Young and the Restless")

Louis Edmonds (Langley Wallingford, "All My Children")

Clint Ritchie (Clint Buchanan, "One Life to Live")

Robert S. Woods (Bo Buchanan, "One Life to Live")

James Mitchell (Palmer Cortlandt, "All My Children")

Jerry verDorn (Ross Marler, "Guiding Light")

1980- **Eric Braeden** (Victor Newman, "The Young and the Restless")

Maeve Kinkead (Vanessa Lewis, "Guiding Light")

William Roerick (Henry Chamberlain, "Guiding Light")

Anne Sward (Lyla Perretti, "As the World Turns")

1981- **Michael Damian** (Danny Romalotti, "The Young and the Restless")

Peter Simon (Dr. Ed Bauer, "Guiding Light")

Sharon Wyatt (Tiffany Hill Donely, "General Hospital")

1982- **Christopher Templeton** (Carol Evans, "The Young and the Restless")

1983- **Lauralee Bell** (Cricket Blair Romalotti, "The Young and the Restless")

David Canary (Adam/Stuart Chandler, "All My Children")

Linda Dano (Felicia Gallant, "Another World")

Tina Sloan (Lillian Raines, "Guiding Light")

Lauren-Marie Taylor (Stacey Donovan, "Loving")

The 20 Hottest Young Stars

Steve Burton	Jason, "General Hospital"
Alicia Coppola	Lorna, "Another World"
Kirk Geiger	Kevin, "One Life to Live"
Ricky Paull Goldin	Dean, "Another World"
Susan Haskell	Marty, "One Life to Live"
Alia Korot	Jenna, "Another World"
Nia Long	Kat, "Guiding Light"
Vanessa Marcil	Brenda, "General Hospital"
Judson Mills	Hutch, "As the World Turns"
Patrick Muldoon	Austin, "Days of Our Lives"
J. Eddie Peck	Cole, "The Young and the Restless"
Yvonne Perry	Rosanna, "As the World Turns"
Kelly Ripa	Hayley, "All My Children"
Antonio Sabato, Jr.	Jagger, "General Hospital"
Laura Sisk	Ally, "Loving"
Monti Sharp	David, "Guiding Light"
Allison Sweeney	Sami, "Days of Our Lives"
Heather Tom	Victoria, "The Young and the Restless"
Michael Weatherly	Cooper, "Loving"
Dondre Whitfield	Terrence, "All My Children"

Soap Kin

Do you know which soap stars are related to other famous people?

Robyn Bernard (Terry Brock, "General Hospital")-Sister of Crystal Bernard, star of prime time sitcom "Wings"
Ian Buchanan (ex-Duke, "General Hospital")-Descendent of poet Robert Burns
Kate Collins (ex-Natalie, "All My Children")-Daughter of Michael Collins, pilot of the spacecraft Columbia on the first moon landing

Jeanne Cooper (Kay, "The Young and the Restless")-Mother of Corbin Bernsen, star of "L.A. Law."

Christina Crawford (ex-Joann Kane, "The Secret Storm")-Daughter of Joan Crawford

Stephen Ford (ex-Andy Richards, "The Young and the Restless")-Son of President and Mrs. Gerald Ford

Kaitlin Hopkins (Kelsey, "Another World")-Daughter of Tony Award winner Shirley Knight

Katherine Kelly-Lang (Brooke, "The Bold and the Beautiful")-Her father, Keith Wegeman, played the Jolly Green Giant on television

Christopher Lawford (Charlie Brent, "All My Children")-Son of Peter Lawford and Pat Kennedy Lawford

Georgianne LePierre (Heather Webber, "General Hospital")-Sister of Cher

Judy Lewis (ex-Barbara Vining, "General Hospital")-Daughter of Loretta Young

Gregg Marx (ex-David Banning, "Days of Our Lives")-Grandson of Zeppo Marx, grandnephew of Groucho

Carrie Mitchum (Donna, "The Bold and the Beautiful")-Granddaughter of Robert Mitchum

Kristoff St. John (Neil, "The Young and the Restless")-Son of actor Charles St. John, who starred in the movie *Shaft*

Kin Shriner (Scott, "General Hospital")-Son of comedian Herb Shriner

Erika Slezak (Viki Lord Buchanan, "One Life to Live"-Daughter of Walter Slezak

Ethan Wayne (ex-Storm, "The Bold and the Beautiful")-Son of John Wayne

Real-Life Marriages

*P*erhaps it is because they spend so much time on the set that soap opera actors and actresses often have off-camera love affairs. Few actually make a long-term commitment; but here are the ones who have tied the knot.

Eden Atwood (ex-Staige, "Loving") and **Paul Michael Valley** (Ryan, "Another World")

Leslie Charleson (Monica, "General Hospital") and **Josh Taylor** (ex-Chris, "Days of Our Lives")

Lynn Herring (Lucy, "General Hospital") and **Wayne Northrop** (Roman, "Days of Our Lives")

Susan Keith (Shana, "Loving") and **James Kiberd** (Trevor, "All My Children")

Catherine Hickland (Tess, "Loving") and **Michael Knight** (Tad, "All My Children")

Melissa Reeves (Jennifer, "Days of our Lives") and **Scott Reeves** (Ryan, "The Young and the Restless")

Courtney Sherman (Lynn, "As the World Turns") and **Peter Simon** (Ed, "Guiding Light")

Erika Slezak (Viki, "One Life to Live") and **Brian Davies** (ex-Dick, "All My Children")

Susan Marie Synder (Julie, "As the World Turns") and **Peter Boynton** (ex-Tonio, "As the World Turns")

Hunter Tylo (Taylor, "The Bold and the Beautiful") and **Michael Tylo** (Blade, "The Young and the Restless")

Colleen Zenk-Pinter (Barbara, "As the World Turns") and **Mark Pinter** (Grant, "Another World")

Christiaan Torrez (ex-Stephanie, "One Life to Live") and **Judson Mills** (Hutch, "As the World Turns")

Multi-Media Stars

Many soap opera stars have achieved significant success in theater, film, prime time television, and other areas of the arts. The following is a list of soap opera actors who've won major awards in those areas:

Jed Allan (ex-C.C. Capwell, "Santa Barbara")-Emmy nomination for "Adam-12"

Richard Backus (ex-Carle, "As the World Turns")-Theater World Award and Variety Critics Award for role in the play, "Promenade All"

Scott Thompson Baker (ex-Connor, "The Bold and the Beautiful")-"Star Search" $100,000 Grand Prize Winner, Acting Category

Maggie Burke (Audrey, "As the World Turns")-Author of best-selling book, *An Informed Decision*

Marilyn Chris (Wanda, "One Life to Live")-Obie and Drama Desk Awards for her role in the off-Broadway play "Kaddish"

Irene Dailey (Liz, "Another World")-1964 Drama Critics Award as Best Actress for her role in "The Subject Was Roses"

Patricia Elliott (Renee, "One Life to Live")-Tony Award, Theater World Award and Drama Desk Award for her role in "A Little Night Music"

Susan Flannery (Stephanie, "The Bold and the Beautiful")-Golden Globe Award for her role in the film, "The Towering Inferno"

Dee Hoty (Karen, "As the World Turns")-Tony nomination for her role in "The Will Rogers Follies"

Elizabeth Hubbard (Lucinda, "As the World Turns")-Prime time Emmy for her role in the NBC special, "First Ladies' Diaries"

Peggy McCay (Caroline, "Days of Our Lives")-Prime time Emmy Award, Best Actress, for her guest-starring performance in "The Trials of Rosie O'Neil" 1987

Quinn Redeker (Rex, "The Young and the Restless")-Nominated for an Academy Award for Best Screenplay for "The Deer Hunter"

Rex Smith (Darryl, "As the World Turns")-Theater Award and Tony nomination for his role in "Pirates of Penzance"

Kathleen Widdoes (Emma, "As the World Turns")-Two Obie Awards; Tony nomination for "Much Ado About Nothing"

Celebrities With Roles On Soaps

*J*ust as radio serials often provided a training ground for stage actors, daytime television serials have sent dozens of alumni on to stardom on prime time television and in movies. Famous stars like Warren Beatty and Dustin Hoffman picked up vital paychecks by working on soaps early in their careers. Other performers, such as Judith Light, spent years as daytime stars before becoming prime time stars. The following is a list of celebrities and the roles and shows in which they were seen on daytime TV.

Dame Judith Anderson—Minx Lockridge, "Santa Barbara"
Richard Dean Anderson—Dr. Jeff Webber, "General Hospital"
Dana Andrews—Thomas Boswell, "Bright Promise"
Kevin Bacon—Tim Werner, "Guiding Light"

"All My Children's" most famous fan is Carol Burnett, who once appeared on the soap as Verla Grubbs.

Warren Beatty—"Love of Life"
Bonnie Bedelia—Sandy Porter, "Love of Life"
Tom Berenger—Timmy Siegel, "One Life to Live"
Corbin Bernsen—Kenny Graham, "Ryan's Hope"
David Birney—Mark Elliott, "Love Is a Many Splendored Thing"
Taurean Blackque—Henry Marshall, "Generations"
Linda Blair—"Hidden Faces"
Carol Burnett—Verla Grubbs, "All My Children"
Ellen Burstyn—Dr. Kate Bartok, "The Doctors"
Timothy Busfield—"All My Children"
Rory Calhoun—Judge Judson Tyler, "Capitol"
Dyan Cannon—"For Better or Worse" and Lisa Crowder, "Full Circle"
Dixie Carter—Olivia "Brandy" Henderson, "The Edge of Night"
Nell Carter—Ethel Green, "Ryan's Hope"
Peggy Cass—Sweeney, "The Doctors"
Shaun Cassidy—Dusty Walker, "General Hospital"
Jill Clayburgh—Grace Bolton, "Search for Tomorrow"
James Coco—"Search for Tomorrow"
Dabney Coleman—Dr. Tracy Brown, "Bright Promise"

John Cullum,—"The Edge of Night" and Artie Duncan, "One Life to Live"
Blythe Danner—"Guiding Light"
Ted Danson—Tim Conway, "Somerset"
Sammy Davis, Jr.—Chip, "One Life to Live"
Ruby Dee—Martha Frazier, "Guiding Light"
Dana Delany—"As the World Turns"
Sandy Dennis—Alice Holden, "Guiding Light"
Troy Donahue—Keefer, "The Secret Storm"
Julia Duffy—Penny Davis, "The Doctors"
Olympia Dukakis—Barbara Moreno, "Search for Tomorrow"
Patty Duke—"Kitty Foyle" and Ellen Williams Dennis, "A Brighter Day"
Charles Durning—Lt. Gil McGowan, "Another World"
Christine Ebersole—Maxie McDermont, "One Life to Live"
Morgan Fairchild—Jennifer Phillips, "Search for Tomorrow"
Mike Farrell—Scott Banning, "Days of Our Lives"
Mary Frann—Amanda Peters, "Days of Our Lives"
Morgan Freeman—Roy Bingham, "Another World"

One of young Christian Slater's first roles was as D.J. LaSalle on "Ryan's Hope."

Paul Michael Glaser—Jonas Falk, "Love of Life"

Farley Granger—Earl Mitchell, "As the World Turns"

Lee Grant—Rose Peabody, "Search for Tomorrow"

Charles Grodin—Matt Crane, "The Young Marrieds"

Larry Hagman—Ed Gibson, "The Edge of Night"

Mark Hamill—Kent Murray, "General Hospital"

David Hasselhoff—Bill Foster, "The Young and the Restless"

Wings Hauser—Greg Foster, "The Young and the Restless"

Marg Helgenberger—Siobhan Ryan, "Ryan's Hope"

Catherine Hicks—Dr. Faith Coleridge, "Ryan's Hope"

Hal Holbrook—Grayling Dennis, "A Brighter Day"

Lauren Holly—Julie Chandler, "All My Children"

Celeste Holm—"The Edge of Night"

Robert Horton—Whit McCall, "As the World Turns"

Barnard Hughes—Dr. Bruce Banning, "Guiding Light"

Kim Hunter—Nola Madison, "The Edge of Night"

Kate Jackson—Daphne Harridge, "Dark Shadows"

James Earl Jones—Dr. Jim Frazier, "Guiding Light"

Tommy Lee Jones—Dr. Mark Toland, "One Life to Live"

Raul Julia—Miguel Garcia, "Love of Life"

Mary Page Keller—Amanda Kirkland, "Ryan's Hope"

Kevin Kline—Woody Reed, "Search for Tomorrow"

Ted Knight—"The Clear Horizon"

Don Knotts—Wilbur Peabody, "Search for Tomorrow"

Swoozie Kurtz—"As the World Turns"

Diane Ladd—Kitty Styles, "The Secret Storm"

Carol Lawrence—Angela Eckert, "General Hospital"

Jack Lemmon—"A Brighter Day"

Judith Light—Karen Martin, "One Life to Live"

Hal Linden—Larry Carter, "Search for Tomorrow"

Ray Liotta—Joey Perini, "Another World"

Cleavon Little—Captain Hancock, "Another World"

Tony LoBianco—"Hidden Faces"

George Maharis—Bud Gardner, "Search for Tomorrow"

A Martinez—Cruz Castillo, "Santa Barbara"

Marsha Mason—Judith Cole, "Love of Life"

Lee Meriweather—"The Clear Horizon"

Joana Miles—Linda Driscoll, "A Time for Us"

Donna Mills—Laura Donnelly, "Love Is a Many Splendored Thing"

Demi Moore—Jackie Templeton, "General Hospital"

Henry Morgan—"Search for Tomorrow"

Diana Muldaur—Ann Wicker, "The Secret Storm"

Luke Perry—Ned Bates, "Loving"

One of soap's most celebrated cameos was Elizabeth Taylor's appearance on "General Hospital" as the evil Helena Cassadine.

Regis Philbin—Malachy Malone, "Ryan's Hope"
Michelle Phillips—Ruby Ashford, "Search for Tomorrow"
Phylicia Rashad—Courtney Wright, "One Life to Live"
Christopher Reeve—Benno Harper, "Love of Life"
Eric Roberts—Ted Bancroft, "Another World"
Tony Roberts—Lee Pollock, "The Edge of Night"
Wayne Rogers—Slim Davis, "Search for Tomorrow"
Howard Rollins—Ed, "Another World"
Richard Roundtree—Dr. Daniel Rubins, "Generations"
Meg Ryan—Betsy Stewart Montgomery, "As the World Turns"
Susan Sarandon—Sarah, "Search for Tomorrow" and Patrice Kahlman, "A World Apart"
Roy Scheider—Bob Hill, "The Secret Storm"
Tom Selleck—Jed Andrews, "The Young and the Restless"
Jane Seymour—"Hat," and "Concerning Miss Marlowe"
Martin Sheen—"As the World Turns"
Ann Sheridan—Cathryn Corning, "Another World"
James Sikking—Dr. James Hobart, "General Hospital"
Christian Slater—D.J. LaSalle, "Ryan's Hope"

Sigourney Weaver starred as Avis Ryan on "Somerset."

Jimmy Smits—"All My Children"
Suzanne Somers—"All My Children"
John Stamos—Blackie Parrish, "General Hospital"
Frances Sternhagen—Mrs. Krakauer, "Love of Life" and Jesse Reddin, "The Secret Storm"
Elizabeth Taylor—Helena Cassidine, "General Hospital"
Richard Thomas—Chris Austin, "A Time for Us" and Tom Hughes, "As the World Turns"
Marisa Tomei—Marcy Thompson, "As the World Turns"
Daniel J. Travanti—"General Hospital"
Janine Turner—Laura Templeton, "General Hospital"
Cicely Tyson—Martha Frazier, "Guiding Light"
Blair Underwood—Bobby Blue, "One Life to Live"
Trish Van Devere—Meredith Lord, "One Life to Live" and Patti Barron, "Search for Tomorrow"
Mamie Van Doren—Mamie Van Doren, "General Hospital"
Joyce Van Patten—Janice Turner, "As the World Turns"
Sigourney Weaver—Avis Ryan, "Somerset"
Billy Dee Williams—Dr. Jim Frazier, "Guiding Light"
JoBeth Williams—Brandy Sheloo, "Guiding Light"

William Windom—"A Brighter Day"
Robin Wright—Kelly Capwell, "Santa Barbara"
Efrem Zimbalist, Jr.—Jim Gavin, "Concerning Miss Marlowe"

Weird Stuff

Marilyn Alex ("The Young and the Restless")-Alex spent over a year in a featured storyline without uttering an intelligible word. The reason: She played stroke victim Molly Carter, who could only communicate with facial expressions and garbled speech.

Millette Alexander ("The Edge of Night")-Alexander had the very unusual task of playing three separate roles on the soap—Gail Armstrong, a commercial artist; Laura Hillyer, who was killed in a car crash; and Julie Jamison, Laura's look-alike who showed up right after Laura's death.

Nicolas Coster-Coster's extensive soap resume includes playing the same character on two different soap operas not once, but twice in his career. He portrayed John Eldridge on "Our Private World" and "As the World Turns," and Robert Delaney on "Somerset" and "Another World."

Christopher Cousins ("One Life to Live")-Cousins is an actor who's very skilled at speaking with different dialects, and "One Life to Live's" producers took advantage of that talent when they had him appear in Llanview as British journalist Hudson King, then German film director Heinrich Kaiser, then professional gambler Humberto Calderon, and, finally, as American con man Cain Rogan.

Steve Fletcher (Hank, "Another World")-While he was appearing on "One Life to Live," Fletcher lost a bet to another actor. His payoff? He had to legally change his last name to Blizzard. The embarrassed actor was Steve Blizzard on the credits, on his driver's license and on his credit cards for several years before he finally declared the wager paid in full and legally changed his name back to Fletcher.

Velekka Gray ("The Young and the Restless")-Gray simultaneously portrayed Sharon Reaves and Ruby the manicurist, two characters who weren't related and weren't lookalikes.

Michael Knight ("All My Children")-Knight, who's one of daytime's highest paid actors as Tad Martin on "All My Children," married actress Catherine Hickland (Tess, "Loving") in 1992. Hickland's previous husband was former soap actor David Hasselhoff—who is best known for his role in the prime time series "Knight Rider" as Michael Knight.

Cady McClain ("All My Children")-McClain, who plays Dixie Cooney, landed in the *Guinness Book of World Records* at age nine when she and 499 others became the largest group ever to simultaneously perform the same tap dance routine.

Hunter Tylo ("The Bold and the Beautiful")-Tylo, who now plays Dr. Taylor Hayes, may confuse longtime fans of "All My Children." From 1985 to 1987, she was on that soap— but she was a blonde and was going under the name Deborah Morehart. After that role, she let her hair return to its natural, brown color. After she married Michael Tylo, who had been her costar on "All My Children," she changed her name to Hunter Tylo (Hunter is her real *last* name). Confused?

Soap Tragedies

Soap stars are real people, and sometimes real tragedies strike their lives.

Brenda Benet (Lee Dumonde, "Days of Our Lives")—Benet committed suicide in 1982.

Andrea Evans (ex-Tina, "One Life to Live")—On the CBS newsmagazine show "48 Hours," Evans revealed that she was forced to leave her major role on "One Life to Live" and go into seclusion because she was being stalked by an obsessed and dangerous male fan.

Richard Lawson (Lucas, "All My Children")—Lawson nearly lost his life when he was a passenger on a U.S.Air flight that skidded off an icy runway into the bay at New York's LaGuardia Airport in 1991. Bumped up to first class when recognized as a star, newspapers credited this move with saving his life. A tragedy narrowly averted!

Michael David Morrison (Caleb, "As the World Turns")— Morrison died of an overdose of alcohol, cocaine and opiates at age 33.

Patsy Pease (Ex-Kimberly, "Days of Our Lives")—Pease courageously came forward to admit that she had been physically, sexually and emotionally abused by her mother when she was a child.

Dack Rambo (ex-Grant, "Another World")—Rambo left the show when he was diagnosed with AIDS. This was the second tragedy in his family's life—his twin brother Dirk was killed by a drunk driver at age 25.

Leonard Stabb (Hart, "Guiding Light")—During the summer of 1993, this handsome actor crashed into a tree while hang gliding in upstate New York, ending up in a coma.

Robert S. Woods (Bo, "One Life to Live")—His twin son Dylan died at age one month.

Where To Write To Your Favorite Shows And Stars

Soap operas are anxious to hear what their viewers think about new characters, new storylines and other aspects of the show. Because the volume of fan mail is a reflection of their popularity, soap stars also enjoy receiving mail, and many answer every letter.

You can write to the producers, writers and stars of your favorite shows at the following addresses.

"All My Children"
ABC-TV
77 West 66th Street
New York, NY 10023

"Days of Our Lives"
NBC-TV
3000 West Alameda Avenue
Burbank, CA 91523

"Another World"
NBC-TV
30 Rockefeller Plaza
New York, NY 10112

"General Hospital"
ABC-TV
4151 Prospect Avenue
Hollywood, CA 90027

"As the World Turns"
CBS-TV
51 West 52nd St.
New York, NY 10019

"Guiding Light"
CBS-TV
51 West 52nd St.
New York, NY 10019

"The Bold and the Beautiful"
CBS-TV
7800 Beverly Boulevard
Los Angeles, CA 90036

"Loving"
ABC-TV
77 West 66th Street
New York, NY 10023

"One Life to Live"
ABC-TV
77 West 66th Street
New York, NY 10023

"The Young and the Restless"

CBS-TV
7800 Beverly Boulevard
Los Angeles, CA 90036

Or you can reach them through fan clubs...

"All My Children"

Friends of "All My Children"
c/o Kathy Hudson
132 Ragsdale Street
Kingsport, TN 15205

Julia Barr
Jill Larson
c/o Michaele Saint-Laurent
1410 York Avenue, Apt. 4D
New York, NY 10021

"Another World"

"Another World" Fan Club
c/o Mindi Schulman
1500 Hornell Loop
Apt. 10E
Brooklyn, NY 11239

Tom Eplin Fan Club
c/o Mindi Schulman
1500 Hornell Loop
Apt. 10E
Brooklyn, NY 11239

Ricky Paull Goldin Fan Club
c/o NBC-TV
75 Rockefeller Plaza
New York, NY 10112

Colleen Dion Fan Club
P.O. Box 46609
Los Angeles, CA 90046

"As the World Turns"

"As the World Turns" Fan Club
c/o Deanne Turco
212 Oriole Drive
Montgomery, NY 12549

Judson Mills Fan Club
c/o "As the World Turns"
CBS-TV
51 West 52nd St.
New York, NY 10019

"The Bold and the Beautiful"

"Bold & Beautiful" Fan Club
7800 Beverly Boulevard,
Suite 3371
Los Angeles, CA 90036

Kimberlin Brown Fan Club
c/o John & Joni Buck
"The Bold and the Beautiful"
7800 Beverly Boulevard,
Suite 3371
Los Angeles, CA 90036

Darlene Conley/Sally Spectra Gang
c/o Jodie Rissuto
9 Metcalf Street
Medford, MA 02155

Bobbie Eakes/Jeff Trachta Fan Club
c/o Jean Smith
"The Bold and the Beautiful"
7800 Beverly Boulevard,
Suite 3371
Los Angeles, CA 90036

Michael Fox Fan Club
Dan McVicar Fan Club
c/o Tommy Garrett
P.O. Box 215
New Canton, VA 23123

Katherine Kelly Lang Fan
Club
c/o Amy Farina
109 Hughes Street
East Haven, CT 06512

John McCook Fan Club
c/o Cathy Tomas
"The Bold and the
Beautiful"
7800 Beverly Boulevard,
Suite 3371
Los Angeles, CA 90036

Ronn Moss Fan Club
c/o Mackie Mann
"The Bold and the
Beautiful"
7800 Beverly Boulevard,
Suite 3371
Los Angeles, CA 90036

Hunter Tylo Fan Club
c/o Pat Freeman
P.O. Box 214
Lafayette, AL 36882

"Days of Our Lives"

National Days Fan Club
c/o Polly Hazen
424A Johnson Street
Sausalito, CA 94965

"Days of Our Lives" Fan
Club
NBC-TV
3000 West Alameda Avenue
Burbank, CA 91523

Louise Sorel Fan Club
c/o "Days of Our Lives"
NBC-TV
3000 West Alameda Avenue
Burbank, CA 91523

Matt Ashford Fan Club
c/o "Days of Our Lives"
NBC-TV
3000 West Alameda Avenue
Burbank, CA 91523

Drake Hogestyn Fan Club
c/o "Days of Our Lives"
NBC-TV
3000 West Alameda Avenue
Burbank, CA 91523

Deidre Hall Fan Club
c/o Evelyn Reynolds
9570 Apricot
Alta Loma, CA 91701

Wally Kurth & Judi Evans
Support Group
c/o Anne Whitesell &
Jerry D. Swink
5028 NW 60th Street
Oklahoma City, OK 73122

The Lakeside Assocation
An Organization of
Supporters
for Mary Beth Evans,
Stephen Nichols, and "Days"
37663 Charter Oaks Blvd.
Mt. Clemens, MI 48043

"General Hospital"

Fans of "General Hospital"
c/o Barb Williams
390 Blairwood Circle South
Lake Worth, FL 33467

Kristina Malandro Fan Club
P.O. Box 22625
Indianapolis, IN 46222

Leslie Charleson Fan Club
c/o Krista Dragna &
Kay Marrs
P.O. Box 1503
Covina, CA 91722

Wally Kurth Fan Club
Wally's Friends
P.O. Box 640
Merrick, NY 11566

Anna Lee Fan Club
Cathy Shapiro
c/o "General Hospital"
ABC-TV
4151 Prospect Avenue
Hollywood, CA 90027

Brad Maule Fan Club
c/o "General Hospital"
ABC-TV
4151 Prospect Avenue
Hollywood, CA 90027

Sharon Wyatt Fan Club
c/o Allison Hood
8949 Falling Creek Court
Annadale, VA 22003

Carl Shayne Fan Club
c/o Claire Weisberg
5332 Las Virgenes Road
Ste. #3
Calabasas, CA 91302

John J. York Fan Club
c/o Claire Weisberg
Fan Club Headquarters
4755 White Oak Place
Encino, CA 91316

"Loving"

Lisa Peluso Fan Club
c/o Shana Sickinger
103 W. 80th Street, Apt. 4C
New York, NY 10024

Robert Tyler Fan Club
c/o Carol Dickson
Entertainment
1218 N. Main Street
Glassboro, NJ 08028

"One Life to Live"

"One Life to Live" Fan Club
c/o Carol Dickson
Entertainment
1218 N. Main Street
Glassboro, NJ 08028

Patricia Elliot
c/o Michelle Saint-Laurent
1410 York Avenue, Apt. 4D
New York, NY 10021

Clint Richie Official Fan
Club
c/o Nadine Shanfeld
140 Alexander Avenue
Staten Island, NY 10312

Karen Witter Fan Club
c/o Funky Fan Clubs
P.O. Box 9624
New Haven, CT 06535

"The Young and the Restless"

"Young & Restless" Fan Club
7800 Beverly Blvd.
Suite 3305
Los Angeles, CA 90336

Lauralee Bell Fan Club
Eric Braeden Fan Club
Jerry Douglas Fan Club
Kate Linder Fan Club

c/o "Young & Restless"
7800 Beverly Blvd.
Suite 3305
Los Angeles, CA 90336

Sharon Farrell Fan Club
c/o Gloria Hesse
"Young & Restless"
7800 Beverly Blvd.
Suite 3305
Los Angeles, CA 90336

III

The Characters and Plots

The Most Romantic Couples

Romance is at the core of the appeal of daytime drama. The following are among the most romantic of all soap opera couples.

Cindy and Stuart, "All My Children"
The courtship and marriage of gentle Stuart Chandler and AIDS victim Cindy Parker was perhaps daytime television's most poignant romance, and her eventual death caused tissues to be pulled out all over America.

Erica and Jackson, "All My Children"
Erica has had too many romances to list, but none compared to the sparks of her affair with Jackson Montgomery, brother of her husband, Travis. No viewer will forget her erotic dance dressed as a chambermaid in a Paris hotel room.

Rachel and Mac, "Another World"
Two of soap's most powerful personalities, Rachel and Mac Cory had their problems, but their love survived numerous affairs. They married three times before Mac's death.

Margo and Tom, "As the World Turns"
These two compelling characters shared an emotional love that endured her rape and the subsequent knowledge that she had been infected with the AIDS virus.

Kayla and Steve, "Days of Our Lives"
Steve "Patch" Johnson and Kayla Brady were one of soapdom's most publicized pairs, and they sailed through endless troubled waters to a wedding aboard ship.

Holly and Robert, "General Hospital"
What started as a marriage of convenience slowly turned into love in one of soap's most emotionally satisfying relationships.

The romance between Trucker (Robert Tyler) and Trisha (Noelle Beck) was one of "Loving's" all-time most passionate.

Holly and Roger, "Guiding Light"
Something powerful and primal must be at the core of this attraction that continues to surface despite Roger's evil behavior that's continued over decades.

Ava and Clay/Alex, "Loving"
Ava thought she was marrying Clay, the heir to the Alden fortune, but her passion continued even after she discovered he was an imposter named Alex Masters.

Tina and Cord, "One Life to Live"
Tina survived disasters, that would have felled Hercules, to eventually marry Cord, and even after their divorce, his imprisonment and amnesia, an emotional bond remains.

Eden and Cruz, "Santa Barbara"
The show may be gone from the air, but the memories of the incredible bond between Eden and Cruz Castillo remain. Their communication and trust in each other set a standard for daytime marriages.

Cricket and Danny, "The Young and the Restless"
Among all the power-hungry connivers and schemers on this soap, it's fitting that two honest, good-hearted young people like Cricket and Danny found each other. The glow from their exotic Hawaiian wedding will remain even if the demands of their careers do eventually pull them apart.

The Worst Soap Marriages

No soap opera marriage is all bells and whistles, but some are truly nightmares. Among the worst soap couplings were:

Erica and Adam, "All My Children"
Two of soap's largest egos and most dominant personalities collided when Erica Kane wed Adam Chandler. This coupling would be doomed to failure if they were the last two people on earth.

Cecile and Sandy, "Another World"
Cecile, a charming woman, married Sandy (Mac's illegitimate son) for his money, then fed his drug dependency so she could have an affair with his brother.

Dee and John, "As the World Turns"
A match with the evil Dr. Dixon turned out to be a disaster for Dee when he brutally raped her in the first case of marital rape on a soap opera.

Sally and Clarke, "The Bold and the Beautiful"
Older woman/younger man romances are becoming more common on daytime dramas, but few of these couples have ended up at the altar. One that did, but shouldn't have, was the coupling of the flamboyant Sally Spectra (Darlene Conley) with the handsome and much younger Clarke Garrison (Daniel McVicar). Needless to say, this was not a marriage made in heaven.

Kayla and Jack, "Days of Our Lives"
Jack Devereaux married Kayla Brady for all the wrong reasons, and this disastrous marriage ended with Jack's brutal
rape of his wife. Fortunately, she eventually ended up in the
loving arms of Jack's brother Steve.

Lucy and Alan, "General Hospital"
The friction produced in this short-term match between the
conniving Lucy and the strong-willed Alan generated enough
heat to melt winter snows in Port Charles.

Eleni and Alan-Michael, "Guiding Light"
The villainous Alan-Michael did everything possible to
coerce Eleni into marriage, including hiring a hooker to pose
as Eleni's true love, Frank, and substituting a placebo for her
birth control pills so she would get pregnant. Eventually, she
escaped the marriage and fell into Frank's arms.

Trisha and Jeff, "Loving"
Trisha Alden was still reeling after her beloved husband
Steve was gunned down in a bank robbery when she married
Jeff Hartman. Jeff promptly launched a torrid affair with
Trisha's mom, Gwyneth, and one of their bedroom trysts
ended up on video tape. Of course, that tape surfaced later
when Trisha was about to marry her true love, Trucker.

Dorian and Victor, "One Life to Live"
The young Dorian Cramer married rich and ailing Victor
Lord. When he promptly died under mysterious circumstances, Dorian inherited his fortune and the Lord family
was left with questions about the manner of his death that
have lingered and festered for decades.

Victoria and Ryan, "The Young and the Restless"
At 16, an age when she should have been preparing for the
junior prom, Victoria was seduced by the ambitious Ryan,
then rushed into a marriage that so traumatized her that she
had to undergo therapy for sexual dysfunction at age 16. She
finally divorced this man who was taking money for sleeping
with Nina Kimble.

Soap Weddings

*M*ost soaps average four or five weddings a year. Because soap couples normally don't wed unless they've survived numerous hardships, viewer interest tends to peak when they finally do tie the knot. Producers pull out all the stops to make weddings more and more glamorous—or more and more dramatic. The following are some of the more memorable soap weddings.

The Grandest Weddings

*S*oap opera weddings are among the most spectacular events on commercial television. Among the most memorable are:

Nina and Cliff, "All My Children"
One of soap's most lavish weddings was the 1980 joining of Nina Cortlandt (Taylor Miller) and Dr. Cliff Warner (Peter Bergman), which was taped at Waveny, a huge estate in New Canaan, Connecticut.

Vicky and Grant, "Another World"
Bay City's congressman wed Vicky Frame, Marley's twin, in the social event of many a season.

Jessica and Duncan, "As the World Turns"
The wedding of two of the most attractive and intelligent young couples on soaps was one of the most satisfying moments for "As the World Turns" fans.

Caroline and Ridge, "The Bold and the Beautiful"
It's only fitting that two characters from the most glamorous of all soaps should stage the most elegant of soap weddings. From the arch of flowers under which the couple took their vows to the flock of white doves released at ceremony's end, every touch was exquisite.

Laura Baldwin (Genie Francis) was the bride in the most famous wedding in soap history.

Julie and Doug, "Days of Our Lives"
One of TV's most publicized nuptials, this 1976 wedding saw Doug Williams (Bill Hayes) marry Julie Olsen (Susan Seaforth), the daughter of his widowed former wife Addie Horton Olsen, who had died of leukemia. Hayes and Seaforth had married in real life in 1974.

Luke and Laura, "General Hospital"
Fourteen million viewers tuned into the 1981 wedding of Luke Spencer (Tony Geary) and Laura Baldwin (Genie Francis), creating the largest single audience in televised soap opera history.

Nola and Quint, "Guiding Light"
Nola's (Lisa Brown) elaborate romantic fantasies about her boss, Quint Chamberlain (Michael Tylo), had the two cavorting in every exotic locale from castles to harems. These fun-filled fantasies led to one of soap's most storybook-like weddings that ended with them taking off in a hot air balloon.

Trisha and Trucker, "Loving"
These two lovers had not one, but two weddings—the first, intimate and romantic; the second, a breathtaking Dr. Zhivago-esque fantasy.

Megan and Jake, "One Life to Live"
Hunks don't come any hunkier than Joe Lando, who played Jake, and few heroines are as endearing as Megan (Jessica Tuck). The tortuous trip to the altar endured by this electric couple made the ceremony a special event.

Olivia and Nathan, "The Young and the Restless"
Drucilla did everything she could to steal Nathan from her sister, Olivia, but true love eventually won out. They were married in a ceremony rich with black tradition, only to discover later that the pregnant Olivia was suffering from cancer.

The Most Disastrous Weddings

One of the very first soap opera weddings was the marriage of the widowed Joanne Barron to Arthur Tate on "Search for Tomorrow." They were just about to say "I do" when a woman rushed up to the altar claiming to be Hazel, the wife Arthur thought was dead. (She turned out to be Sue, twin sister of the deceased Hazel.) Countless wedding days have had similar disasters ever since, including the following.

Dixie and Tad, "All My Children"
On the day of their wedding, Tad got into a life-and-death struggle with the evil Billy Clyde, and they both tumbled off a burning bridge. The grieving Dixie didn't learn for years that Tad survived the fall, but suffered from amnesia.

Isabella and John, "Days of Our Lives"
Sometimes brides feel a pang of regret at the altar, but what Isabella felt were labor pains! She interrupted the ceremony, retreated to a private room, and gave birth. Then she was wheeled back down the aisle to say, "I do." (Yes, the father was John.)

Julie and Doug, "Days of Our Lives"
Perhaps the most publicized soap couple of the 1970s, Julie and Doug were about to make it official when a Polynesian princess named Kim rushed in and claimed that she was still Doug's wife because their divorce wasn't legal. Kim had lied, and the couple later wed.

Brenda and Steve, "One Life to Live"
These two lovers made it through the ceremony, but the reception was a blast—a bomb in the wedding cake killed Steve. Talk about a disastrous wedding!

Tina and Cord, "One Life to Live"
Tina and weddings don't seem to mix. She'd been stood up at the altar not once, but twice. She delivered a baby after having fallen over a waterfall in Argentina, and then she showed up to disrupt Cord's wedding to another woman by claiming the baby was his (it wasn't). So it was only fitting that Tina's long-awaited wedding to Cord should be interrupted by *another* woman claiming Cord was already married to her!

Gina and Lionel, "Santa Barbara"
These two were playing the parts of the bride and groom being married in a play—without realizing the minister was authentic and the ceremony was real. Lionel was just about to kiss his bride when the police showed up and arrested her on a murder charge.

Marriage-Go-Round

arriage and divorce are everyday occurrences on soap operas, but when it comes to totaling up the number of marriages of any one particular character, only Erica Kane can compete in the class of real-life "I doers" like Elizabeth Taylor and Zsa Zsa Gabor! Among the current characters with four or more marriages are the following (#1 is the first spouse ever married).

Jill Abbott, "The Young and the Restless"
1. Brock Reynolds
2. Phillip Chancellor
3. Stuart Brooks
4. John Abbott

Nikki Abbott, "The Young and the Restless"
1. Greg Foster
2. Kevin Bancroft
3. Victor Newman
4. Jack Abbott

Asa Buchanan, "One Life to Live"
1. Olympia
2. Samantha (Sam) Vernon
3. Pamela
4. Delilah Ralston
5. Becky Lee
6. Renee Divine

Bo Buchanan, "One Life to Live"
1. Delila Ralston
2. Didi O'Neill
3. Sarah Gordon
4. Cassie Callison

Adam Chandler, "All My Children"
1. Erica Kane
2. Brooke English
3. Dixie Cooney

Delila Ralston (Shelly Burch) was married to both Asa and Bo Buchanan on "One Life to Live."

4. Gloria Marsh

Rachel Cory, "Another World"
1. Russ Matthews
2. Ted Clarke
3. Steve Frame
4. Mac Cory
5. Mac Cory
6. Mac Cory

Dr. John Dixon, "As the World Turns"
1. Dee Stewart
2. Kim Reynolds
3. Ariel Aldrin
4. Lucinda Walsh

Audrey Hardy, "General Hospital"
1. Steve Hardy
2. Tom Baldwin
3. Jim Hobart
4. Steve Hardy

Bob Hughes, "Another World"
1. Lisa Miller
2. Sandy McGuire
3. Jennifer Ryan
4. Miranda Marlowe
5. Kim Reynolds

Lisa Mitchell, "As the World Turns"
1. Bob Hughes
2. An elderly Chicago millionaire
   (she was married and widowed off camera)
3. Dr. Michael Shea
4. Grant Coleman
5. Whit McColl
6. Earl Mitchell

Erica's Weddings

*E*rica Kane is daytime television's Zsa Zsa Gabor, racking up a grand total of seven weddings. Many sources report that she wedded writer Mike Roy, a great love of her life who was tragically murdered. But "All My Children" does not consider their spiritual coupling to be a legal wedding. Her official weddings were:

1. **Jeff Martin,** a medical intern who got upset when Erica had a legal abortion without telling him.

2. **Phil Brent** finally succumbed to Erica after she became pregnant with his child, but when she had emotional problems after a miscarriage, he went back to his previous wife, Tara.

3. **Tom Cudahy,** an ex-football star, married Erica after a whirlwind courtship, but they broke up when she took off for Hollywood rather than settle down and have children.

4. **Adam Chandler,** whom Erica admired primarily for his wealth, was the man she turned to as husband number four after her true love, Mike Roy, went off to Tibet. This stormy marriage ended when Roy came back to town.

5. **Travis Montgomery** married Erica and they had a baby girl, Bianca. When Erica discovered that Travis had been involved in kidnapping Bianca, she left him and began an affair with his brother, Jackson.

6. **Travis Montgomery** was also husband number six when Erica was forced to choose between Travis and Jackson. However, she continued to see Jackson, resulting in a sixth divorce.

7. **Dimitri Marick,** a handsome businessman, became husband number seven in 1993.

As Erica Kane, Susan Lucci seems to wear wedding gowns about as frequently as the rest of us don bathing suits.

AND THE ONES THAT GOT AWAY

Among Erica's more memorable lovers were:

• **Jason Maxwell,** head of New York modeling agency, tempted Erica with glamour while she was married to Jeff Martin (husband #1), but Maxwell wouldn't leave his wife. Maxwell was accidentally murdered by Erica's mother, Mona.

• **Nick Davis,** owner of the Chateau, was the real father of Phil Brent (husband #2), Erica's ex-husband. But their torrid affair ended when Nick reneged on his promise to marry her and left town.

• **Brandon Kingsley** was head of Sensuelle Cosmetics, and his job offer to Erica ended her marriage to Tom (husband #3). Erica became engaged to Kingsley, even though he wasn't divorced from his wife.

• **Kent Bogard,** heir to Sensuelle's biggest competitor, wooed Erica away from Kingsley. When she discovered he was having an affair with a woman who claimed to be Erica's sister, Erica accidently killed him. She was sentenced to die in the electric chair, but she was pardoned when the truth came out that it was really self-defense.

• **Jeremy Hunter** was the man Erica turned to after Mike Roy's death, but he left her for Natalie Cortlandt.

• **Jackson Montgomery,** a lawyer and brother of Travis (husband #5), combined with Erica for a white-hot affair that saw her do a sensational seductive dance dressed as a chambermaid in a Paris hotel.

The Name's Familiar, But I Can't Place The Face

The turnover rate on soap operas is incredible. Sometimes the actors want to move on, and sometimes the show wants to get rid of a performer. One way to deal with the situation is to eliminate the character. But some characters are so crucial to the plot that they are constantly recast—in one case, twelve different actors have played a role! The following is a list of characters who've been portrayed by four or more different performers.

Character	Actors
Charlie Brent, "All My Children"	Ian Washam
	Brian Lima
	Josh Hamilton
	Robert Duncan
	Charles Van Eman
	Christopher Lawford

Jeff Martin, "All My Children"	Charles Frank
	Christopher Wines
	Robert Perault
	James O'Sullivan
	Jeffrey Byron
	John Tripp
Jamie Frame, "Another World"	Seth Holtzein
	Aiden McNulty
	Tyler Mead
	Brad Bedford
	Bobby Doran
	Tim Holcum
	Richard Bekins
	Stephen Yates
	Laurence Lau
	Russell Todd
Alice Matthews, "Another World"	Jacqueline Courtney
	Susan Harney
	Wesley Ann Pfenning
	Vana Tribbey
	Linda Borgeson
	Jacqueline Courtney
Marian Randolph, "Another World"	Jeanne Beirne
	Lora McDonald
	Tracey Brown
	Loriann Ruger
	Jill Turnbull
	Tiberia Mitri
	Ariane Munker
	Adrienne Wallace
	Beth Collins
Michael Randolph, "Another World"	Dennis Sullivan
	John Sullivan
	Christopher Corwin
	Tim Nissen
	Tom Rogers
	Tom Sabota, Jr.
	Glenn Zachar
	Christopher J. Brown
	Lionel Johnston

Dee Stewart, "As the World Turns"	Simone Schachter
	Jean Malla
	Glynnis O'Connor
	Marcia McClain
	Heather Cunningham
	Jacqueline Schultz
	Vicky Dawson
Susan Stewart, "As the World Turns"	Connie Scott
	Diana Walker
	Jade Rowland
	Leslie Perkins
	Judith Bancroft
	Marie Masters
Tom Hughes, "As the World Turns"	James Madden
	Frankie Michaels
	Richard Thomas
	Paul O'Keefe
	Peter Link
	Peter Galman
	C. David Colson
	Tom Tammi
	Justin Deas
	Jason Kincaid
	Gregg Marx
	Scott Holmes
Michael Horton, "Days of Our Lives"	Bobby Eilbacher
	Eddie Rayden
	Stuart Lee
	Alan Decker
	John Amour
	Dick DeCoit
	Wesley Eure
	Paul Coufos
	Michael Weiss
Scotty Baldwin, "General Hospital"	Johnny Whitaker
	Teddy Quinn
	Tony Campo
	Don Clarke
	Johnny Jensen
	Kin Shriner

Hope Bauer, "Guiding Light"	Jennifer Kerschner
	Paula Schwartz
	Elissa Leeds
	Tisch Raye
	Robin Mattson
	Katherine Justice
	Elvera Roussel
Freddie (Rick) Bauer, "Guiding Light"	Albert Zungallo
	Gary Hannoch
	Robbie Berridge
	Phil MacGregory
	Michael O'Leary
Cathy Craig, "One Life to Live"	Cathy Burns
	Amy Levitt
	Jane Alice Brandon
	Dorrie Kavanaugh
	Jennifer Harmon
Dorian Cramer, "One Life to Live"	Nancy Pinkerton
	Claire Malis
	Robin Strasser
	Elaine Princi
	Robin Strasser
Danny Wolek, "One Life to Live"	Neail Holland
	Eddie Moran
	Tim Waldrip
	Steven Culp
	Ted Demers
	Josh Cox
	Michael Palance
Jill Foster, "The Young and the Restless"	Brenda Dickson
	Bond Gideon
	Deborah Adair
	Brenda Dickson
	Jess Walton

The Face's Familiar, But I Can't Place The Name

No doubt you remember a number of your current soap favorites from other shows. Following is a list of actors and actresses who are veterans of at least four different shows.

Actor	Characters
Marla Adams	Bell Clemens, "The Secret Storm" Maria Clegg, "Capitol" Beth Logan, "The Bold and the Beautiful" Helen Mullin, "Generations" Dina Abbott Mergeron, "The Young and the Restless"
Jed Allan	Ace Hubbard, "Love of Life" Paul Britton, "The Secret Storm" Don Craig, "Days of Our Lives" C.C. Capwell, "Santa Barbara"
John Aniston	Eric Richards, "Days of Our Lives" Edouard Aleata, "Love of Life" Martin Tourneur, "Search for Tomorrow" Victor Kiriakis, "Days of Our Lives"
Richard Backus	Jason Saxton, "Lovers and Friends" Jason Saxton, "For Richer, For Poorer" Ted Bancroft, "Another World" Barry Ryan, "Ryan's Hope" Dr. Russ Elliot, "As the World Turns" Carl Eldridge, "As the World Turns"
Peter Brown	Greg Peters, "Days of Our Lives"

Robert Lawrence, "The Young and the Restless"
Roger Forbes, "Loving"
Charles Sanders, "One Life to Live"
Blake Hayes, "The Bold and the Beautiful"

Leslie Charleson — Pam, "A Flame in the Wind"
Alice Whipple, "As the World Turns"
Iris Garrison, "Love Is a Many Splendored Thing"
Monica Quartermaine, "General Hospital"

Darlene Conley — Rose DeVille, "The Young and the Restless"
Edith Baker, "Days of Our Lives"
Louise, "Capitol"
Trixie, "General Hospital"
Sally Spectra, "The Bold and the Beautiful"

John Considine — Dr. Brian Walsh, "Bright Promise"
Philip Chancellor, "The Young and the Restless"
Vic Hastings, "Another World"
Reginald Love, "Another World"

Nicolas Coster — Matt Steele, "Young Dr. Malone"
Paul Britton, "The Secret Storm"
John Eldridge, "Our Private World"
John Eldridge, "As the World Turns"
Robert Delaney, "Somerset"
Robert Delaney, "Another World"
Anthony Makana, "One Life to Live"
Steve Andrews, "All My Children"
Lionel Lockridge, "Santa Barbara"

Jacqueline Courtney — Viola Smith, "Edge of Night"
Ann Lee, "Our Five Daughters"
Alice Matthews Frame, "Another World"
Pat Ashley, "One Life to Live"
Diane Winston, "Loving"

Augusta Dabney — Tracey Malone, "Young Dr. Malone"
Laura Baxter, "Another World"

	Ann Holmes, "As the World Turns"
	Betty Kahlman Barry, "A World Apart"
	Barbara Norris, "Guiding Light"
	Carolyn Chandler, "General Hospital"
	Theodora Van Alen, "The Doctors"
	Isabelle Alden, "Loving"

Jane Elliot	Madge Sinclair, "A Flame in the Wind"
	Carrie Todd, "Guiding Light"
	Cynthia Prest, "All My Children"
	Angelica Deveraux, "Days of Our Lives"
	Tracy Quartermaine, "General Hospital"

David Forsyth	T.J. Canfield, "Texas"
	Burke Donovan, "As the World Turns"
	Hogan McCleary, "Search for Tomorrow"
	Dr. John Hudson, "Another World"

Susan Seaforth Hayes	Dorothy Bradley, "General Hospital"
	Carol West, "The Young Marrieds"
	JoAnna Manning, "The Young and the Restless"
	Julie Williams, "Days of Our Lives"

James Horan	Denny Hobson, "Another World"
	Sky Witney, "Edge of Night"
	Brett Madison, "General Hospital"
	Creed Kelly, "All My Children"
	Clay Alden, "Loving"

Elizabeth Hubbard	Anne Benedict Fletcher, "Guiding Light"
	Carol Kramer, "Edge of Night"
	Dr. Althea Davis, "The Doctors"
	Lucinda Walsh Dixon, "As the World Turns"

Fiona Hutchison	Sheila, "As the World Turns"
	Molly Patterson, "Guiding Light"
	Gabrielle Medina, "One Life to Live"
	Jenna Bradshaw, "Guiding Light"

Elizabeth Lawrence	Francie Brent, "The Road of Life"
	Constance Johnson, "Edge of Night"
	Betty Kahlman Barry, "A World Apart"

	Virginia Dancy, "The Doctors" Myra Nurdoch Sloan, "All My Children"
Robert Lupone	Chester Wallace, "Ryan's Hope" Tom Bergman, "Search for Tomorrow" Zach Grayson, "All My Children" Neal Cory, "As the World Turns" Leo Sharpe, "Guiding Light"
Larkin Malloy	Schuyler Whitney, "Edge of Night" Kyle Sampson, "Guiding Light" Travis Montgomery, "All My Children" Clay Alden, "Loving"
Robin Mattson	Hope Bauer, "Guiding Light" Heather Weber, "General Hospital" Delia Ryan, "Ryan's Hope" Gina DeMott Capwell, "Santa Barbara"
Peggy McCay	Vanessa Dale, "Love of Life" Susan Garrett, "The Young Marrieds" Iris Fairchild, "General Hospital" Caroline Brady, "Days of Our Lives"
Judith McConnell	Augusta McCloud, "General Hospital" Valerie Conway, "As the World Turns" Miranda Bishop, "Another World" Eva Vasquez, "One Life to Live" Sophia Capwell, "Santa Barbara"
Beverlee McKinsey	Julie Richards/Martha Donnelly, "Love Is a Many Splendored Thing" Emma Frame Ordway, "Another World" Iris Cory Carrington, "Another World" Iris Cory Carrington, "Texas" Alexandra Spaulding, "Guiding Light"
Mark Pinter	Dr. Tom Crawford, "Love of Life" Mark Evans, "Guiding Light" Brian McColl, "As the World Turns" Dan Hollister, "Loving" Grant Harrison, "Another World"
Elaine Princi	Miranda Marlowe, "As the World Turns" Linda Anderson/Madame X,

"Days of Our Lives"
Dr. Kate Winograd, "Days of Our Lives"
Dorian Lord Callison, "One Life to Live"

Rosemary Prinz
Penny Hughes, "First Love"
Penny Hughes, "As the World Turns"
Amy Tyler, "All My Children"
Dr. Julie Franklin, "How to
Survive a Marriage"

Gil Rogers
Ray Gardner, "All My Children"
Dr. Martin Brandt, "The Doctors"
Brent Kenwood, "Search for Tomorrow"
Hawk Shayne, "Guiding Light"

Tina Sloan
Kate Cannell, "Somerset"
Patti Baron, "Search for Tomorrow"
Dr. Olivia Delaney, "Another World"
Lillian Raines, "Guiding Light"

Jim Storm
Larry Wolek, "One Life to Live"
Gerard Stiles, "Dark Shadows"
Sean Childers, "The Secret Storm"
Mick Powers, "The Doctors"
Neil Fenmore, "The Young and the
Restless"
Bill Spencer, "The Bold and the
Beautiful"

Michael Tylo
Peter Belton, "Another World"
Quint Chamberlain, "Guiding Light"
Matt Conelly, "All My Children"
Charlie Prince, "General Hospital"
Blade, "The Young and the Restless"

Nicholas Walker
Brad Huntington, "The Doctors"
Sam Clegg III, "Capitol"
Jimmy O'Herleihy, "General Hospital"
Max Holden, "One Life to Live"
Frank, "Santa Barbara"

Kathleen Widdoes
Jill Malone, "Young Dr. Malone"
Rose Perrini, "Another World"
Una MacCurtain, "Ryan's Hope"
Emma Snyder, "As the World Turns"

Double Plays

As a soap opera viewer, you're no doubt used to seeing a favorite character portrayed by different performers. And it's also not unusual for a performer to return to a soap as a twin or a "look-alike" of his or her former character. But it's a lot rarer for a performer to return to a soap to play an entirely different character. Following is a list of soap's double-players.

ANOTHER WORLD
John Considine, Jr.-Vic Hastings/Reginald Love
Beverlee McKinsey-Emma Ordway/Iris Carrington

AS THE WORLD TURNS
Jean Mazza-Annie Stewart/Dee Stewart
Glynnis O'Connor-Dee Stewart/Margo Hughes

DAYS OF OUR LIVES
John Aniston-Eric Richards/Victor Kiriakis
Eileen Barnett-Brooke Hamilton/Stephanie Woodruff

EDGE OF NIGHT
Millette Alexander-Gail Armstrong/Laura Hillyer/Julie Jamison

GENERAL HOSPITAL
Ed Platt-Dr. Miller/Wyatt Chamberlain

GUIDING LIGHT
Jordan Clarke-Dr. Tim Ryan/Billy Lewis
Fiona Hutchison-Molly Patterson/Jenna Bradshaw
William Roerick-Dr. Bruce Banning/Henry Chamberlain

ONE LIFE TO LIVE
Christine Jones-Sheila Rafferty/Pamela Buchanan
Lee Patterson-Joe Riley/Tom Dennison
Anthony Ponzini-Vince Wolek/Charlie Smith

THE YOUNG AND THE RESTLESS
Rod Arrants-Jeff/Dr. Stew Lassiter
Velekka Gray-Sharon Reeves/Ruby
Quinn Redeker-Nick Reed/Rex Sterling

Twins

*I*f you glance at the list of annual daytime Emmy Award winners in this book, you'll get the idea that playing twins on a soap is a springboard to success in acting. In the world of daytime drama, multiple births—and, especially, secret evil twins—are nearly as common as normal siblings, with mysterious "look-alikes" a close second. Following are some of soap's most famous twins and look-alikes.

Francesca James played twins Kitty and Kelly Cole on "All my Children."

Victoria Love/Marley Hudson, "Another World"-Ellen Wheeler won a 1986 Emmy playing these twins; Anne Heche later played the same role—and won a 1991 Emmy.

Adam/Stuart Chandler, "All My Children"-David Canary is the only actor to win four daytime Emmys, perhaps because he's playing twins.

Lisa Miller/Ruth Hadley, "As the World Turns"-Eileen Fulton got to play Lisa's look-alike—but only as a corpse!

Although her character wasn't a twin, Erika Slezak had great fun portraying Nikki Smith, the evil split personality of Viki Buchanan.

Bo/Mitch, "Days of Our Lives"-Robert Kelker-Kelly played both roles, but Mitch's voice was supplied by actor Larry Hayden.

Marlena/Samantha Evans, "Days of Our Lives"-Deidre Hall's real-life twin, Andrea Hall Lovell, played Marlena's evil counterpart.

Luke Spencer/Bill Eckert, "General Hospital"-These two look-alikes were supposedly cousins.

Brandon Lujack/Nick Henry, "Guiding Light"-Nick Henry is also another look-alike cousin.

Grace/Gillian Forrester, "One Life to Live"-Grace was the good twin and Gillian the murderess of this pair, who were played by real twins, Cary and Camille More.

Bo Buchanan, "One Life to Live"-This character was brought back into the story when Robert S. Woods returned to the cast by introducing a mysterious "faux Bo," a man masquerading as the son of Asa.

Déjà Vu!

"Wow, that face sure looks familiar." If you're a soap fan and you're uttering those words, chances are that you are seeing a once-familiar character reappear—maybe with a brand new identity. The following are some of the *strangest* returns of some all-time favorite stars.

KISSING COUSINS

As Luke Spencer, Anthony Geary was the male half of perhaps the most famous of all soap couples, "General Hospital's" Luke and Laura. He left the show in the early 1980s to pursue other opportunities, but he never found anything that elevated him to the plateau of popularity he'd achieved as Luke. In February, 1992, Geary returned to the soap as Bill Eckert, Luke Spencer's look-alike cousin. An engineer with a mysterious past (what else?), Eckert seemed to be biding his time until something important happened.

Anthony Geary struggles for his life in a story of murder and intrigue upon his return to "General Hospital."

That "something" occurred in October, 1993, when Genie Frances rejoined the show for the resurrection of Luke and Laura. Shortly afterwards, Bill Eckert faded into the sunset.

THE LONG-LOST TWIN

In 1983, "Guiding Light" introduced Vincent Irizarry as Lujack, son of the wealthy Alexandra Spaulding. His romance with Beth Raines (Judith Evans) was hugely popular. But he left the show in 1985 when Lujack was killed in an explosion. When Irizarry went back to "Guiding Light" in 1992, the writing team couldn't find a way to put him back together. So he appeared as newspaper reporter Nick McHenry, a Lujack look-alike. And wouldn't you know, it turns out that Nick was Lujack's long-lost twin brother, stolen at birth by his natural father and sold to an American couple.

KIDNAPPED!

In 1986, Deidre Hall left her role as Marlena Evans Brady on "Days of Our Lives" after eleven years. To explain her departure, Marlena was seen going down in a fiery plane crash, leaving Roman a distraught widower. In 1992, Roman had just proposed to Isabella when, lo and behold, Marlena returned. The explanation? She'd survived the crash but had been held hostage on a deserted island for six years!

YET ANOTHER CRASH SURVIVOR

Also in 1986, Emma Samms left her role as Holly Sutton Scorpio on "General Hospital" to star on the prime time drama, "Dynasty." Shortly afterwards, her soap hubby, Tristan Rogers (Robert Scorpio) also departed. Rogers returned three years later—alone. To explain the absence of his spouse, viewers were told Holly died in a plane crash. Then, in 1992, Emma Samms came back. You probably won't believe it, but she missed the fatal flight! But on the way home from the airport, she was in a car crash and ended up in a coma that lasted almost exactly as long as Deidre Hall's imprisonment on that deserted island. What a coincidence!

THE EVIL TWIN

Robert S. Woods left his role as Bo Buchanan on "One Life to Live" for a role on "Days of Our Lives." To explain Woods' departure, the storyline had Bo getting on a plane to Arizona for the funeral of his ranch foreman and simply deciding not to return to Llanview. When Woods became disenchanted with "Days," he asked for his old role back. Since there is nothing interesting about simply getting back on a plane, Woods first returned as Bo's evil twin—as the producers put it, the "faux Bo." The only way to stop this scoundrel was for the "real Bo" to fly back to stop his treachery.

RESURRECTION

The boldest of all returns took place on "Guiding Light." As the dashing but dastardly Roger Thorpe, Michael Zaslow was perhaps the leading soap villain of the 1970s. Then, in 1980, Roger fled to the Dominican Republic after deliberately setting a fire that killed a baby. Chased through the jungle, he slipped on the edge of a high cliff, held on for a moment with one hand, then plunged into the abyss to his death. Zaslow went on to other roles, including the pianist spy David Rinaldi on "One Life to Live." In 1990, "Guiding Light" approached him about playing another character, but he wanted to return to his old role. After agonizing over a way to bring Roger back to life, the writers came up with a simple but stunning solution—ignore the death. Roger Thorpe was simply resurrected, and slipped back into the plot as his old, evil self!

Don't I Know You From Somewhere?

Almost all soap characters stick pretty close to their fictional homes—after all, how would you go about finding your way from Bay City to Corinth? But a handful have visited other soaps.

Steve Hardy, "General Hospital"
In 1969, the Chief of Staff was called to Llanview, home of "One Life to Live," to examine Viki Lord's ill sister, Meredith. Meredith later died when she was surprised by a burglar.

Mike and Hope Bauer, "Guiding Light"
Mike and his daughter Hope left Springfield in 1966 to visit "Another World's" Bay City.

Sheila Grainger, "The Young and the Restless"
This demented nurse left Genoa City in 1993 to go to Los Angeles where she met and married Eric Forrester. The Genoa City victims of her cruelty, Lauren Fenmore and Brad Carlton, came to "The Bold and the Beautiful" hot on her trail.

Jeremy Hunter, "All My Children"
After numerous love affairs, this artist left Pine Valley to take a position as Dean of Humanities at "Loving's" Alden University in Corinth.

Dinah Lee and Hannah Mayberry, "Loving"
Dinah Lee went on vacation to Pine Valley, home of "All My Children," but when she was beaten by Carter Jones, her sister Hannah arrived to rescue her, then they returned to Corinth.

If Memory Serves Me Right...

Doctors tell us that true amnesia is very rare in the real world—it's a nearly one-in-a-million occurrence. But on soap operas, losing one's memory is a time-honored tradition. In case you've forgotten, refresh your memory with some major characters who've forgotten who *they* are.

Tad Martin, "All My Children"
Everyone thought Tad was killed falling off that bridge during his struggle with villainous Billy Clyde. But wouldn't you know it, Tad survived but forgot who he was and ended up in California thinking he was Ted Orsini, son of wine-making mama Nola Orsini. And, coincidentally, the wine business took him back to his home, Pine Valley.

Rachel Cory, "Another World"
Rachel was kidnapped by the evil Carl Hutchins. During her rescue by Mac, she stepped in the way of a bullet. The result: amnesia.

Kim Hughes, "As the World Turns"
Kim left Oakdale to decide which of her two loves she should marry. She finally decided, but on the way back home, she was caught up in a tornado, hit her head and—you guessed it—developed amnesia and forgot who she chose to marry.

Stephanie Forrester, "The Bold and the Beautiful"
After Eric and Brooke were married, Stephanie was so upset that she had a stroke which erased all of her memory. She wandered the streets, finally befriending some homeless people who lived on a street corner. Sally eventually found her digging through garbage and brought her back home. When she regained her memory, she visited the streets to assist her former, homeless friends.

Mickey Horton, "Days of Our Lives"
While recovering from triple-bypass surgery, Mickey had a stroke that wiped out his memory when his son (who wasn't

really his son) turned against him. Not knowing who he was, he left the hospital and Salem, wandering until he found a farm where he met Maggie, his true love.

Edward Quartermaine, "General Hospital"
As far as anyone knew, Edward was killed in a plane crash. But—surprise!—he was discovered living like a king on an island in the Caribbean, having forgotten that he was really a family patriarch in Port Charles.

Felicia Jones, "General Hospital"
Felicia recently returned from not her first, but her second bout of amnesia. This latest one (caused by an auto accident) occurred to explain her return in 1992 after the actress left the show a year earlier to spend more time with her new baby.

Trucker McKenzie, "Loving"
Trucker rescued Trisha from the evil Giff, but in the process fell off the belfry. After life-saving brain surgery, there were evidently a few bats left over—he'd forgotten everything, including who he was.

Ashley Abbott, "The Young and the Restless"
Ashley is another character who's had two bouts of amnesia. The first came when she discovered John wasn't her real father; the shock was so great it wiped out her memory and she ended up waiting tables at a truck stop. The second bout came after an abortion she had when she believed Victor was going back to his wife, Nikki. This time she wandered the streets and was taken to an asylum.

Soap Scum

One of the essential ingredients for a riveting soap opera is a dastardly and devious villain or villainess. These characters whom we love to hate provide the emotional spice that keeps us watching week after week. Following is a list of soap's most prominent human scum.

ALL MY CHILDREN
Billy Clyde Tuggle (Matthew Cowles)-This dastardly, low-class crook periodically returned to Pine Valley to wreak havoc until he was killed falling off a bridge in a struggle with Tad Martin.

Ray Gardner (Gil Rogers)-The father of Tad Martin and Jenny Gardner was a rapist and blackmailer who also returned to town from time to time to execute his evil plots.

Langley Wallingford (Louis Edmunds)-This con man, whose real name was Lenny Vlasic, cheated and connived to marry Phoebe and separate her from her money before he eventually settled down and became more benign.

Palmer Cortlandt (James Mitchell)-The wealthy head of Cortlandt Electronics went to any means to exert his power and wage his personal war against Adam Chandler.

Adam Chandler (David Canary)-Another rich, unscrupulous man who would do anything in the world to get his way—including bribing a psychiatrist to have his perfectly sane wife, Dixie, committed to an asylum so he could have custody of their son.

ANOTHER WORLD
Iris Carrington (Beverlee McKinsey)-This illegitimate daughter of Mac Cory is one of soap's classic villainesses.

Cecile dePoulignac (Nancy Frangione)- This femme fatale with the exotic name maneuvered her way into a marriage with Sandy Cory, among other misdeeds.

Willis Frame (John Fitzpatrick)-Steven Frame's evil brother connived with his almost equally evil sister Janice to cause trouble for the good and well-intentioned.

AS THE WORLD TURNS
Lisa Miller (Eileen Fulton)-As soap opera's premiere villainess, Miller has been among the most hated characters on television since she arrived in Oakdale in 1960.

Dr. John Dixon (Larry Bryggman)-Although the not-so-good doctor has toned down his act in recent years, his past treacheries include kidnapping and rape.

James Stenbeck (Anthony Herrera)-This evil businessman did battle with Dr. John Dixon.

Douglas Cummings (John Wesley Shipp)-Murder was just one of the crimes this most dastardly modern villain has committed.

THE BOLD AND THE BEAUTIFUL
Sheila Forrester (Kimberlin Brown)-As a mad nurse, Kimberlin Brown is the Eileen Fulton of the early 1990s.

DAYS OF OUR LIVES
Alex Marshall (Quinn Redeker)-This evil businessman was a prime source of trouble between 1979 and 1987.

Stephano DiMera (Joe Mascolo)-This gangster was so bad that Mascolo was twice voted Villain of the Year in the *Soap Opera Digest* Awards.

Victor Kiriakis (John Aniston)-This father of Bo is one of today's leading doers of evil deeds.

GENERAL HOSPITAL
Bobbie Spencer (Jackie Zeman)-Luke Spencer's sister used her brother (and his ties to organized crime) to get her way.

Jane Elliot (Tracy Quartermaine)-Nothing stood in the way of this powerful businesswoman who is Alan's sister and was once married to Paul.

John Aniston (Victor, "Days of Our Lives") was a dual Soap Opera Digest Award Winner (Outstanding Actor, Outstanding Villain) in 1986.

Jackie Zeman was one of the major soap opera villainesses of the 1970s and 1980s in her role as Bobbie Spencer on "General Hospital."

Scott Baldwin (Kin Shriner)-When his teenage romance with Laura was broken up by Luke, Baldwin turned to conniving and revenge for solace.

Lucy Coe (Lynn Herring)-Villainy with a touch of humor has marked this long-standing character.

GUIDING LIGHT
Roger Thorpe (Michael Zaslow)-This ruthless businessman is rivaled only by Eileen Fulton's Lisa Miller in the pantheon of all-time great soap villains.

Alan-Michael Spaulding (Rick Hearst)-This powerful businessman is a conniver who will do anything to get his way.

LOVING
Dane Hammond (Anthony Herrara)-Hammond tried to destroy the Alden family after he was fired from Alden Enterprises.

Alex Masters (Randolph Mantooth)-Masters masqueraded as the long missing Clay Alden before his first wife showed up to ruin his plan.

Clay Alden (Larkin Malloy)-Alden set out to destroy his family after learning that Cabot Alden was not his real father.

ONE LIFE TO LIVE
Dorian Cramer (Robin Strasser)-Dorian married the elderly, wealthy Victor Lord, who died under mysterious circumstances, and she has been conniving ever since.

Marco Dane (Gerald Anthony)-This gangster caused all kinds of trouble before departing for Port Charles.

Carlo Hesser (Thom Christopher)-This mob boss lived for revenge and crime.

Alex Hesser (Tonja Walker)-Carlo's widow has vowed revenge for her the person who killed her husband.

THE YOUNG AND THE RESTLESS

Brad Eliot (Tom Hallick)-A former surgeon who had to quit after an injury made his hands useless, Eliot turned bitter and vengeful.

Jill Abbott (Brenda Dickson, Jess Walton)-This former hairdresser connived her way to wealth and power.

Victor Newman (Eric Braeden)-This powerful businessman got his way at any cost.

The Ten Dumbest Plots

One of the basic tenets of writing any kind of fiction, from novels to a television series, is that "life is not a story." While real human behavior produces incidents beyond the most bizarre imaginations of writers, the routine of everyday life is not fast-paced or dramatic enough to sustain the interest of soap viewers. Fans of daytime have come to accept as routine certain stock plot devices, like characters coming back from the dead. But in their quest for higher ratings, sometimes soaps go over the edge, creating some of the dumbest possible plots.

GET THEE TO A NUNNERY

When "Days of Our Lives" began, Tommy Horton, the oldest son of Dr. Tom Horton and his wife Alice, was missing in action in Korea. A few years later, brother Bill Horton left Salem for a while after a personal crisis and returned with Dr. Mark Brooks, a young man he'd happened to meet on his travels. Brooks, who had suffered amnesia and had undergone plastic surgery after being burned and tortured by the North Koreans, fell in love with Bill's sister Marie. Guess what? Dr. Mark Brooks turned out to be the missing Tommy Horton. Mortified by having fallen in love with her brother, Marie ran off to a convent and became a nun. Years later, Marie left the convent to search for her illegitimate daughter Jessica, who was so freaked out she developed a split personality.

HE WAS A LITTLE BIG

"As the World Turns" created a storyline that had police-woman Margo Montgomery and lawyer Tom Hughes chasing all over Europe after the head of a major international drug cartel, who went by the highly original name "Mr. Big." After numerous narrow escapes, Margo and Tom were imprisoned in Mr. Big's lair, a house of horrors. Finally, the dynamic duo nailed Mr. Big—who turned out to be a dwarf. Crimefighting also stirred a few emotions, as Margo and Tom became a couple.

MOM'S A SNAKE

On "All My Children," after Brooke English's father died suddenly (he was Phoebe's brother), she and her husband Tom Cudahy discovered that he had been a runner for a vicious drug smuggling cartel. A mysterious figure called the Cobra told the two that if they didn't continue her father's job, the cartel would murder Brooke's mother, Peg English. Brooke struggled to keep the secret from her unknowing mother as the Cobra attempted to murder her. Brooke finally discovered that *Peg* was really the Cobra—the head of the drug ring—and her father had been the innocent pawn. Then, apparently to alleviate her anguish over the fact that her mother tried to kill her, Brooke discovered a secret letter written by her father before his death that said Peg wasn't her real mother.

THE ICE MAN COMETH

Science fiction entered the world of "General Hospital" when Alex Quartermaine smuggled a gigantic diamond called the Ice Princess into the country. It turned out that the evil Mikos Cassadine had concocted a plot to rule the world by building a machine that could send Port Charles—or any other location—into a permanent deep freeze. The Ice Princess was, of course, required to operate the device. Luke, Laura and Robert stowed away on the Cassadine yacht to stop the plan. Eventually, Luke killed Mikos and discovered the one password that saved the world.

THE ULTIMATE IDENTITY CRISIS

When Wayne Northrop left the role of detective Roman Brady on "Days of Our Lives" to take a role on the prime time soap "Dynasty," Drake Hogestyn took over as Roman. When Marlena Brady returned to Salem after being held prisoner on a desert island, she fell back in love with her "husband." It was then decided that actor Northrop was returning to "Days of Our Lives," and viewers suddenly discovered that Roman wasn't really Roman. Instead, he was a hit man named John Black, who had masqueraded as Roman. And—talk about coincidences—the real Roman had also been held prisoner for six years. And to further muddle the mess, John Black's real identity turned out to be Forrest Alamain, who was supposed to be dead. Sometimes, it seems, you really don't know the man you marry!

WILD WEST

Soap operas are always recycling old plots, but "One Life to Live" created a whole new standard of "old" when it sent Clint Buchanan and his wife Viki back to the Old West, in 1988. Clint (who was also named Clint back in time) eventually fell in love with Miss Ginny, a schoolteacher played by Erika Slezak, who also played Viki. Unfortunately, neither Roy Rogers nor Gene Autry showed up in this six month-long fantasy story.

NOW YOU'RE KIN, NOW YOU'RE NOT

When incest is the subject of a storyline, things can get pretty complicated, as they did on "As the World Turns." It began when it was revealed that Iva Snyder had a child out-of-wedlock after being raped at age thirteen by her cousin Josh—who later turned out *not* to be her cousin. That child, Lily, was living in Oakdale, and she fell in love with Holden, Iva's brother. Despite the intense sparks between them, Holden broke off the romance when he found out that Lily was his niece. Then mother Emma disclosed that Iva had really been adopted, so Holden and Lily weren't related by blood after all. Soaps being soaps, the two didn't rush into each other's arms. At one point, Holden got drunk, then slept with his brother's wife Julie believing it was Lily. After all the scandals, Holden and Lily finally did get married, then got divorced.

LAND OF THE LOST

Movie-goers have often thrilled at the exploration of fabulous lost cities in remote locations, from the mountains of Tibet to the sands of North Africa to the jungles of Africa. But soaps can't transport their entire casts on location for months, so when "One Life to Live" decided to incorporate a lost city into their storyline, it turned out to be right near Llanview, a suburb of Philadelphia. The exploration of this lost city, named Eterna, took over a year, during which time soap credibility (a precious commodity anyway) flew straight out the window.

THE HUMAN HAMSTER

Many people make the wrong choice for their first spouse, but "The Young and the Restless" character Brad Carlton evidently made one of the worst. He kept all knowledge of his first marriage from Traci Abbott, his second bride. Then, out of the blue, his crazy first wife, "Trapper" Lisa Mansfield, took him captive and kept him in a giant cage for months while she slowly tortured him. Eventually, Lauren Fenmore and Jack Abbott spotted Lisa on the ski slopes and rescued poor Brad—who was promptly divorced by Traci. Wonder how long it took before he stopped trying to press a bar to get his food pellets?

ROLL OVER, BOGART

Parody is a difficult art form, which is why skits on such shows as "Saturday Night Live" are only a few minutes long. Endless is a good word for the "Another World" parody of 1940s detective films called "The Case of the Broken Heart." Filmed in black-and-white, this storyline starred character Cass Winthrop (Stephen Schnetzer) as detective Cass A. Nova (get it?), who was hired by ex-love Francesca Kinkaid to find her stolen heart (get it again?).

A Day In The Life Of A Soap

One veteran soap opera actor described his job as "an under-rehearsed opening night, every day of the year." While prime time production teams tape 22 to 25 original shows per year on a schedule of one show per week, a soap opera production team tapes one show per day, 5 days per week, 52 weeks per year. This schedule would be impossible to meet without the utmost professionalism and teamwork. Although working for a soap opera may seem glamorous, it can also be grueling. Check out this schedule!

Early Morning

Cast members arrive at the studio by 7 or 7:30 a.m. But not every member of the cast comes in every day. How often each performer works is a function of contract and storyline. Soap's leading stars are paid a yearly salary and are guaranteed a certain number of weeks off. Most other cast members are paid by the show, and they sign contracts guaranteeing them a certain average number of shows per week or per year. Non-contract performers work when they're told to work. Performers involved in "hot" storylines get more work than those whose characters are "on the back burner." The intense competition for air time is one reason that soap opera performers are more accessible to the press and more accommodating to fans than are prime time performers.

The performers show up to work in the a.m. having spent the previous night memorizing as much as 50 or 60 pages of dialogue. Each day's script is the end result of a six- to twelve-month long process that began when the head writer and producers sat down to make notes for the serial's "bible," or long range story planning guide. As the stories take shape, they are first broken down by weeks, then show by show. When the scenes that will make up each day's show are finalized, writers create the dialogue that the actors will speak on camera.

First thing each morning, the performers gather for a read-through of the script with the director of that day's show. On most shows, a director is responsible for one show per week. During the read-through, the director tells the actors how each scene should be played, the performers add their input, and rough spots in the dialogue are worked out.

While the read-through is in progress, stage crews prepare the sets for the day's shooting. Most shows have a number of permanent sets, with others constructed for short-term use. One or more members of the production team is in charge of making sure that everything is in the same place when a setting is used for more than one day of a continuing scene.

Late Morning

Still in their street clothes, the performers move to the sets for what is called "blocking"—that is, a walk-through of the physical movement that will take place on camera. Camera angles and lighting are worked out while the actors go through their movements. Blocking a scene between just two characters can go very quickly, but large party scenes that involve lots of extras can take hours. After blocking, the actors absorb notes and suggestions from the directors and producers.

Before they're actually on the set, the performers review their dialogue, read their mail, play games, make telephone calls, exercise, even take naps. Younger actors keep busy doing school work. Lunch is normally eaten in the dressing rooms or in the studio cafeteria.

Early Afternoon

By early afternoon, the performers have gotten the day's costumes from the "ready" room and have gone through make-up. The studio PA calls them to the set. With the directors and the producers in the control booth, they go through a dress rehearsal and the scene is timed. Notes containing final suggestions and instructions are passed from the control room to the performers, and any adjustments required for time purposes are made. Make-up is touched up and costumes are readjusted.

Then the actual taping begins. While the tape is stopped if mistakes are made or if the control room sees a problem, it generally progresses much more smoothly than the taping of a prime time show. After the director and the producers are satisfied with the scene, shooting is moved to the next set.

Late Afternoon

Half-hour shows normally complete the day's shooting by mid-afternoon, while hour-long shows can easily run into the early evening. Twelve-hour days aren't uncommon, and complicated episodes can extend that time even longer. No matter what time the cast members leave, most go home to memorize another huge chunk of dialogue for the following day.

Even performers who don't have a call the next day have a busy agenda. Many schedule acting, dancing, exercise or voice lessions while they audition for commercials, plays, prime time series guest spots, movies and other work. Although the major stars of daytime make a good salary, the average performer depends on such moonlighting jobs to make ends meet. In addition to talent, a requirement for success as an actor or actress is a big appetite for hard work.

The Soaps: What Does The Future Hold?

The soap opera genre is now six decades old, and for the past decade many television observers predicted the demise of this dowager, citing the cancellations of long-running soaps such as "Search for Tomorrow" and critically acclaimed shows such as "Ryan's Hope" and "Santa Barbara." It appeared that the vast increase in the number of women in the workforce and the competition from dozens of cable channels might send ratings plummeting to fatal depths.

Those dire projections haven't come true. The last three or four years have seen a resurgence of interest in daytime drama that has occurred for a number of reasons. First, new production teams installed at the helm of many of the older soaps have revitalized shows that seemed to have seen their better days. Second, stars such as Deidre Hall, Anthony Geary, Genie Francis and Michael Zaslow have returned to daytime, providing former viewers with a reason to tune in again. Third, the video cassette recorder has allowed working men and women to keep up with their favorite soaps—in fact, "All My Children" is the most frequently taped of all television shows.

The result is that the beginning of 1994 finds the ten remaining shows alive and competing vigorously for viewers. But since the status quo never lasts very long in the volatile medium of television, soap production teams must continue to innovate to survive and grow. Looking into the crystal ball, here's what we see in the future of daytime drama.

• Much more intermingling of the casts of each network's soaps. As we write, the production team behind "The Young and the Restless" and "The Bold and the Beautiful" have set forth story lines that involve dozens of cross-overs of characters between the two shows over the next year. At ABC, a number of characters have begun to move between "All My Children" and "Loving." This trend, which is enthusiastically greeted by viewers, is sure to continue.

• A reversal of the "one way" sign on the highway that has led so many daytime stars on to careers in prime time or movies. The stability of long-running roles on soaps is appealing at a time when prime time shows come and go with lightning speed. Look for major prime time personalities and film stars to make more than cameo appearances.

• Twenty-four hour availability of soap programming. Interactive TV is just over the horizon, and one of the first services to be offered is sure to be round-the-clock access to soap operas. By punching in a few codes on a remote control, you will be able to watch any episode of "The Young and the Restless," "All My Children" or any other soap at any time you choose. This service will greatly expand daytime's audience and, consequently, daytime's budgets.

• More remote shoots and more elaborate plots. Higher budgets will allow storylines that are worldwide in scope and feature larger casts (with characters borrowed from sister soaps.)

• A strong return to family values. America in the 1990s is a more traditional society than the America in the turbulent 1960s, 1970s, 1980s. Soap operas began in this country's kitchens and living rooms where the focus was on the ties between husband and wife, parent and child, brother and sister. By going back to this timeless theme, soaps will keep viewer interest into the twentieth century.

The conclusion: The critics are wrong. Soaps will not only survive, but thrive. For decades to come, we'll be reveling in the loves, lusts and lives of daytime drama.

IV

Bios of Your Favorite Soap Stars

RACHEL AMES

BORN: November 2; Portland, Oregon

HEIGHT: 5'6"

EYES: Blue

STATUS: Married to actor Barry Cahill

CHILDREN: Christine, Susan

GRANDCHILDREN: Jocelyn, Mark

AWARDS: Emmy nomination, Best Actress, 1974, 1975; Best Supporting Actress, 1978

Ames was born in Portland, Oregon to actor Byron Foulger and actress Dorothy Adams. As a child, she performed with her parents while attending University High School in Los Angeles and U.C.L.A. After college, she became a contract performer at Paramount Pictures and made her film debut in "When Worlds Collide." She had numerous roles in plays, including "Broadway Jones," "The Circle," "King of Hearts," "The Immortalist," "Mary Rose," "Golden Boy" and "Cradle Song" (with her father). She made her television debut in 1959 when she joined the cast of the San Francisco-based police show, "Lineup," as Police Officer Sandy McAllister (the show was later syndicated under the name "San Francisco Best").

In 1964, Ames joined the cast of the fledgling soap "General Hospital," and today she is one of the longest running performers in the history of soap opera.

In her spare time, she plays tennis and enjoys gardening.

Audrey Martin
"General Hospital"

Shortly after her character was created, Audrey married Dr. Steve Hardy, Chief of Staff of General Hospital (played by John Beradino, the show's only remaining original cast member). By the time she divorced Hardy, married and divorced two other men, and remarried Hardy, Ames' character was at the very heart of the show.

JOHN ANISTON

BORN: July 24; Crete

HEIGHT: 6'3"

EYES: Brown

STATUS: Married to a Sherry Rooney

CHILDREN: Jennifer, Alexander

OTHER SOAP ROLES:
Eric Richards, "Days of Our Lives"
Edouard Aleata, "Love of Life"
Martin Tourneur, "Search for Tomorrow"

AWARDS: Outstanding Lead Actor and Outstanding Villain, *Soap Opera Digest* Award, 1986

*A*niston spent his early childhood on his native island of Crete. After moving to the United States, Aniston pursued his education, but had trouble defining his goals. He received a B.A. in theater arts from Penn State, then went on to get a B.S. in biology from the University of California at Northridge. After a tour of duty in U.S. Navy Intelligence, Aniston decided to devote himself to acting.

Aniston won many stage roles, in addition to appearances in such feature films as "Love With a Proper Stranger" and "What a Way to Go." His first daytime role, as Eric Richards on "Days of Our Lives," lasted less than a year. After a series of guest starring roles on such series as "Kojak," "That Girl" and "Toma," he got the part of Edouard Aleata in "Love of Life." In 1979, he switched to "Search for Tomorrow," where he starred for five years. In 1985, he made a triumphant return to "Days of Our Lives" as Victor Kiriakis.

Aniston met his second wife, actress Sherry Rooney, when both were on "Love of Life," and they have adopted a son, Alexander. Aniston's daughter from a previous marriage, Jennifer Aniston, had starring roles in the NBC sitcom "Ferris Bueller" and the Fox sitcom "Molloy." Aniston enjoys tennis, skiing and cabinet making.

Victor Kiriakis
"Days of Our Lives"

Powerful crime boss Victor Kiriakis, the father of Bo Brady (by Caroline Brady) and Isabelle Toscano, appeared in Salem in 1985, and his impact as a villain was so impressive that John Aniston garnered two *Soap Opera Digest* Awards the next year. His character has romanced a number of the show's leading ladies, most recently the mysterious Kate Roberts.

MATTHEW ASHFORD

BORN: January 29; Davenport, Iowa

EYES: Brown

STATUS: Married to Christina Saffran

CHILDREN: Grace

OTHER SOAP ROLES:
Drew Ralston, "One Life to Live"
Cagney McCleary, "Search for Tomorrow"

AWARDS: *Soap Opera Digest* Award, Outstanding Villain, 1989; Outstanding Super Couple (with Melissa Reeves), 1991; Best Wedding (with Melissa Reeves), 1992; Outstanding Comic Performer, 1993.

Ashford was born in the Midwest, and moved East with his family to Fairfax, Virginia as a teenager. After high school, he enrolled in the North Carolina School of Arts in Winston-Salem to study acting. Afterwards, he performed with the Ragamuffin Magic and Mime Company of Myrtle Beach, South Carolina, then toured in "The Member of the Wedding."

His big break came early in his career, when he won the part of Drew Ralston on "One Life to Live" in 1982. He moved on to "Search for Tomorrow" until that soap was canceled in 1986. Shortly afterward, he landed the juicy role of Jack Deveraux on "Days of Our Lives." The breadth of that role is demonstrated by the fact that he has won *Soap Opera Digest* Awards for Outstanding Villain and Outstanding

Comic Performer—the latter an area in which his magic and mime training no doubt came in handy.

Ashford married choreographer Christina Saffran in 1987, and their first child was born in 1992. He enjoys theater and listening to music. He's also very interested in Buddhist philosophy.

Jack Deveraux
"Days of Our Lives"

Ashford followed Joseph Adams and James Acheson in the role of money-hungry Jack Deveraux in 1987. Deveraux married Kayla Brady, but she divorced him and married Steve "Patch" (as in eye patch) Johnson in 1988. Deveraux was a villain, but his long romance and marriage to TV anchorwoman Jennifer turned him into the kind of appealing character that allowed Ashford to win the Oustanding Comic Performer Award.

JULIA BARR

BORN: February 8;
Fort Wayne, Indiana

HEIGHT: 5'1"

EYES: Blue

STATUS: Married to Dr.
Richard Hirschlag

CHILDREN: Allison,

OTHER SOAP ROLES:
Reenie Szabo, "Ryan's Hope"

AWARDS: Emmy Award, Outstanding Supporting Actress, 1990; Emmy nomination, Outstanding Lead Actress, 1980, 1981, 1991, 1993; *Soap Opera Digest* Award nomination, Outstanding Lead Actress, 1992

*E*nglish always wanted to be an actress, and she was active in community theater while growing up. She performed in student productions while at Purdue

University, then got her first professional job appearing with Van Johnson in "Our Town." She moved to New York, juggling acting jobs with other means of employment that included working for an answering service. In 1976, she got the role of Reenie Szabo on "Ryan's Hope," and the exposure led to her winning the role of Brooke English on "All My Children" later the same year.

Seventeen years later, she's one of daytime drama's best known and admired actresses. She took a short leave from "All My Children" in 1981-1982, during which time she appeared with Katherine Hepburn and Dorothy Louden in the play "West Side Waltz" and performed in the film "I, the Jury."

During that break, she also married oral surgeon Dr. Richard Hirschlag, her second husband. Their daughter was born in 1984. In her spare time, she enjoys the theater and collecting snow domes. She and her husband are active in their daughter's school.

Brooke English
"All My Children"

In 1976, Barr became the third Brooke English, niece of Phoebe Wallingford and editor of Tempo Magazine. She was married to Tom Cudahy in a stormy relationship that lasted several years. Then she married Adam Chandler in a marriage that was tormented by the couple's inability to have a baby. She finally left Adam and later became pregnant by Tad Martin. After nearly losing the baby in an auto accident, she gave birth to Jamie. She married Tad after he returned to Pine Valley with amnesia.

BERNARD BARROW

BORN: December 30; New York, New York

HEIGHT: 6'0"

EYES: Brown

STATUS: Married to Joan Kaye

OTHER SOAP ROLES:
Earl Dana, "Where the Heart Is"

Dan Kinkaid, "The Secret Storm"
Johnny Ryan, "Ryan's Hope"

AWARDS: Emmy Award, Outstanding Supporting Actor, 1991; Emmy nomination, Outstanding Supporting Actor, 1979, 1988, 1992

*F*ew people in the theater have had as distinguished a performing and academic career as Barrow. He was born in New York City, and he began his show business career as a child actor on radio. After high school, he received his B.A. from Syracuse University, his masters degree from Columbia University and his Ph.D in theater history from Yale Univeristy. From 1955 to 1992, he taught and directed student performances at Brooklyn College.

In the 1950s and 1960s Barrow performed in numerous regional productions, touring companies and off-Broadway productions. He has played featured roles in the motion pictures "Serpico," "Rachel, Rachel," "Glass Houses," "Claudine" and "The Survivors." In 1969, he got his first daytime role in the short-lived serial, "Where the Heart Is." He then spent five years on "The Secret Storm," after which he joined the original cast of the new daytime serial, "Ryan's Hope," in the central role of patriarch Johnny Ryan. Barrow received two Emmy nominations for this role, which he played until the soap ended in 1989. He then moved on to his current role as retired sanitation worker Louie Slavinsky on "Loving."

After so many years of acting, Barrow's main interest remains the theater, and he still loves performing. Among his many guest appearances on television are roles as the judge who performed two of prime time television's most publicized weddings—Valarie Harper and David Groh on "Rhoda" and Bea Arthur and Bill Macy on "Maude." He has been married to actress Joan Kaye for almost 30 years.

Louie Slavinsky
"Loving"

Louis Slavinsky, a retired sanitation worker, moved on to Corinth and soon fell in love with the wealthy Kate Rescott, mother of Ava. He remained by Kate's side while she recovered from cancer surgery, then married her.

PATRICIA BARRY

BORN: November 16; Davenport, Iowa

HEIGHT: 5'6"

EYES: Brown

STATUS: Married to Philip Barry

CHILDREN: Miranda Barry, Stephanie Agnew

OTHER SOAP ROLES:
Addie Horton Olson Williams, "Days of Our Lives"
Peg English, "All My Children"
Sally Gleason, "Guiding Light"

One of the most experienced performers on daytime television, Patricia Barry attended Stephens College where she became interested in the theater. She moved to New York to study acting and soon got her first Broadway role in "Pink Elephant" (with Steve Allen). She moved on to many other roles on Broadway, in touring productions and in Los Angeles.

Her television credits total more than 2,000 appearances, including roles on almost every major series of the last three decades. Among others, she has guest-starred on "Perry Mason," "Gunsmoke," "The Untouchables," "77 Sunset Strip," "Maverick," "Three's Company," "Thriller," "Hitchcock," "Columbo," "Dallas," "Knots Landing" and "Hunter." Her TV movie appearances include "The Hard Road," "The Wicked Scheme of Jebel Deeks," "Golden Nuggets," "First You Cry," "The Devil You Say" and "She Woke Up." Her feature film appearances include "Send Me No Flowers," "Kitten With a Whip," "Dear Heart," "American Gigolo," "Twilight Zone—The Movie," "War Dancing" and "Sea of Love."

Barry's first soap role was as Addie Horton Olson Williams on "Days of Our Lives." She was so popular that Addie's on screen death (in an automobile accident) produced a flood of protest letters from viewers. She moved on to play the scheming Peg English in "All My Children" and the colorful ex-madam-turned-entrepreneur Sally Gleason in "Guiding Light." These days, she portrays Isabelle Alden on "Loving."

Outside of performing, Barry is the president of Women in

Films, a founder of the First Woman's Bank, founding president of the American Film Institute Associates, vice president of the John Tracy Clinic, a member of the Foreign Film Committee of the Academy of Motion Pictures, a member of the Blue Ribbon Panel of the Academy of Television Arts & Sciences, a member of the Women's Committee of the Screen Actors Guild and special advisor to the president of Stephens College. Her husband is TV producer Philip Barry. Their daughter Miranda is also a TV producer, and daughter Stephanie owns a daycare center.

Isabelle Alden,
"Loving"

Barry recently replaced Augusta Dabney as Isabelle Alden, widow of Cabot Alden, mother of Clay Alden, and the matriarch of the Alden family. Isabelle is a manipulator who is always involving herself in everyone else's business.

LAURALEE BELL

BORN: December 22; Chicago, Illinois

HEIGHT: 5'6"

EYES: Blue

STATUS: Single

*B*ell comes from one of soap's leading families: father William Bell co-created "Another World" and with her mother, Lee Philip Bell, created "The Young and the Restless" and "The Bold and the Beautiful." Her mother was also a Chicago talk show host who won several local Emmy awards.

Lauralee was always captivated by show business. She took acting, dance and voice lessons in addition her school work. She made her first appearance at age nine as an extra on "The Young and the Restless," and at age thirteen she had her very first line as Cricket. Bell spent the entire summer before her senior year in high school working on the show. Her character was very well received, and she eventually joined the show full time.

Bell is extremely interested in the problems of young people, and she's active in ChildHelp U.S.A. Because of her exposure to the behind-the-scenes mechanics of daytime drama, she's interested in writing and production. In her spare time, she enjoys tennis, needlepoint and shopping.

Cricket Blair Romalotti
"The Young and the Restless"

Cricket Blair was first introduced as a high school student, who then went on to become a lawyer. She's married to rock singer Danny Romalotti, but a conflict in careers has caused increasing tension.

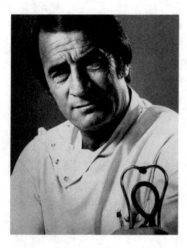

JOHN BERADINO

BORN: May 1;
Los Angeles, California

HEIGHT: 5'11"

EYES: Brown

STATUS: Married to Marjorie Binder

CHILDREN: Katherine, John

AWARDS: Emmy nomination, Best Daytime Actor, 1974, 1975, 1976

Beradino, one of soap's most durable stars, had also had one of the most unusual careers. He grew up in Los Angeles, and was successful as a child actor, even appearing in the famous "Our Gang" movies. But as a teenager, it was his athletic prowess that won him honors. After graduating from high school, he received a football scholarship to attend the University of Southern California. In his sophomore year, he switched to baseball and was named the team's most valuable player. In 1939, he was signed by the St. Louis Browns. His professional baseball career was interrupted when he served in World War II, but he returned to the major leagues after his discharge. He was a member of the Cleveland Indians team that won the 1948 world series, and he continued to play until a leg injury ended his career in 1953.

At that point, Beradino returned to acting. He made his television debut in an episode of "Superman" in 1955, and went on to starring roles in the series "The New Breed" and "I Led Three Lives." He guest-starred on "The Untouchables," "Cheyenne" and "Laramie." Then, on April 1, 1963, he appeared on the very first broadcast of "General Hospital." On the same date in 1993, he celebrated his thirty year anniversary as the only remaining original cast member. He may have appeared in more televised episodes of a soap opera than any other actor.

Beradino is married to Marjorie Binder and has two grown children. Tennis is his major athletic outlet, and he also enjoys writing.

Dr. Steve Hardy
"General Hospital"

General Hospital is the meeting ground for the core "family" on which the soap opera has centered for thirty years and, as Chief of Staff, Dr. Steve Hardy has been the family's patriarch. He met and married nurse Audrey March early in the show's run, but she divorced him after the death of their baby. After two subsequent marriages and divorces, Audrey remarried Steve, and their relationship has endured.

PETER BERGMAN

BORN: June 11; Guantanamo, Cuba

HEIGHT: 6'1"

EYES: Blue

STATUS: Married to Mariellen Bergman

CHILDREN: Connor, Clare

OTHER SOAP ROLES:
Dr. Cliff Warner, "All My Children"

AWARDS: Emmy Award, Outstanding Lead Actor, 1991, 1992; Emmy nomination, Outstanding Lead Actor, 1983,

1990, 1993; *Soap Opera Digest* Award, Outstanding Lead Actor, 1992

This tall, blue-eyed star was born into a military family that moved nine times before he started the eighth grade. Bergman always loved working with his hands, so it wasn't until college that he decided to pursue acting. He worked in construction for a year to earn his tuition to the American Academy of Dramatic Arts in New York. He performed in a number of off-Broadway plays and appeared in several television commercials before he won his role on "All My Children" in 1980. He was such an immediate success that the magazines *Daytime TV* and *Soap Opera Digest* named him "The Most Promising Young Actor in Daytime Television" for 1980.

The low point in his career came ten years later, when he was written out of "All My Children." But shortly afterward, "The Young and the Restless" executive producer Bill Bell hired him to replace Terry Lester as Jack Abbott on the top-rated soap. Again, he was immediately popular, receiving an Emmy nomination in his first year and the coveted Emmy Award the next two years.

The attention he's received in daytime television has led to Bergman's starring roles in six prime time, made-for-television movies, including "Palimino" and "Woman on the Ledge." In his spare time, Bergman is an accomplished piano player and he enjoys doing carpentry, plumbing and electrical work around his Los Angeles home.

Jack Abbott
"The Young and the Restless"

Jack Abbott, the son of John Abbott, founder of Jabot Cosmetics, was married to Patty. He divorced her and married Nikki, an ex-stripper who was also the ex-wife of powerful business magnate Victor Newman. Jack left Nikki when she was unable to rid herself of her feelings for Victor, and he is constantly caught up in battles for control of Jabot.

ERIC BRAEDEN

BORN: April 3;
Kiel, Germany

HEIGHT: 6'1"

EYES: Brown

STATUS: Married to Dale
Braeden

CHILDREN: Christian

AWARDS: *Soap Opera Digest* Award, Outstanding Actor,
1989

*B*raeden was born Han Gudegast, the son of a
German Army officer. As a teenager, he was a star
athlete, excelling in track and field and soccer.
After graduating from high school he moved to the United
States, where he drifted for a while, working at several jobs.
Then he and a friend became the first people to ever success-
fully travel up and down Idaho's infamous Salmon River.
The two then went to Los Angeles to try to market a docu-
mentary film they made of the adventure.

In California, Gudegast discovered a market for German
actors. He made his television debut as Captain Hans
Dietrich of the German Afrika Corps in the World War II
series "The Rat Patrol." He also appeared in the movie
"Operation Eichman." He soon changed his name to Eric
Braeden (Braeden was his family's home village in
Germany). He went on to guest-star in numerous TV series
and played roles in films, including the cult favorite
"Colossus: The Forbidden Project," "The Ultimate Chase,"
"Honeymoon with a Stranger," "A Hundred Rifles" and
"Escape From the Planet of the Apes." In 1980, he made his
daytime debut as Victor Newman on "The Young and the
Restless," and he quickly became one of the most popular
leading men on the most highly-rated daytime drama.

In his private life, Braeden was a founder of the German-
American Cultural Society and sits on the German-American
Advisory Board with such distinguished Americans as Dr.
Henry Kissinger, General Alexander Haig and Washington
Post publisher Katherine Graham. Braeden, who is married

to his college sweetheart, enjoys being athletic, and likes soccer, running, tennis and skiing.

Victor Newman
"The Young and the Restless"

Ruthless businessman and head of Jabot Cosmetics, Victor Newman has been married to Julie, Nikki and Ashley, and is father to Victoria and Nicholas. But he and Nikki have never lost their attraction to each other. Recently, Victor was kidnapped and presumed dead, setting off a power struggle for his empire before he reemerged.

JOSEPH BREEN

BORN: July 5; Mount Kisco, New York

HEIGHT: 6'1"

EYES: Hazel

STATUS: Divorced

CHILDREN: Catlin, Meghan, Devon

OTHER SOAP ROLES:
Dr. Will Jeffries, "Guiding Light"
Paul Slavinsky, "Loving"

*B*reen was born and raised in Westchester County, a New York City suburb. A neighbor, Broadway actor Robert Rounseville, encouraged the teenage Breen to develop his singing talent, and he responded by acting in school plays. After a brief stay at Oberlin College in Ohio, Breen enrolled in the American Academy of Dramatic Arts in New York. After appearing in several off-Broadway and touring productions, he won the role of Jean-Michael in the Broadway production of the smash hit, "La Cage aux Folles."

After touring in the same play, he returned to New York and took singing and acting at the Julliard School.

In 1987, he joined the cast of "Guiding Light" as Dr. Will Jeffries, who married Mindy Lewis in 1988. Breen moved on to "Loving" in 1989 to portray mobster Paul Slavinsky, who was later paralyzed. In 1992, he joined "As the World Turns."

In his spare time, Breen continues to train as an opera singer, a passion he would like to pursue professionally. He writes plays and he also enjoys gardening, carpentry and spending time with his three daughters.

Scott Eldridge
"As the World Turns"

Scott Eldridge is Lisa Mitchell's son, and he shares her penchant for creating trouble.

KIMBERLIN BROWN

BORN: June 29; Hayward, California

HEIGHT: 5'6"

EYES: Hazel

STATUS: Married to Gary Petzer

OTHER SOAP ROLES:
Danielle Steele, "Santa Barbara"

AWARDS: Emmy nomination, Outstanding Supporting Actress, 1992; *Soap Opera Digest* Award, Outstanding Villain/Villainess, 1993

This Hayward, California beauty began modeling at age nine, when she was discovered by Nina Blanchard. As a teenager she won the Miss La Mesa and Miss California competitions. After briefly attending college, she modeled in Europe for a year and in the Orient for six months.

After returning to the U.S., Brown guest-starred in such television series as "Matt Houston," "T.J. Hooker" and "Hawaiian Heat." She had a recurring role on "Santa Barbara" and also appeared on "Capitol." In 1989, she was cast as nurse Sheila Carter on "The Young and the Restless," where she soon became one of soap's most treacherous women. In 1992, William Bell moved her character to "The Bold and the Beautiful"; a year later, she was involved in major storylines on both soaps at the same time. For her herculean labors, Brown received a 1992 Emmy nomination and a 1993 *Soap Opera Digest* Award. She's also found the time to appear in the feature films "Who's That Girl," "Eye of the Tiger" and "18 Again."

Brown is married to Gary Petzer. She's active in the Free Arts Clinic and the City of Hope. In her spare time, she enjoys traveling, scuba diving, snow skiing, water skiing and mountain climbing.

Sheila Carter
"The Bold and the Beautiful"
"The Young and the Restless"

Sheila Carter, a nurse who is also one of the most devious soap villains of recent years, made her debut on "The Young and the Restless" in 1989. She exited that show when she was believed killed in a raging inferno that leveled the Michigan farmhouse where she was holding Lauren and her mother, Molly, prisoner. Then she surfaced on "The Bold and the Beautiful," where she recently married Eric Forrester.

LARRY BRYGGMAN

BORN: December 21; Concord, California

HEIGHT: 6'0"

EYES: Blue

STATUS: Divorced

CHILDREN: Michael, Jeffrey, Heidi

AWARDS: Emmy Award, Outstanding Lead Actor, 1984, 1987; Emmy nomination, Outstanding Lead Actor, 1990

*B*ryggman studied acting at the City College of San Francisco, and shortly afterward began a significant stage career that included roles in "Ulysses In Nighttown" (with Zero Mostel), "The Lincoln Mask," "Checking Out," "The Basic Training of Pavlo Hummer" (with Al Pacino) and "Richard III" (also with Pacino).

In 1969, Bryggman was cast in "As the World Turns." His reputation as one of daytime's finest actors grew as he garnered two Emmy awards for Outstanding Lead Actor. In his time off from the show, he had roles in the films "...And Justice For All" and "Hanky Panky," and he also appeared in the TV productions "Trail of Panther 13," "The Witches of Salem," "A Celebration for William Jennings Bryan" and "Strike Force." He continues to perform in off-Broadway and in regional productions.

Bryggman has three grown children. In his spare time, he enjoys sports, reading and music.

Dr. John Dixon
"As the World Turns"

Dr. John Dixon, Chief of Staff of Oakdale Hospital, has been one of soap's leading villains for more than two decades. He's been married several times, most recently to Lucinda, and he's the father of Andy, Duke and Margo. In one memorable storyline, he was arrested and tried for marital rape of his then-wife, Dee.

DAVID CANARY

BORN: August 25; Elmwood, Indiana

STATUS: Married to Maureen Canary

CHILDREN: Lisa, Chris, Kate

OTHER SOAP ROLES:
Steve Frame, "Another World"

AWARDS: Emmy Award, Outstanding Lead Actor, 1986, 1988, 1989, 1991; *Soap Opera Digest* Award, Outstanding Villain, 1990; *Soap Opera Digest* Award, Outstanding Lead Actor, 1992

*C*anary was raised in Ohio, where his high school football talent won him an athletic scholarship to the University of Cincinnati. In college, he studied at the Cincinnati Conservatory of Music. Following graduation, he went to New York and made his stage debut in the play "Great Day in the Morning" (with Colleen Dewhurst). His next role was a command performance—but the command came from Uncle Sam. After a tour of duty in the Army, he resumed his stage career in San Francisco.

He first came to national attention when he was cast in the role of Russ Gehring on the prime time serial, "Peyton Place." He moved on to "Bonanza," where he played Candy, the ranch foreman. After "Bonanza" ended in 1973, he guest-starred in numerous television series and appeared in the films "Hombre," "The St. Valentine's Day Massacre," "End of a Dark Street" and "In a Pig's Eye." In 1981, he moved back to New York and, after two years on "Another World," won the part of Adam Chandler on "All My Children." He is the only daytime performer to win four Emmy Awards.

Canary and his wife Maureen were married in 1982. They have two children, and Canary has another daughter from a previous marriage. He continues to perform on stage during his breaks from "All My Children," and he devotes considerable time to playwriting.

Adam/Stuart Chandler
"All My Children"

The wealthy, ruthless Adam Chandler had a fiery and memorable marriage to Erica Kane in his early days in Pine Valley. He has lost and regained his fortune, caused havoc in the love lives of others, fathered Adam, Jr. by Dixie, and, most recently, married Gloria shortly before he was paralyzed in an automobile accident.

The gentle, naive Stuart Chandler couldn't be more different from his twin brother. His courtship and marriage to Cindy, who was dying of AIDS, was one of soap's most poignant love affairs of the last decade.

MACDONALD CAREY

BORN: March 15; Sioux City, Iowa

STATUS: Divorced

AWARDS: Emmy Award, Outstanding Actor, 1974, 1976; Emmy nomination, Outstanding Actor, 1968, 1973, 1975; *Soap Opera Digest* Award, Outstanding Actor in a Mature Role, 1978, 1979, 1984, 1985

*B*orn in Iowa in 1913, Carey was a serious student who received a masters degree from the University of Iowa. He moved to New York in 1938, where he found work on Broadway and in such radio serials as "Stella Dallas," "John's Other Wife," "Just Plain Bill," "Ellen Randolph," "Woman in White" and "Young Hickory." He put his career on hold to serve in the Marine Corps in World War II, but after his discharge he signed with Paramount Pictures. Carey appeared in more than fifty films, including Alfred Hitchcock's "Shadow of a Doubt." He starred in the 1956 TV series "Dr. Christian" and the 1959 series "Lock Up," and he guest-starred on TV series such as "Lassie," "Ben Casey," "Outer Limits," "G.E. Theater," "U.S. Steel Hour" and "Mr. Novak."

On November 8, 1965, Carey appeared in the very first episode of "Days of Our Lives." One of the most distinguished of all daytime performers, Carey has received two Emmy and four *Soap Opera Digest* Awards.

In his personal life, Carey emerged from a decades-long battle with alcoholism and has been sober since the early 1980s. In his spare time, he continues his forty-year practice of karate. A father of six, he is also an accomplished poet who has published three volumes of his work.

Dr. Tom Horton
"Days of Our Lives"

From the very first episode of "Days of Our Lives," Dr. Tom Horton's voice has entoned, "Like sands through the hourglass, so are the days of our lives." He is the patriarch of the Horton family, and, together with his wife, Alice, has served as the wise and calm emotional center of the show.

PHILIP CAREY

BORN: July 15; Hackensack, New Jersey

HEIGHT: 6'4"

EYES: Blue

STATUS: Single

*V*eteran actor Philip Carey was born in New Jersey, but raised in the Long Island towns of Rosedale and Malverne. The strapping 6'4", blue-eyed youth enlisted in the U.S. Marines, seeing action in both World War II and the Korean War. In between, he studied acting at the University of Miami.

After his military service, he began his acting career in stock theater productions. During a performance of "Over 21" in Sayville, Long Island, he was seen by a representative of Warner Brothers, who invited him to take a screen test. Shortly afterward, he won a role in the John Wayne movie, "Operation Pacific," launching a long film career. Under contract for periods of time to both Warner Brothers and Columbia Pictures, Carey appeared in such famous films as "Springfield Rifle" (with Gary Cooper), "The Long Gray Line" (with Tyrone Power), "Mr. Roberts" (with Henry Fonda), and "Pushover" (with Fred MacMurray and Kim Novak). In prime time television, he had the title role in the series "Philip Marlowe," the role of Captain Parmalee in the western "Laredo" and acted as host of "The Untamed World." He guest starred on "All in the Family," "Little House on the Prairie," "Police Woman" and "Gunsmoke." He has also toured in stage productions of many plays, including "All My Sons" and "Cyrano de Bergerac." In the late 1970s, Carey joined the cast of "One Life to Live" as Texas oil millionaire Asa Buchanan, a role he's played ever since.

In his spare time, Carey is an accomplished horseman who has appeared in many rodeos. He also enjoys playing golf.

Asa Buchanan
"One Life to Live"

Asa Buchanan is a wealthy Texas businessman who moved to Llanview in 1979 with his son, Clint. He married Olympia and raised her son Bo as his own. He later married Sam, Delilah, Pamela, Becky Lee and Renee, a former madam.

CRYSTAL CHAPPELL

BORN: August 4; Silver Spring, Maryland

HEIGHT: 5'6"

EYES: Brown

STATUS: Divorced

*C*happell grew up in a nomadic family. Her parents would purchase an old home, then the entire family would work to rebuild it so it could be sold at a profit. After graduating from high school in Maryland, she became sort of an intellectual wanderer, beginning her college studies in computer science, then switching to journalism, then finally to acting. After performing in the finals of the National College Theater Festival at the Kennedy Center in Washington, she studied acting in the West Indies, then moved to New York.

After a tough period, during which she did day work on "All My Children," she moved to Los Angeles. After a week-long cameo on "Santa Barbara" (as a drug dealer who was killed), she was offered the role of Carly on "Days of Our Lives." She and costar Peter Reckell had great chemistry on-camera, and she quickly became a daytime star in her own right.

Chappell continues to perform on stage during her breaks from daytime work. When she has time, she enjoys running, scuba diving, tennis, skiing, hiking and music. She's also a cat lover.

Dr. Carly Manning
"Days of Our Lives"

Carly Manning was the mother of Nicholas, and had a nasty break-up with his father, Lawrence. She was hired to care for Victor after he had a stroke, and he fell in love with her. She accepted his marriage proposal because his son, Bo, who she really loved, wouldn't declare his love for her. But after Carly learned Victor had plotted to kill Bo, she divorced him and married Bo in a Mayan ceremony. Their marriage, however, was tainted by the chemistry still lingering between Carly and Lawrence.

LESLIE CHARLESON

BORN: February 22; Kansas City, Missouri

STATUS: Divorced

OTHER SOAP ROLES:
Pam, "A Flame in the Wind/A Time For Us"
Alice Whipple, "As the World Turns"
Iris Garrison, "Love is a Many Splendored Thing"

AWARDS: Emmy nomination, Outstanding Lead Actress, 1980, 1982, 1983

*A*s a young girl, Charleson's primary interest was horses. But as a teenager, she also fell in love with acting. After being named Outstanding Theater Arts student in her Bennett College graduating class, she moved to New York to continue her studies. It didn't take long before she was cast as Pam in the new daytime serial "A Flame in The Wind," which was soon renamed "A Time For Us." When that soap was canceled in 1966, she moved on to "As the World Turns." Her next role, as Iris Garrison in "Love is a Many Splendored Thing," produced her first Emmy nomination in 1970.

That same year, she left that role and New York to move to Los Angeles. For the next seven years, she guest-starred on such shows as "Adam 12," "Barnaby Jones," "The Streets of San Francisco," "Medical Center," "Marcus Welby, M.D.," "Ironside" and "Happy Days." She appeared in the theatrical movie "Day of the Dolphin" and the television movies

"The Black Box Murders" and "The Norming of Jack 2-3-4." Then, in 1977, she was offered the role of Monica Quartermaine on "General Hospital." Charleson's fine work as Monica for more than sixteen years has won her two additional Emmy nominations and the adoration of "General Hospital" fans.

Her co-star on "General Hospital," Anna Lee, reawakened her interest in horses. Charleson owns an Andalusian horse, which she rides in such events as the Rose Bowl Parade. She is also a fund-raiser for the Cystic Fibrosis Foundation.

Monica Quartermaine
"General Hospital"

Dr. Monica Bard, a skilled heart surgeon, arrived in Port Charles and soon married Jeff Webber, but she was also attracted to his brother, Rick Webber. After divorcing Jeff, Monica met Dr. Alan Quartermaine. Although they hated each other at first, but they eventually married. Their ongoing love-hate relationship has resulted in a long-term but very stormy relationship.

DARLENE CONLEY

BORN: July 18; Chicago Heights, Illinois

HEIGHT: 5'7"

EYES: Green

STATUS: Divorced

CHILDREN: Raymond, Theodore, William

OTHER SOAP ROLES:
Rose DeVille, "The Young and the Restless"
Edith Baker, "Days of Our Lives"
Louie, "Capitol"
Trixie Monahan, "General Hospital"

AWARDS: Emmy nomination, Outstanding Supporting Actress, 1991

hicago-born Conley got her first break at age 15 when she was cast in the touring production of "The Heiress" with Basil Rathbone. After completing two years of college, she moved to New York, where she performed in such plays as "The Night of the Iguana" (with Richard Chamberlain) and "The Baker's Wife." Her first movie role was in the Alfred Hitchcock classic "The Birds."

Her illustrious career includes film appearances in "Lady Sings the Blues," "Play It As It Lays," "Valley of the Dolls," "Faces," "Minnie and Moscowitz" and "Tough Guys." Conley's roles in TV movies include "The Fighter," "Robert Kennedy and His Times," "The Choice," "Return Engagement" and "The President's Plane Is Missing." She's had guest appearances on "Gunsmoke," "The Cosby Show," "Murder, She Wrote," "Cagney and Lacey," "Little House on the Prairie" and "The Mary Tyler Moore Show."

Her daytime career began when she played Rose DeVille on "The Young and the Restless." After short-term roles on three other soaps, she was hired once again by Bill Bell for "The Bold and the Beautiful." The role has already garnered her one Emmy nomination.

Conley is the divorced mother of three grown sons. She volunteers in an AIDS hospice, contributes her talents to theater organizations and enjoys art.

Sally Spectra
"The Bold and the Beautiful"

Sally Spectra is the flamboyant, even wild, head of Spectra Fashions. She's the mother of Macy and Clarke, Jr., and she has been involved with Jack.

JEANNE COOPER

BORN: October 25; Taft, California

HEIGHT: 5'6"

EYES: Blue

STATUS: Divorced

CHILDREN: Corbin, Colin, Caren

AWARDS: *Soap Opera Digest* Editors' Award for Lifetime Achievement; *Soap Opera Digest* Award, Outstanding Lead Actress, 1989; Emmy nomination, Outstanding Lead Actress, 1990, 1991, 1992

After studying theater at the College of the Pacific and the Pasadena Playhouse School, Cooper started working with the Civic Light Opera Company and the Revue Theater of Stockton, California. She caught the attention of talent scouts for Universal Pictures and was signed as a contract player. Before long, she made her film debut in "Redhead from Wyoming" and had her first starring role opposite Glenn Ford in "The Man from the Alamo." She has also appeared in "The Boston Strangler," "Tony Rome," "All American Boy," "The Glory Guys," "Kansas City Bomber," and "Let No Man Write My Epitaph." She had regular roles on the TV series "Maverick" and as Mrs. Douglas on "Bracken's World" (for which she was nominated for a prime time Emmy).

In 1973, Cooper joined the cast of the new soap "The Young and the Restless." She has been a fixture on daytime television ever since, garnering not only three Emmy nominations and a *Soap Opera Digest* Award, but also a lifetime achievement recognition from *Soap Opera Digest*. She has continued to appear as a guest star on other TV shows. Her more than 400 appearances include one as the mother of Corbin Bernsen, her real-life son, on "L.A. Law." This role earned her a second prime time Emmy nomination.

In her spare time, she dotes on her five grandchildren. She also contributes her time to a host of charitable organizations.

Katherine Chancellor Sterling
"The Young and the Restless"

The wealthy socialite Kay Chancellor had a penchant for alcohol and for younger men, both vices against which she waged a long battle. This lively and vibrant woman even had an on-air face lift (which featured tape of Jeanne Cooper's real-life face-lift). She's currently married to Rex Sterling.

ALICIA COPPOLA

BORN: April 12; Huntington, New York

HEIGHT: 5'8"

EYES: Brown

STATUS: Single

AWARDS: *Soap Opera Digest* Award, Outstanding Leading Younger Actress, 1993

*C*oppola, who was born on Long Island, had her comfortable world disrupted at age 12 when her father was diagnosed with brain cancer. For eleven years he fought the disease before succumbing in 1991. Even though she graduated from the prestigious Kent prep school, Coppola never felt like she fit in. For college, she chose New York University in Manhattan, where she studied philosophy.

After she graduated from college, she met a model from the Elite agency, who arranged an interview for her. That led to a 13-week job on MTV's game show, "Remote Control." Coppola found she loved being in front of the camera and she began going to auditions. To her surprise, she was hired by "Another World."

The most frequent question Coppola is asked is if she's any relation to famous director Francis Ford Coppola. Because family records are non-existent, all she knows is that both families are from Naples, Italy.

Lorna Devon
"Another World"

Lorna, the music manager of D&M Enterprises, is the daughter of Felicia Gallant and is the half-sister of Jenna. She had to deal with the death of her father, Lucas, in a plot line that eerily mirrored Coppola's personal life.

IRENE DAILEY

BORN: September 12; New York, New York

HEIGHT: 5'6"

EYES: Blue-green

STATUS: Single

OTHER SOAP ROLES:
Pamela Stewart, "Edge of Night"

AWARDS: Emmy Award, Outstanding Actress, 1979

*D*ailey's father was the manager of New York City's Roosevelt Hotel, and she and her brother, Dan, were introduced to the theater and theater people at an early age. In 1941, she made her stage debut in "In Out of the Frying Pan." She went on to star in scores of plays, including "Desire Under the Elms," "Night of the Iguana," "Goodwoman of Setzuan," "Andorra," "The Subject Was Roses," "Rooms," "The Cavern," "Threepenny Opera," "Mother Courage," "The Effect of Gamma Rays of Man-in-the-Moon Marigolds," "The House of Blue Leaves," "Look Homeward Angel," "Company," "Long Days Journey Into Night," "Rio Grande" and "Lost in Yonkers." She's received a number of awards for her stage work. She also appeared in several films, including "Five Easy Pieces" (with Jack Nicholson) and "The Amityville Horror." Her prime time TV appearances include "Ben Casey," "The Naked City," "Twilight Zone," "Doctor Kildare" and "Perry Mason."

Dailey's first daytime drama was "Edge of Night." In 1974, she took over a role on "Another World." She has been a central character ever since, and her work was recognized with an Emmy award in 1979.

Throughout her career, Dailey has taught acting at such institutions as Princeton, Purdue, Northwestern, the North Carolina School of the Arts and the School of the Actors Company. She has recorded three albums and has written several stage plays.

Liz Matthews
"Another World"

When "Another World" premiered in 1964, Liz Matthews was the wife of William Matthews, one of two brothers in the soap's central family. William soon died, and attention shifted to the Corys, the Frames and other families. Liz Matthews continues as a confidante to younger characters and as a sometime rival to the scheming Rachel Cory.

MICHAEL DAMIAN

BORN: April 26; San Diego, California

HEIGHT: 5'10"

EYES: Blue

STATUS: Single

Damian was the youngest of nine children in a very musical family. As a child, he was tutored in the piano by his mother, a classical pianist, but he soon turned to more hip music. With his brothers and sisters, he toured and recorded as The Weirz. Eventually, he went out on his own and his first single, "She Did It," was a Billboard Top 100 hit. An appearance on "American Bandstand" brought him to the attention of the producers of "The Young and the Restless," who hired him in 1981.

Since then, Damian has combined recording with his daytime TV work. Many of his songs have debuted on "The Young and the Restless." His albums include Michael Damian, Love is a Mystery, Where Do We Go From Here and Dreams of Summer. His hit singles include "Rock On," which sold over 500,000 copies, and "Was It Nothing At All," which won a Broadcast Music Industry Award as one of the most performed songs of 1990. Most of his songs are produced by two of his brothers.

In his spare time, Damian enjoys going to the movies and playing golf. He devotes considerable time to persuading young people to say no to drugs.

Danny Romalotti
"The Young and the Restless"

Heartthrob Danny Romalotti, the son of Rex Sterling, is a successful rock singer whose music is frequently featured on the show. He's married to Cricket, but their marriage has been strained by their very different work schedules.

STUART DAMON

BORN: February 5; Brooklyn, New York

HEIGHT: 6'2"

EYES: Brown

STATUS: Married to Deirdre Ottewill

CHILDREN: Jennifer, Christopher, Christina

AWARDS: Emmy nomination, Outstanding Actor, 1981, 1982, 1983

The son of Russian immigrants, Damon enjoyed entertaining as a child, but he got a degree in psychology at Brandeis University in preparation for his enrollment in law school. However, a role in a summer stock production caused a delay in his plans that eventually became permanent. He spent several years touring with musical productions until he got his first Broadway role in the chorus of "Irma La Douce." He eventually worked his way into a featured role, and he later received the Theater World Award for Most Promising Performer of the Year for his role in "The Boys From Syracuse." A role in the television production of Rogers and Hammerstein's "Cinderella" led to the offer to star in a British television series "The champions." Partially because he was married to British actress Deirdre Ottewill, he accepted.

Damon spent twelve years in England doing both stage and television work. He and his family returned to the U.S. in 1977 and just two months later, he won a role on

"General Hospital." His work has earned him three Emmy nominations, and he continues to be a central character on this highly rated show.

Damon devotes a lot of time to raising money for the Juvenile Diabetes Foundation, a cause close to his heart because his son Christopher (one of his three children) suffers from diabetes. He also enjoys playing golf, watching sports and working around the house.

Dr. Alan Quartermaine
"General Hospital"

Alan Quartermaine is the son of Edward and Lila and the brother of Tracy. His career as a surgeon was cut short by an injury that affected his use of his hands. His long-term marriage to Monica has been very turbulent. He and Monica are the parents of A.J., and Alan fathered Jason in an affair with Susan Moore, who was later murdered.

LINDA DANO

BORN: May 12; Long Beach, California

HEIGHT: 5'7"

EYES: Hazel

STATUS: Married to Frank Attardi

OTHER SOAP ROLES:
Gretel Cummings, "One Life to Live"
Cynthia Haines, "As the World Turns"

AWARDS: Emmy Award, Outstanding Lead Actress, 1993; Emmy nomination, Outstanding Supporting Actress, 1992

After Dano received a degree in art from the University of California at Long Beach, she soon began working as a model. The exposure led to a three-year contract with 20th Century Fox. She was given a starring role as Angela in the briefly aired series "The Montefuscos," and she guest-starred on "Peyton Place," "The Rockford Files," "Emergency," "C.H.I.P.S.,"

"Charlie's Angels," "Barney Miller," "The Hardy Boys," "The Fess Parker Show" and "Braken's World."

In 1978, she joined the cast of "One Life to Live," then moved to "As the World Turns" in 1981. In 1983, she found a more permanent home on "Another World." She has gained recognition, receiving an Emmy nomination in 1992 and the coveted Emmy Award for Outstanding Lead Actress in 1993.

While on "Another World," Dano was co-host of the talk show "Attitudes," for which she received a 1989 Emmy nomination. She also operates her own fashion consulting firm, Strictly Personal Ltd. She also co-authored a romance novel, *Dreamworld*, under her TV name, Felicia Gallant. Married to advertising executive Frank Attardi, she loves antiques and devotes time to charitable activities.

Felicia Gallant
"Another World"

Felicia Gallant is a novelist turned TV talk show hostess. She was married to Zane Lindquist. After their marriage ended, she married Lucas, by whom she had a daughter, Lorna. She's also the adoptive mother of Lucas's daughter, Jenna. She recently emerged triumphant from a harrowing battle with alcoholism that was waged after Lucas died.

DOUG DAVIDSON

BORN: October 24; Glendale, California

HEIGHT: 6'0"

EYES: Blue

STATUS: Married to Cindy Fisher

CHILDREN: Calyssa, Caden

AWARDS: *Soap Opera Digest* Award, Outstanding Hero, 1990, 1991; *Soap Opera Digest* Award, Outstanding Supporting Actor, 1992

avidson grew up in La Canada-Flintridge, and he discovered his interest in acting early in high school. He attended Occidental College, with a double major of theater and marine biology. He supported himself by doing magazine and catalog modeling when he could find the work, and by a series of odd jobs that included tending bar and driving a cab. He eventually landed a number of national television commercials.

His big break came totally by accident. In 1979 he was visiting a friend on the set of "The Young and the Restless" when he was noticed by the producers. Shortly afterward he was hired, and he soon became one of the most popular actors on daytime. He won three *Soap Opera Digest* Awards in three years' time. During his breaks, he's appeared in the movie "Fraternity Row" and in the television films "I'll Take Manhattan" and "The Initiation of Sarah." He's also served as master of ceremonies of the Miss California Pageant and co-host of the Kenny Rogers Cerebral Palsy Telethon.

Davidson is married to actress Cindy Fisher and has two young children. In his spare time, he enjoys waterskiing, camping, scuba diving, running, karate and playing the bagpipes.

Paul Williams
"The Young and the Restless"

The dashing Paul Williams runs his own detective agency, a job which frequently involves him with other people's business. He is the ex-husband of Lauren Fenmore. His secretary, Lynne, is secretly in love with him; April, the mother of his illegitimate child, recently returned to town; and he has grown closer to Cricket as her marriage to Danny falters.

EILEEN DAVIDSON

BORN: June 15, 1960; Artesia, California

HEIGHT: 5'7"

EYES: Blue

STATUS: Single

OTHER SOAP ROLES:
Ashley Abbott, "The Young and the Restless"
Kelly Capwell, "Santa Barbara"

avidson, the youngest of seven children, was a teenager when she was discovered by a photographer who persuaded her to model. At age nineteen, she moved to Los Angeles where she began taking acting classes between modeling assignments. After getting her feet wet in student films, she won the role of Ashley Abbott on "The Young and the Restless" at age twenty-two. She left that show in 1988, and then starred with John Voight in the feature film "Eternity." The leading role of J.J. "Bullet" Bingreedies in the short-lived 1990 prime time series "Broken Badges" followed.

In 1991, she joined the cast of "Santa Barbara" as Kelly Capwell. After that show was canceled, she was hired by "Days of Our Lives."

Davidson has been very active in organizations devoted to solving the problems of the inner-city. In her spare time, she enjoys music, dancing, painting and her many pets.

Kristen Blake
"Days of Our Lives"

Kristen Blake is a bleeding-heart social worker who was introduced as a love interest for John Black.

JAMES DEPAIVA

BORN: October 8; Hayward, California

HEIGHT: 6'0"

EYES: Blue

STATUS: Married to Misty Rowe

CHILDREN: Dreama Marie

OTHER SOAP ROLES:
Small roles on "Days of Our Lives" and "General Hospital"

While growing up in Livermore, California, DePaiva wanted to be a musician, and he played electric bass with bands that crossed the music spectrum from punk rock to country-western. At the same time, he took acting classes at a community college and performed in several community theater productions.

Finally, after eight years as a professional musician, he decided to devote himself exclusively to acting. He moved to Los Angeles to study with famed drama coach Stella Adler. His big break came when he was cast as a waiter who pursued Holly Scorpio (Emma Samms) on "General Hospital." When he left the show in 1987, he auditioned for "One Life to Live" and won the major role of Max Holden. DePaiva has also appeared as a guest star on "Simon and Simon" and in the TV movie "Commitment to Excellence." He has also performed in several California theater productions. He left the role of Max in 1990, appearing in commercials and the PBS series "Mathnet," but returned to the cast in 1991.

In 1986, DePaiva married second wife Misty Rowe, an actress who appeared in "Hee Haw." He has a black belt in kung fu, which he practices to stay in shape. He and his wife spend as much time as possible with their young daughter and their three dogs at their California home.

Max Holden
"One Life to Live"

The dapper Max Holden has been manipulating and romancing the ladies of Llanview since 1987. He has been involved in a long-term relationship with Luna, who has saved his life twice.

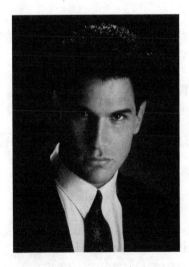

DON DIAMONT

BORN: December 31; New York, New York

HEIGHT: 6'1"

EYES: Hazel

STATUS: Single

OTHER SOAP ROLES: Carlo Forenza, "Days of Our Lives"

$\mathcal{B}$ orn on New Year's Eve, Diamont established a pattern of achieving excellence from an early age. In high school, he was a top student and a star athlete. His plans for college were permanently halted when he was discovered by a modeling agency, which sent him to work in Europe. He later returned to the U.S. to do more modeling and to study acting with the renowned Nina Foch.

His break came in 1984 with a short-term role as Carlo Forenza on "Days of Our Lives," which led to his being named "Best Newcomer" by Daytime T.V. Magazine. In 1985, he was hired by "The Young and the Restless." In addition to playing Brad on "Y&R," he continues to do commercials and has appeared on the series "The Fall Guy."

Diamont enjoys traveling, football, tennis, basketball, boxing, swimming, karate, skiing and working with stained glass. He also does considerable charitable work with such organizations as the American Cancer Society and the Juvenile Diabetes Foundation.

Brad Carlton
"The Young and the Restless"

Brad Carlton is an ambitious man who rose from the lowly position of groundkeeper to a high-powered assistant to Victor Newman. He married Traci in 1986 and they later had a baby, Colleen, but his devotion to his job led to their divorce and, later, a failed attempt at reconciliation.

FRANK DICOPOULOS

BORN: January 3; Akron, Ohio

HEIGHT: 6'1"

EYES: Green

STATUS: Married to Teja Anderson

$\mathcal{D}$ icopoulos was an outstanding high school student and athlete who enrolled in Ohio's prestigious Kenyon College in a pre-med program. Outside the classroom, he was a three sport athlete who set a NCAA Division III high hurdles track record; but inside the classroom, drama classes derailed his intended medical career.

After graduation he moved to Texas, where he juggled odd jobs while modeling and acting.

He first came to national attention in the MTV documentary "Wild Rides." After stints as host of ESPN's "On the Move" and the "Miss Teenage America Pageant," Dicopoulos moved to California. He appeared on "The Young and the Restless," "Capitol" and "General Hospital," as well as on the prime time series "Hotel," "The Tracey Ullman Show," "Silver Spoons," "Dynasty" and "Falcon Crest." In 1987, he landed his current role of Frank Cooper on "Guiding Light," and daytime stardom soon followed.

Dicopoulos married Teja Anderson, an actress who had also appeared on "Guiding Light," in October, 1990. He is very involved in environmental organizations Greenpeace and the Rainforest Alliance. He also enjoys sports, music, theater, films, art and pets.

Frank Cooper
"Guiding Light"

Frank Cooper, Buzz and Nadine's son, is a detective, as is his sister, Harley. He has recently fallen in love with Eleni, the mother of his baby, who divorced Alan-Michael.

COLLEEN DION

BORN: December 26, 1964; Newburgh, New York

HEIGHTS: 5'6"

EYES: Brown

STATUS: Divorced

OTHER SOAP ROLES:
Evie Stone, "Search for Tomorrow"
Cecelia Sowolsky, "Loving"
Felicia Forrester, "The Bold and the Beautiful"

*D*ion was born in the Hudson River town of Newburgh, New York, the youngest of four children, and she was raised in a suburb of Chicago. She began modeling at age 15 when she won a local contest in a department store, and she soon became a busy print and commercial model in

New York. She studied acting between modeling assignments, and at age 20 she won a role on "Search for Tomorrow." Later she spent eighteen months on "Loving."

She then moved to Los Angeles, guest-starring on "Santa Barbara," "Divorce Court" and "Equal Justice," while also appearing in the films "Fatal Charm" and "Lucas." Then she landed the role of Felicia Forrester on "The Bold and the Beautiful." When that role ended, she auditioned for three different soap roles before accepting an offer from "Another World."

In her spare time, Dion enjoys crafts, especially ceramics. She also loves to ice skate, rollerskate, ride horses and cook.

Brett Gardner
"Another World"

Brett Gardner, who lives in Bay View Court, is a beautiful young architect who is working on renovating Bay City. She recently entered a relationship with Ryan, but is also attracted to Matt.

JERRY DOUGLAS

BORN: November 12; Chelsea, Massachusetts

HEIGHT: 6'1"

EYES: 1 blue, 1 brown

STATUS: Married to Kymberly Douglas

CHILDREN: Avra, Jodaman

*D*ouglas, born and raised in Boston, earned a degree in economics from Brandeis University, but he soon decided to pursue a career in the theater. He studied acting in New York with Uta Hagen, and after some stage roles, moved to California. In the 1970s, he guest-starred on a number of television shows, including "The F.B.I.," "Police Story," "The Greatest American Hero," "The Rockford Files," "Harry O.," "House Calls" and "The Streets of San Francisco." His made-for-television movies include "Crash," "Walton's Mountain" and "Night Watch."

In 1982, he took over a role on "The Young and the

Restless." He soon became a well-established daytime personality. He has taught soap opera seminars at colleges and universities, and he has produced and performed in "The Other Side of Daytime," a musical variety show featuring other daytime personalities. He has also appeared in the movies "Looker," "Mommie Dearest" and "Avalanche."

He met his wife Kymberly, a Michigan television news anchorwoman, while hosting a Muscular Dystrophy telethon, and they were married in 1985. Douglas is active in the Variety Clubs, and in his spare time enjoys golf, reading, sports and theater.

John Abbott
"The Young and the Restless"

John Abbott is the founder of Jabot Cosmetics and the father of Jack, Ashley and Traci. He's married to Jill, a much younger woman who was once seduced by his son Jack. Jill recently gave birth to a son exactly nine months after she slept with Victor.

BOBBIE EAKES

BORN: July 25; Warner Robins, Georgia

HEIGHT: 5'5"

EYES: Hazel

STATUS: Married to David Steen

*E*akes was born the youngest of five outgoing and talented daughters in a military family. Singing was a family tradition, and she toured regionally with her sisters as the "Eakes Girls." Another tradition in her family was entering beauty pageants, and Eakes achieved great success. She was Miss Georgia TEEN, and she won the national talent competition on the way to being named First Runner-up. While she was attending the University of Georgia, she was named Miss Georgia and was a top ten finalist in the Miss America competition.

She left college after two years to pursue a singing and

acting career in Los Angeles. She guest-starred on the prime time series "Cheers," "The Wonder Years," "Laverne and Shirley," "Full House," "Jake and the Fatman," "21 Jump Street," "Comedy Break," "Werewolf" and "Falcon Crest." She also joined the all-girl band "Big Trouble," which did a song on the soundtrack of the Sylvester Stallone movie "Over the Top." In 1989, she joined the cast of "The Bold and the Beautiful." She also changed direction in her musical career, and she's now recording as a country singer.

She married writer/actor David Steen in 1992. In her limited spare time, she enjoys cooking and decorating.

Macy Alexander Forrester
"The Bold and the Beautiful"

Macy is the daughter of Sally Spectra, who is active in her mother's business. Her separation from Thorne Forrester triggered a serious drinking problem and threatened her health and well-being.

LOUIS EDMUNDS

BORN: September 24; Baton Rouge, Louisiana

HEIGHT: 6'0

EYES: Blue

HAIR: White

STATUS: Single

OTHER SOAP ROLES:
Rick Hampton, "Young Dr. Malone"
Roger Collins/Joshua Collins/Edward Collins, "Dark Shadows"

AWARDS: Emmy nomination, Outstanding Supporting Actor, 1984, 1985, 1986

*E*dmunds' first love was singing, and he sang as a soprano in choirs as a teenager. He went on to study both voice and theater at Pittsburgh's Carnegie

Mellon University. He graduated during World War II and spent three years in the U.S. Navy. After the war, he moved to New York where he began a distinguished stage career that included roles in "Otherwise Engaged," "Candide," "Passage to India," "Fire," "Maybe Tuesday," "The Importance of Being Ernest," "Ernest in Love," "Under Milkwood," "The Interview," "Billy Budd," "Dearest Enemy," "The Three Sisters" and "Antony and Cleopatra."

He made his daytime debut on "Young Dr. Malone" in 1962, and he was a regular on the cult soap hit "Dark Shadows" from 1966 to 1971. Since 1979, he has been a cast member of "All My Children." In his time off from daytime, Edmunds has developed a cabaret act, given concerts and appeared in several regional musical productions. He has also had roles in the films "The Exterminator," "The House of Dark Shadows," "The Fifth Arm" and "Come Spy With Me."

In his spare time, Edmunds enjoys cajun cooking and going to the theater.

Langley Wallingford
"All My Children"

Wallingford was really a con artist known as "Lucky Lenny" who came to Pine Valley pretending to be a professor. He courted the wealthy widow Phoebe Tyler, intending to steal her money. After their marriage, he pursued affairs, including one with Phoebe's maid Opal Gardner. However, he unexpectedly fell in love with Phoebe, and they have remained married ever since.

BETH EHLERS

BORN: July 23; Queens, New York

HEIGHT: 5'4"

EYES: Blue

STATUS: Divorced

AWARDS: Emmy nomination, Outstanding Actress in a Supporting Role, 1992, 1993; *Soap Opera Digest* Award nomination for Outstanding Younger Actress, 1992, 1993

*B*eth Ehlers grew up in New York City and began her pursuit of an acting career at age nine, appearing in several television and radio commercials during her childhood. After a year at Syracuse University, she returned to New York to pursue her career. She snagged a role as student Mia Braithwaite on the short-lived 1985 prime time dramatic series, "Best Times." She's appeared in the Jon Cryer movie, "Hiding Out," as well as David Bowie's "The Hunger." Her TV movies include "Family Reunion" with Bette Davis, "In Defense of the Kids" and "Mystery on Fire Island." In 1987, she joined the cast of "Guiding Light."

In real life, Ehlers married Dr. William Parsons in 1991. But when her character fell in love with fellow police officer A.C. Mallet, Ehlers found herself falling in love with Mark Derwin, who plays Mallet. She later divorced Parsons. In her spare time, she likes to read and travel.

Harley Cooper
"Guiding Light"

Harley Davidson Cooper, a policewoman, is the daughter of Buzz and Nadine Cooper and sister of Frank, a detective. In 1989, Harley Cooper was married to businessman Alan-Michael Spaulding, whom she later divorced. She has been involved in a long-term relationship with A.C. Mallet, also a police officer.

PATRICIA ELLIOTT

BORN: July 21; Gunnison, Colorado

HEIGHT: 5'5"

EYES: Blue

STATUS: Divorced

AWARDS: *Soap Opera Digest* Award nomination, Outstanding Supporting Actress, 1992

*A*s a child growing up in Denver, Elliott was a self-described "constant show-off." After a brief stint working in the public relations office at Harvard

University, she traveled to England to enroll in the London Academy of Music and Dramatic Arts. She returned to the U.S. in 1973 to make her Broadway debut as the Countess Charlotte in Stephen Sondheim's "A Little Night Music." This role won her a coveted Tony Award, a Theater World Award, and a Drama Desk Award.

She later earned another Tony nomination for her performance in the Pulitzer-prize winning play "The Shadow Box." Her other starring Broadway roles include parts in "The Elephant Man" (with David Bowie) and "A Month of Sundays" (with Jason Robards). In addition, she has had numerous roles in off-Broadway and touring productions. Her television guest starring roles include "Kate and Allie," "Spencer: For Hire," "St. Elsewhere" and "Hill Street Blues." She has appeared in the TV movies "Sometimes I Don't Like My Mother," "The Ladies," "The Cartier Heist," "The Adams Chronicles" and "Man Without a Country," as well as the theatrical films "Somebody Killed Her Husband," "Natural Enemies" and "Morning, Winter, Night." Her role on "One Life to Live" is her first on a daytime serial.

Elliott is a board member (along with Frances Sternhagen and Tony Randall) of "Plays for Living," an organization which produces inspirational plays performed at schools, shelters, prisons, churches and corporations. These plays focus on such issues as alcoholism, drug abuse, homelessness and AIDS. She enjoys bike-riding, race-walking, meditation and swimming with dolphins.

Renee Divine Buchanan
"One Life to Live"

Elliott replaced Phyllis Newman in the role of Renee Divine, a former madam who married oil baron Asa Buchanan in 1988. She later divorced Asa, and she now owns the Palace Hotel.

TOM EPLIN

BORN: October 25, 1960; Hayward, California

HEIGHT: 5'10"

EYES: Blue

STATUS: Married to Courtney Gibbs

om Eplin grew up in California, then studied for three years at the American Conservatory Theater in San Francisco. After performing in a number of theatrical productions, including "Bus Stop" and "Bent," he went on to guest-starring roles on "The Facts of Life," "240 Robert" and "Private Practice." He also appeared in the films "Discovery Bay," "Sunset Strip" and "Enchanted Evening."

In 1985, he was cast in "Another World." He left the soap the following year, then returned in 1988. Eplin is also a producer of the film "Delta Fever" and the TV pilot "Odd Jobs." He continues to study acting and conducts acting seminars.

Eplin was formerly married to actress Ellen Wheeler, but is now married to former Miss U.S.A. Courtney Gibbs. In his spare time, he enjoys race car driving, skydiving, scuba diving and flying his airplane.

Jake McKinnon
"Another World"

Jake McKinnon was married to Marley McKinnon, Vicky's twin sister. He was involved in a long love affair with Paulina Cory while he was attempting a takeover of Cory Publishing.

JUDI EVANS

BORN: July 12; Montebello, California

HEIGHT: 5'4"

EYES: Blue

STATUS: Married to Robert Eth

OTHER SOAP ROLES:
Beth Raines, "Guiding Light"
Adrienne Kiriakis, "Days of Our Lives"

AWARDS: Emmy Award, Outstanding Supporting Actress, 1984

$\mathcal{E}$vans' early childhood was spent in a world that many children dream about—the circus. From age two to age eight, she traveled throughout the western United States with her father, a trapeze artist and occasional ringmaster; and her mother and her three older brothers, all jugglers. Evans herself performed as a tiny clown in a wig, floppy shoes and colorful make-up. She turned to other pursuits when her family settled in Monterey Park, California—planning a career in medicine. But the old performing bug took hold of her after she graduated from high school and she studied acting at a community college.

Less than a year after her college graduation, she won the role of sensitive Beth Raines on "Guiding Light." After garnering an Emmy Award for that role in 1984, she moved to "Days of Our Lives" from 1986 to 1990. She also appeared in the television movie "Dreams of Gold."

One of the reasons Evans took a role on "Another World" in 1990 was her marriage to Robert Eth, who is in the men's footwear business in New York where "Another World" is produced. In her spare time, she loves horseback riding, scuba diving, skiing, working out on the trapeze, casino gambling and poker.

Paulina Cory
"Another World"

Judi Evans replaced Cali Timmons as the illegitimate daughter of the late Mac Cory, founder of Cory Publishing. This sexy siren's stormy love affair with Jake McKinnon has been a focus of "Another World" for two years.

SUSAN FLANNERY

BORN: July 31;
New York, New York

EYES: Blue

STATUS: Single

OTHER SOAP ROLES:
Dr. Laura Horton, "Days of
Our Lives"

AWARDS: Emmy Award, Outstanding Lead Actress, 1975

*F*lannery was born in New York City, received a bachelor's degree in theater from Stephens College, then went on to do graduate work at Arizona State. She was discovered by producer Irwin Allen and made her television debut in "Voyage to the Bottom of the Sea." She also appeared in the TV movies "Women in White" and "Anatomy of Seduction" and she was nominated for an Emmy for her performance in the miniseries "The Moneychangers." She also won a Golden Globe Award for her performance in the feature film "The Towering Inferno."

Her soap career began in 1966 when she was cast as Dr. Laura Horton on "Days of Our Lives." She ended her stint on that show by winning an Emmy in 1975. From 1980 to 1982, she played press agent Leslie Stewart on the prime time soap "Dallas." In 1987, she returned to daytime as an original cast member of "The Bold and the Beautiful."

Behind the scenes, Flannery has co-produced the cable soap opera "New Day in Eden" and she serves as a director of "The Bold and the Beautiful." She is a licensed pilot, a gourmet cook and she keeps in shape by swimming and playing tennis.

Stephanie Forrester
"The Bold and the Beautiful"

Stephanie is the strong-willed ex-wife of Eric and mother of the Forrester children. She still loves her ex-husband, who recently married Sheila. She continually battles to keep control of Forrester Creations in the family.

GENIE FRANCIS

BIRTH: May 26; Englewood, New Jersey

HEIGHT: 5'5"

EYES: Blue

STATUS: Married to Jonathan Frakes

OTHER SOAP ROLES:
Diane Colville, "Days of Our Lives"
Ceara Connor, "All My Children"

AWARDS: *Soap Opera Digest* Award, Outstanding Lead
Actress, 1981

*F*rancis was the daughter of actor and drama teacher
Ivor Francis and she made her television debut on the
prime time series "Family" at age thirteen. The next
year, she was hired for the role of Laura Webber on "General
Hospital." Laura was the teenage bride of Scotty Baldwin
when she was raped by Luke Spencer. Then she fell in love
with Luke. Their 1981 television wedding was the most publicized event in soap opera history, landing Francis and Tony
Geary (Luke) on the cover of Newsweek.

That same year, Francis left the show, but she returned
briefly as Laura in 1983 and in 1984. In 1983, she starred
as Tyger Hayes in "Bare Essence," a mini-series that continued as scheduled series for a few months. In 1986, she
starred in the mini-series "North and South" and its sequel.
She also guest-starred on "Hotel" and "Murder, She Wrote."
In 1987, she returned to daytime on "Days of Our Lives,"
then moved to "All My Children" in 1990. She left "All My
Children" in 1992 and the next year made a much-publi-
cized return to the role of Laura on "General Hospital."

Francis is married to actor Jonathan Frakes, a star of the
hit syndicated series "Star Trek: The Next Generation." She
enjoys the theater and playing with her many pets.

Laura Vining Webber Baldwin Spencer
"General Hospital"

Laura was the daughter of Dr. Leslie Webber, who gave her
up for adoption to the Vinings, then later took custody when
she married Rick Webber. Laura was married to Scott
Baldwin when she was raped by then-bad guy Luke Spencer.
Their subsequent courtship and marriage made them the
most famous couple in the history of daytime drama. Laura
supposedly died when Francis left the show in 1981, but she
reappeared when the actress returned to the show briefly in
1983 and in 1984. Her dramatic reappearance in Port
Charles in the fall of 1993 represented yet another of the
most publicized of all soap plot developments.

EILEEN FULTON

BORN: September 13;
Ashville, North Carolina

HEIGHT: 5'2"

EYES: Hazel

STATUS: Single

AWARDS: *Soap Opera Digest* Editor's Award, 1990

*B*orn Margaret Elizabeth McLarty, Fulton was born and raised in North Carolina, where she attended Greensboro College and majored in drama and music. She moved to New York where, as a struggling actress, she did everything from selling hats at Macy's to posing for the covers of True Confessions magazine. Eventually, she began to win stage roles in such plays as "Abe Lincoln in Illinois," "Sabrina Fair," "Any Wednesday," "Cat on a Hot Tin Roof" and "The Owl and the Pussycat." She has also appeared in the films "Girl of the Night" and "My Friend Alex."

In 1960, Fulton was hired by "As the World Turns" in a temporary role as a walk-on date for character Bob Hughes. However, she made such a vivid impression that she soon became a star of the show. In the 1960s, she was so well-known that she had to hire bodyguards to protect her. In 1965, CBS created a prime time soap called "Our Private World" for her character, but the show only lasted a few weeks. Fulton left "As the World Turns" briefly in 1983, but then returned. During her long stint on daytime, she has also appeared in a number of stage productions and has continued to sing in nightclubs and to record. She has also been featured in many commercials.

Fulton devotes her spare time to a variety of community service activities, including UNICEF and the March of Dimes.

Lisa Mitchell
"As the World Turns"

Lisa Mitchell (she was Lisa Miller in 1960) was daytime television's first famous villainess. One of the most hated characters because of her penchant for breaking up marriages and causing mayhem, she has had almost 40 romances, six marriages, murder trials, amnesia, been kidnapped, and been involved in foreign intrigue. She's now the co-owner of Fashions and the Argus, and she's the mother of Tom Hughes.

MAUREEN GARRETT

BORN: August 18; Rocky Mount, North Carolina

HEIGHT: 5'7"

EYES: Brown

STATUS: Single

OTHER SOAP ROLES:
E.J. Ryan, "Ryan's Hope"

AWARDS: Emmy nomination, Outstanding Supporting Actress, 1991

Garrett, the daughter of an Army officer, spent her childhood moving around the U.S. and Europe. She attended college at Germany's Universitat Munchen as well as Temple and Villanova Universities in Philadelphia. Her daytime career began on "Guiding Light" in 1976. She left the show in 1981, joining "Ryan's Hope" in the role of E.J. Ryan.

In 1982, she left acting entirely to run an art and architectural furniture business on eastern Long Island. She performed in numerous theatrical productions, including "Les Laisons Dangereuses," "As You Like It" and "Quartermain's Terms." In 1989, she rejoined "Guiding Light" in her original role.

Garrett is fluent in German and French. She enjoys yoga and swimming.

Holly Thorpe
"Guiding Light"

Holly was married to Ed Bauer then divorced him before entering into a nightmarish marriage with the evil Roger Thorpe. She eventually shot him and went on trial for his murder. But Roger reemerged to cause further havoc until apparently falling from a cliff to his death in 1981. Holly also left the show at that time. But she returned in 1989, a year after Roger returned. Not learning from past mistakes, she once again became involved in a dangerous triangle with Ed and Roger.

ANTHONY GEARY

BORN: May 29, 1947; Coalville, Utah

HEIGHT: 6'0"

EYES: Blue

STATUS: Single

OTHER SOAP ROLES: David Lockhart, "Bright Promises" George Curtis, "The Young and the Restless"

AWARDS: Emmy Award, Outstanding Lead Actor, 1982; Emmy nomination, Outstanding Lead Actor, 1981, 1983; *Soap Opera Digest* Award, Outstanding Actor, 1980, 1981, 1982

Geary grew up in Utah and won a scholarship to study theater at the Unversity of Utah. He was discovered by Jack Albertson, who hired him to play his son in a touring production of "The Subject Was Roses." Geary moved to California, where he supported himself with a number of temporary jobs until he began to land guest-starring roles on such television series as "Room 222," "All in the Family," "Starsky and Hutch," "The Mod Squad," "Barnaby Jones," "Marcus Welby," "The Six Million Dollar Man" and "The Streets of San Francisco."

His daytime career began with short stints on "Bright Promises" and "The Young and the Restless." In 1978, he was hired by "General Hospital" and he went on to become a daytime superstar. He left that show in 1984 to pursue film and prime time television work. His film appearances include "Johnny Get Your Gun," "Educated Heart,"

"Ammo," "The Whistle Stop Girl" and "Scorchers." His TV movies include "Intimate Strangers," "Sins of the Past," "The Great Pretender" and "Do You Know the Muffin Man?" He returned to "General Hospital" in a new role in 1991 and in 1993 he was reunited with Genie Francis. Geary writes screenplays and fiction and he also enjoys traveling.

Luke Spencer and Bill Eckert
"General Hospital"

Luke Spencer came from a shady background (his sister Bobbie was a prostitute) and he was involved with the mob until he met Laura. Their love affair changed his life and he began to straighten out, working with intelligence agent Robert Scorpio and getting involved in legitimate business deals. He ended up being elected mayor of Port Charles before he and Laura left the city and disappeared in 1984.

RICKY PAULL GOLDIN

BORN: January 5; San Francisco, California

HEIGHT: 5'10"

EYES: Brown

STATUS: Single

OTHER SOAP ROLES:
Rick, "Ryan's Hope"

AWARDS: *Soap Opera Digest* Award, Outstanding Younger Leading Actor, 1992

With both of his parents in show business, Goldin spent his youth as a nomad, graduating from a high school that was the twenty-second school he attended. He knew he wanted to be an actor and his career got off to a fast start with theater roles in the London production of "The Magic Show," the Broadway production of "On Golden Pond" and several off-Broadway shows. He moved to Los Angeles, starring in ABC Afterschool Specials "The Movie Star's Daughter," "Words to Live By," "The

Third Dimension" and "The Rocking Chair Rebellion." Goldin had a starring role on the short-lived 1985 sitcom, "Hail to the Chief" and he guest-starred on "MacGyver," "Kate and Allie," "Baywatch" and "Alf." His feature film appearances include "Piranha II," "Lambada—Set the Night On Fire," "Mirror, Mirror" and "Pastime."

Goldin had a brief role on "Ryan's Hope," but his leap to daytime stardom came when he moved to New York to take the role of Dean Frame on "Another World." He has become one of the most prominent younger leading men on the soaps. Goldin is also currently the host of "Street Match" on ABC.

Goldin is always very involved in music. He wrote a love song which was used on "Another World" and he has filmed music videos. He loves animals and has pets that range from a dog to a boa constrictor.

Dean Frame
"Another World"

Young musician Dean Frame, who's Frankie's cousin, is half owner of D&M Enterprises. He's been involved with Jenna, who is having his child.

DEIDRE HALL

BORN: October 31; Milwaukee, Wisconsin

STATUS: Married to Steve Sohmer

OTHER SOAP ROLES: Barbara Anderson, "The Young and the Restless"

AWARDS: Emmy nomination, Outstanding Lead Actress, 1984, 1985; Emmy nomination, Outstanding Supporting Actress, 1980; *Soap Opera Digest* Award, Outstanding Lead Actress, 1982, 1983, 1984, 1985; *Soap Opera Digest* Award, Outstanding Contribution to Daytime Drama, 1986

*H*all was born in Wisconsin but raised in Lake Worth, Florida. She studied psychology at Palm Beach Junior College while earning money as a model and as a disc jockey at an all-women's radio station. She moved to California and continued her studies at Los Angeles Community College. She played Sally on the TV series "Emergency" and guest-starred on "Perry Mason" and "Columbo."

From 1973 to 1975, she played Barbara Anderson on "The Young and the Restless." In the 1976-1977 TV season, she was a female newspaper reporter who turned into the superhero Electric Woman on the prime time show "The Krofft Supershow." Also in 1976, she was hired to play Dr. Marlena Evans on "Days of Our Lives." She soon became a major star of that show, earning three Emmy nominations and five *Soap Opera Digest* Awards. She left daytime to star as Jessie Witherspoon on the prime time series "Our House," which lasted until 1988. She appeared on "Murder, She Wrote," "Wiseguy," "Circus of the Stars" and "The Bob Hope Comedy Special," as well as in the television movies "And the Sea Will Tell," "A Reason to Live," "Take My Daughters, Please" and "For the Very First Time." In 1991, she returned to "Days of Our Lives."

Hall wed her third husband, Steve Sohmer, and they made headlines when they had their first child through a surrogate mother. Hall appears in many commercials and she operates two video companies.

Dr. Marlena Evans Brady
"Days of Our Lives"

Dr. Marlena Evans, a psychiatrist, was first married to Don Craig. She was apparently murdered by serial killer "The Salem Strangler," but the victim turned out to be her twin sister, Samantha. In the early 1980s, she married police detective Roman Brady. In 1986, she was apparently killed again, this time in a fiery plane crash. Six years later, just as Roman was proposing to Isabella, she reappeared, having been kept prisoner on a desert island. When Wayne Northrop, who had originally played Roman, returned to the show, it was explained to the audience that the current Roman was really an imposter named John Black. Marlena then became involved in a romantic triangle between Roman and John.

RICK HEARST

BORN: January 4;
Queens, New York

HEIGHT: 5'10"

EYES: Brown

STATUS: Married to Donna
Smoot

CHILDREN: Nicholas

OTHER SOAP ROLES:
Scott Banning, "Days of Our Lives"

AWARDS: Emmy Award, Outstanding Younger Actor, 1991;
Emmy nomination, Outstanding Younger Actor, 1992

*H*earst was born in New York City, but moved frequently after his parents divorced. From a very early age, he loved performing and he eventually won an acting scholarship to the University of Texas. After two years, he moved to New York to train at the Circle in the Square Professional Workshop. He appeared in a Circle in the Square production of "Spring Awakening" and in the films "Crossing the Line" and "Brain Damage."

His big break came when he was hired to play Scott Banning on "Days of Our Lives." He left the show after a year, then was hired by "Guiding Light" shortly afterward. He was an immediate success, winning an Emmy in 1991.

Hearst is married to Donna Smoot, whom he met at the University of Texas, and they have a young son. He and fellow "Guiding Light" cast member Morgan Englund have a rock band called 2C that performs in New York clubs. Hearst also enjoys karate.

Alan-Michael Spaulding
"Guiding Light"

Alan-Michael Spaulding is a powerful and manipulative businessman who was recently divorced from Eleni, but still wants to be a part of her life.

LYNN HERRING

BORN: September 22; Enid, Oklahoma

HEIGHT: 5'7"

EYES: Hazel

STATUS: Married to Wayne Northrop

CHILDREN: Hank

OTHER SOAP ROLES:
Lisanne Gardener, "Days of Our Lives"

AWARDS: Emmy nomination, Outstanding Supporting
Actress, 1989, 1991; *Soap Opera Digest* Award, Outstanding
Villainess, 1989, 1991, 1992

*H*erring seldom had a chance to unpack her suit-
case as a child; as the daughter of an Air Force
officer, she went to fifteen different schools in ten
states and Puerto Rico. After high school, she enrolled in
Louisiana State University (where she has family). While
there she won the 1977 Miss Virginia title and was runner-
up in the 1978 Miss U.S.A. competition. After receiving her
degree in psychology, Herring opted for modeling instead of
academics. After a year of modeling and theater study in
New York, she moved to California, where she split her time
between show business and graduate school.

Her first big part was in the movie "Roller Boogie" and
she went on to TV appearances in "Riptide," "Arthur
Hailey's Hotel," "T.J. Hooker" and "The Colbys." In 1986,
she was hired for a thirteen week role on "General Hospital,"
but impressed the producers so much that she was soon
offered a contract. She went on to garner two Emmy nominations and three *Soap Opera Digest* Awards. In 1992, she
left "General Hospital" for "Days of Our Lives," but she
soon regretted the decision, and six months later her character Lucy was back in Port Charles.

Herring married "Days of Our Lives" star Wayne
Northrop (Roman Brady) in 1981. In 1991, she gave birth to
their son, Hank. In her spare time, she enjoys horseback riding on her ranch, raising her animals, skiing, tennis and
crossword puzzles.

Lucy Coe
"General Hospital"

Lucy Coe has been one of daytime's most seductive villainesses since her introduction in 1986. However, she has been trying to reform, most recently by volunteering to carry a baby for Scott and the dying Dominique.

DRAKE HOGESTYN

BORN: September 29; Fort Wayne, Indiana

EYES: Brown

STATUS: Married to Victoria Hogestyn

*H*ogestyn wanted to be a dentist, but other temptations got in his way. After winning a baseball scholarship to the University of South Florida, he was offered a contract by the New York Yankees organization. He decided to forego dental school to play third base in the minor leagues. After an injury ended his baseball career, he decided to be an actor.

His big break came when he was one of just 30 winners among 75,000 people who entered a talent competition conducted by Columbia Pictures. He went on to appear on a number of television shows, then was offered a starring role as Brian on the prime time series "Seven Brides for Seven Brothers." Then, in 1986, he moved to daytime when he was hired by "Days of Our Lives."

Hogestyn continues to enjoy the national pastime as a member of the Hollywood All Stars Baseball team. His wife and four children keep him busy and entertained the rest of the time!

John Black
"Days of Our Lives"

Hogestyn first played police detective Roman Brady, husband of Marlena. But when actor Wayne Northrop returned to the show, it was revealed that a man named John Black had been masquerading as Roman. John went on to marry Isabella, who died, but he and Marlena still had a strong romantic attraction.

SCOTT HOLMES

BORN: May 30; West Grove, Pennsylvania

HEIGHT: 5'9"

EYES: Hazel

STATUS: Married to Pamela Holmes

CHILDREN: Taylor

OTHER SOAP ROLES:
David Greenberg, "Ryan's Hope"

*H*olmes' first love was music. His father bought him a piano when he was five and he learned to play and sing. He was a member of the Pennsylvania state choir and played trumpet in the state band. He majored in music and drama while a student at Catawaba College in North Carolina. After appearing in a touring production of "Godspell," he joined the Pittsburgh Civic Light Opera Company for a year. He went on to appear on Broadway in "Grease," "Evita," "The Rink" and "Jerome Kern Goes to Hollywood." He also toured in "Evita," "Nightclub Confidential" and "Shanandoah."

His first daytime role was David Greenberg on "Ryan's Hope," which he played from 1984-1985. In 1987, he was hired by "As the World Turns."

Holmes is married to Pamela Holmes, whom he met in college and they have a young son, Taylor. He continues to perform in night clubs. In his spare time, he likes sports, including baseball, basketball, swimming and vollyball.

Tom Hughes
"As the World Turns"

Holmes is the twelfth actor to portray Tom Hughes, son of Bob Hughes and Lisa Mitchell and grandson of Nancy McCloskey. After returning from Vietnam, he became hooked on drugs, but eventually reformed. He has a long-term marriage to Margo.

ELIZABETH HUBBARD

BORN: November 22; New York, New York

HEIGHT: 5'5"

EYES: Blue

STATUS: Divorced

CHILDREN: Jeremy

OTHER SOAP ROLES:
Anne Benedict Fletcher, "Guiding Light"
Carol Kramer, "Edge of Night"
Dr. Althea Davis, "The Doctors"

AWARDS: Emmy Award, Outstanding Leading Actress, 1974; Emmy nomination, Outstanding Leading Actress, 1986, 1987, 1988, 1989, 1990, 1991, 1992

Hubbard was born in New York City, graduated from Radcliffe College, then studied at the prestigious Royal Academy of Dramatic Arts in London, where she received a high honor, the silver medal. She had played major roles in many Broadway plays, including "Joe Egg," "Children! Children!," "Present Laughter," "Dance a Little Closer," "I Remember Mama," "A Time for Singing," "Look Back in Anger" and "The Physicist." Her off-Broadway roles include "War and Peace," "Uncle Vanya," "The Boys from Syracuse," "The Threepenny Opera," "Blithe Spirit" and "Macbeth." She has co-starred in the Oscar-winning film "Ordinary People," as well as in "The Bell Jar" and "I Never Sang For My Father." She received a prime time Emmy Award for her performance in the NBC special, "First Ladies' Diaries."

Hubbard's daytime career began with short roles on "Guiding Light" and "Edge of Night." From 1964-1982, she portrayed Dr. Althea Davis on "The Doctors" for which she won a 1974 Emmy as Outstanding Leading Actress. When that show was canceled, she joined the cast of "As the World Turns." With seven consecutive Emmy nominations, she has established herself as one of daytime television's most distinguished and honored performers.

When she's not working, Hubbard enjoys writing, the theater and traveling.

Lucinda Walsh Dixon
"As the World Turns"

Head of World Wide, Lucinda Walsh Dixon is a hard driving businesswoman who often seems to have a heart of stone. She's the ex-wife of John and she raised Lily, whose natural mother is Ida.

VINCENT IRIZARRY

BORN: November 12; Queens, New York

HEIGHT: 5'9"

EYES: Brown

STATUS: Divorced

CHILDREN: Siena

OTHER SOAP ROLES:
Brandon Lujack, "Guiding Light"
Scott Clark, "Santa Barbara"

AWARDS: Emmy nomination, Outstanding Younger Leading Man, 1986

The young Irizarry was a classically-trained pianist who studied at the Berklee College of Music in Boston. After appearing in some student productions, he decided to devote himself to acting. In 1979, he won a scholarship to the famous Lee Strasberg Theater Institute in New York and he also studied jazz and dance.

His theater credits in New York include roles in "The Death of Von Richtoven" and "Lennon" (with Paul McCartney). In 1982, he was an instant sensation when he joined "Guiding Light" as Lujack, a rebel with a cause. Still at the peak of popularity, Irizarry left the show in 1985. He appeared in the TV mini-series "Echoes in the Darkness" and "Lucky/Chances," the TV movies "Firefighters" and

"The Circus" and guest-starred on "L.A. Law" and "Mancuso." In 1988, he began a three year stint as Dr. Scott Clark on "Santa Barbara." Finally, in 1991, he returned to "Guiding Light."

Irizarry is divorced from actress Signy Coleman (Hope, "The Young and the Restless"), with whom their young daughter lives. He spends a lot of his time away from the show visiting Siena. Much of the rest of his spare time is devoted to music, writing and photography.

Nick McHenry
"Guiding Light"

Nick McHenry is the look-alike cousin of Lujack, the rebel-with-a-cause who created a sensation from 1982 - 1985. McHenry is Alexandra's son, a journalist who has been involved in a triangle with Mindy and Eve.

JOANNA JOHNSON

BORN: December 31; Phoenix, Arizona

HEIGHT: 5'7"

EYES: Blue

STATUS: Single

OTHER SOAP ROLES:
Caroline Spencer, "The Bold and the Beautiful"

*J*ohnson was born in Phoenix, where her father was a produce broker. Her ambition was to become a director, not an actor. She attended the film school at the University of Southern California, where she directed several student films. After graduation, she wrote and directed medical training films for the Hospital Satellite Network. To learn more about how actors think and respond, she enrolled in acting classes with Darryl Hickman and at the Shakespeare Workshop. Soon, she made her professional debut on "The New Mike Hammer." She appeared in the film "Killer Party" and on the TV shows "Twilight Zone" and "Riptide."

She was hired to play Caroline Spencer on "The Bold and

the Beautiful" in 1987. That role ended in 1990, but she rejoined the cast the following year as Karen Roberts. She is also pursuing her original ambition of becoming a major film director.

Johnson is active in the charities Angel Food and the Family Assistance Program. She enjoys jogging, horseback riding, tennis, boxing and weightlifting.

Karen Roberts
"The Bold and the Beautiful"

Karen Roberts is the look-alike sister of Caroline Spencer. She was the other woman in Thorne and Macy's marriage.

MELINA KANAKAREDES

BORN: April 23; Akron, Ohio

HEIGHT: 5'7"

EYES: Green

STATUS: Married to Peter Constantinides

Kanakaredes was born in Akron, Ohio and from the time she played Becky Thatcher in a musical production of "Tom Sawyer" at age eight, she knew she wanted to be an actress. She attended Ohio State for a year, then transferred to Point Park College, where she graduated cum laude in musical theater. She was also Miss Columbus and first runner-up in the Miss Ohio contest.

Her first professional work was as a print and television model. After moving to New York, she appeared in the stage productions "State of the Art," "Evita," "42nd Street," "Romeo and Juliet" and "Candide." After a bit part on "One Life to Live," she auditioned for her role on "Guiding Light," for which she imitated her grandmother's Greek accent.

In her spare time, Kanakaredes volunteers with the Starlight Foundation. She enjoys swimming and she remains close to her family.

Eleni Cooper
"Guiding Light"

The beautiful young Eleni Andros was brought from Greece by her uncle to marry Frank Cooper. She fell in love with Frank at first sight, despite his chilly attitude toward her. Alan-Michael Spaulding fell in love with her and they married. When Frank did finally fall in love with her, she had his baby, and she divorced Alan-Michael.

SUSAN KEITH

BORN: September 30; Milwaukee, Wisconsin

HEIGHT: 5'3"

EYES: Blue

STATUS: Married to James Kiberd

OTHER SOAP ROLES:
Samantha Vernon, "One Life to Live"
Cecile de Poulignac, "Another World"

A native of Wisconsin, Keith enrolled in Barat College in Lake Forest, Illinois to study speech therapy. However, she soon decided that she'd rather be an actress, so she transferred to the Goodman School of Drama in Chicago. Just before her graduation, she was offered the role of Samantha Vernon on "One Life to Live" and she moved to New York to take it.

After leaving the ABC soap, she originated the role of Cecile de Poulignac on "Another World." In 1983, she took the role of Shana Sloane on the fledgling soap "Loving." Keith left the show in 1989, but strong audience demand made her decide to return the next year.

Keith met her husband, James Kiberd, on the set of "Loving" when he played Mike Donovan. In her spare time, she enjoys hiking, ice skating, bowling, tennis and Tai Chi. She is also an animal lover, and is the proud owner of a bluepoint Siamese cat named Caliban and a dog named Omen.

Shana Vochek
"Loving"

A lawyer, Shana is the strong-willed, beautiful, illegitimate daughter of Cabot Alden. She fell in love with Father Jim Vochek and he eventually left the priesthood to marry her. After they divorced and remarried, Jim and their infant daughter were killed in a plane crash. Shana offered to pay Leo to father a child with her and they fell in love.

JAMES KIBERD

BORN: July 6; Providence, Rhode Island

HEIGHT: 6'0"

EYES: Brown

STATUS: Married to Susan Keith

OTHER SOAP ROLES:
Mike Donovan, "Loving"
Dustin Marlowe, "Another World"

AWARDS: *Soap Opera Digest* Award, Outstanding Lead Actor, 1982

*F*rom early childhood, Kiberd showed great talent as an artist. As a student at the University of Pennsylvania, he jumped from undergraduate school to the Graduate School of Fine Arts as a sophomore. He eventually left school to study and work in Europe. Upon his return to the United States, he took up residence in an artist's colony in Rockland County, New York. His work received wide recognition from such organizations as the New York State Council on the Arts and the National Endowment for the Arts. He was also executive director of an organization that sought to promote bilingual cultural and artistic traditions.

In 1980 Kiberd began performing with a local repertory company. After a number of stage appearances, he joined the cast of the new soap "Loving" as troubled Vietnam veteran Mike Donovan. In 1989, he took over the part of Trevor on "All My Children."

Kiberd is married to actress Susan Keith (Shana, "Loving"). He continues to pursue his art and he also enjoys the theater.

Trevor Dillon
"All My Children"

Trevor Dillon, a policeman, had a long relationship with Natalie. He was tricked into marrying her sister, Janet, who masqueraded as Natalie after kidnapping her and hiding her in a well. Trevor finally married Natalie, but their love tragically ended when she died in an automobile accident.

MICHAEL E. KNIGHT

BORN: May 7; Princeton, New Jersey

HEIGHT: 6'1"

EYES: Blue

STATUS: Married to Catherine Hickland

AWARDS: Emmy Award, Outstanding Younger Leading Actor, 1986, 1987; Emmy nomination, Outstanding Younger Leading Actor, 1985

*K*night was born in New Jersey, but raised in California, where his father was a teacher at a boy's prep school. He studied theater at the prestigious Wesleyan University in Middletown, Connecticut, graduating in just three years. He studied further at the Circle in the Square Theater in New York, then did stage work until he was hired by "All My Children" in 1982. He was nominated for an Emmy Award in 1985 and won Emmys the next two years. In addition to his soap role, Knight guest-starred on "Matlock," did the television film "Charles and Diana" and had roles in the movies "Date With an Angel" and "Baby It's You."

Knight married soap actress Catherine Hickland (Tess, "Loving") in 1992. He loves the theater and continues to perform on stage.

Tad Martin
"All My Children"

Knight was the third actor to portray Tad Martin, the illegitimate son of Opal Gardner and the adopted son of Dr. Joe

Martin and his wife, Ruth. Tad was a manipulator and conniver who once had affairs with the wealthy Marion Colby
and her daughter at the same time. After a long and stormy
courtship, he married Hillary Wilson, but he left town—and
the show—after she discovered some of his deceptions. He
returned in 1988, only to fall off a bridge on the day of his
scheduled marriage to Dixie in 1990. But in 1993, a Ted
Orsini showed up in Pine Valley. He turned out to be Tad
Martin, who had suffered from amnesia since falling from
the bridge.

KATHERINE KELLY LANG

BORN: June 25; Los Angeles, California

EYES: Blue

STATUS: Married to Skott Snider

CHILDREN: Jeremy, Julian

OTHER SOAP ROLES:
Gretchen, "The Young and the Restless"

AWARDS: *Soap Opera Digest* Award nomination,
Outstanding Heroine, 1990

*L*ang was born in Los Angeles to a show business
family—her father, a former Olympic ski jumper,
played the Jolly Green Giant in TV commercials;
her mother was an actress; and her grandfather, Charles
Lang, was a cinematographer. After graduating from Beverly
Hills High School, she made her film debut (with another
first-timer, Patrick Swayze) in "Skate Town U.S.A." She also
appeared in "Evilspeak," "The Nightstalker" and "Delta
Fever," and she guest-starred on "Happy Days," "Magnum
P.I.," "The Last Precinct," "Crazy Like a Fox" and "First
and Ten."
  She made her debut in the brief role of Gretchen on "The
Young and the Restless." Having made an impression on
producer William Bell, she was given the role as Brooke

Logan when "The Bold and the Beautiful" debuted in 1987. She has since become one of soaps' most popular and glamorous leading ladies, winning the 1990 *Soap Opera Digest* Award for Outstanding Heroine.

She is married to director Skott Snider and has two young children. She owns several Arabian horses and competes in long-distance endurance races. She also enjoys tennis, surfing, skiing, mountain biking and jogging.

Brooke Logan Forrester
"The Bold and the Beautiful"

Brooke, a talented and beautiful scientist, has given birth to children by Eric Forrester (Eric, Jr.) and his son Ridge Forrester (Bridget). She has been involved in a long-term struggle to dominate Forrester Creations.

JILL LARSON

BIRTH: October 7; Minneapolis, Minnesota

HEIGHT: 5'8"

EYES: Blue

STATUS: Divorced

OTHER SOAP ROLES:
Judith Clayton, "As the World Turns"
Ursula Blackwell, "One Life to Live"

AWARDS: Emmy nomination, Outstanding Supporting Actress, 1991

Although her father was an aerospace engineer and her mother was an interior decorator, Larson always wanted to be an actress and she got her first professional job when she was ten. She received a Bachelor of Fine Arts degree from New York City's Hunter College, then spent two years in the Circle in the Square Professional Acting Program.

She went on to a number of theatrical productions, including "The Glass Menagerie," "Life With Father,"

"Romantic Comedy," "Agnes of God" and "Gypsy." She also guest-starred on "Kate and Allie" and "The Equalizer." After stints on "As the World Turns" and "One Life to Live," she snared the part of Opal on "All My Children" in 1989.

In her spare time, Larson produces plays and films. She is a yoga enthusiast and she enjoys cooking, carpentry, hiking and skiing.

Opal Cortlandt
"All My Children"

Larson replaced Dorothy Lyman, who won two Emmy Awards as the flamboyant Opal Gardner. Gardner's rags-to-riches story began when she arrived in Pine Valley with her daughter, Jenny. She took a job as housekeeper for the Wallingfords and, after an affair with Langley, blackmailed Phoebe into putting up the money so she could open a beauty parlor. Over the years, she opened a chain of beauty parlors and eventually became the wife of wealthy Palmer Cortlandt. Opal is also the mother of Tad Martin (by the no-good Ray Gardner) and, recently, Peter Cortlandt.

JEAN LECLERC

BORN: July 7; Montreal, Canada

HEIGHT: 6'0"

EYES: Brown

STATUS: Single

OTHER SOAP ROLES:
Jean Marc Gauthier, "The Doctors"
Peter Russo, "One Life to Live"
Jeremy Hunter, "All My Children"

*L*eClerc was a pre-med student at the University of Quebec who only dabbled in acting until a featured role in a prime time Canadian Broadcasting Corporation series led to his decision to abandon his medical studies. He soon got roles in productions of playrights from Shakespeare to Beckett at theaters in the U.S. and Canada. A major change in his career came when he won the title role in a Broadway production of "Dracula." He added credits in American theater and television, including guest appearances on "T.J. Hooker," "The Greatest American Hero" and "The Devlin Connection."

His daytime career began with short-term roles on "The Doctors" and "One Life to Live." In 1985, he joined the cast of "All My Children" as Jeremy Hunter. Seven years later, in an unusual move, his character moved from Pine Valley to Corinth, "Loving's" hometown. LeClerc has also continued to perform on stage and in Canadian television productions.

LeClerc has the honor of serving as the national fund-raising chairman of the Cystic Fibrosis Foundation. His hobby is restoring antiques and historic houses. He owns a restored 1820 flour mill outside of Montreal, a residence which boasts a waterfall in the living room.

Jeremy Hunter
"Loving"

Jeremy Hunter first appeared on "All My Children" as a monk sent from Tibet to watch over Erica Kane, who had gone to a monastery to recover from her grief over Mike's death. Jeremy and Erica were an item, but never married. Jeremy (who became a world famous artist) later married Natalie, divorced her and married Ceara. After Ceara's death left him a widower, Hunter moved to Corinth to become Dean of Humanities at Alden University and begin an affair with Stacey.

NIA LONG

BORN: October 30; Brooklyn, New York

HEIGHT: 5'2"

EYES: Brown

STATUS: Single

*L*ong was born in Brooklyn, lived a short time in Iowa after her parents divorced, then moved to South Central Los Angeles with her artist/singer mother. She got her first professional job at age 12 when she landed a role on a Sunday night television special. Although roles dried up when she was in high school, Nia was so confident that she was going to be a success that she was voted "Biggest Ego" in her high school graduating class.

Her big break came when she was cast as Brandi in a low budget film by recent college graduate director John Singleton. The film, "Boyz N the Hood," was a critical and box office smash. Shortly afterward, Long became only the third black performer to become a contract player on "Guiding Light." She went on to star as Whoopi Goldberg and Ted Danson's daughter in the comedy film "Made in America."

Long is also an accomplished singer and dancer and she has formed her own production company called Go Girl Productions. She also has a weakness for chocolate and shopping.

Kathryn "Kat" Speakes
"Guiding Light"

Kat Speakes is the rebellious young daughter of Hampton and Gilly Speakes who has had a relationship with David, a man convicted of murder.

SUSAN LUCCI

BORN: December 23; Westchester County, New York

HEIGHT: 5'3"

EYES: Dark brown

STATUS: Married to Helmut Huber

CHILDREN: Liza, Andreas

AWARDS: 14 consecutive Emmy nominations, Outstanding Actress, 1978, 1981-1993; *Soap Opera Digest* Award, Outstanding Actress, 1993; *Soap Opera Digest* Award, Outstanding Contribution to Daytime Television, 1988

*L*ucci was born to a Swedish mother and an Italian father in suburban New York City. She was an honor student and a cheerleader in high school and went on to Marymount College and the Yale School of Drama. Shortly after she began her career, she auditioned for the role of Tara Martin on "All My Children," but was cast as bratty teenager Erica Kane. She has since become America's best-known soap star. Even though she has never won an Emmy Award, her incredible total of 14 nomination reflect the consistent high level of her performances over two decades.

During breaks in her soap schedule, Lucci has starred in the television movies "Lady Mobster," "Mafia Princess," "Invitation to Hell," "Anastasia," "Secret Passions," "The Woman Who Sinned," "Double Edge" and "The Bride in Black." Her sole film role was in "Young Doctors in Love." She has appeared as a spokesperson for several major companies, most recently Ford, and she sells her own line of hair care products. She has hosted "Saturday Night Live" and is frequently interviewed on celebrity shows.

Lucci married former restaurateur Helmut Huber in 1969, and he now serves as her manager. She devotes her spare time to skiing, tennis, traveling and her teenage children.

Erica Kane
"All My Children"

Erica Kane is the archetypal soap opera femme fatale, who would do anything or say anything to get her man. She started causing trouble in the very beginning of the show's run, when her attempt to break up the relationship of Phil Brent and Tara Martin by revealing the secret of his parentage resulted in Phil's father's death and Phil's amnesia. Over the next twenty-three years, she married eight times, had many affairs and wreaked havoc in dozens of relationships. Along the way, she's encountered her long-lost father, long-lost brother, long-lost real and pretend half-sisters and, most recently, her long-lost daughter Kendall. She's also the mother of Bianca.

CADY McCLAIN

BORN: October 13; Burbank, California

HEIGHT: 5'3"

EYES: Blue

STATUS: Single

AWARDS: Emmy Award, Outstanding Ingenue, 1991; Emmy nomination, Outstanding Younger Actress, 1992; Emmy nomination, Outstanding Supporting Actress, 1993; *Soap Opera Digest* Award, Outstanding Heroine, 1991

*M*cClain had an eventful childhood: at age 9, she joined 499 other tap dancers to enter the Guiness Book of World Records as the largest group to perform the same tap dance routine simultaneously; at age 10, she was filming her first commercial (for Band-Aids) when a horse stepped on her foot and broke her toe. Undeterred, she devoted herself to acting after graduating from high school at age 16. She guest-starred on such TV shows as "St. Elsewhere," "Cheers," "Spencer: For Hire" and "Lou Grant." She appeared in the films "My Favorite Year," "Simple Justice" and "Pennies From Heaven," along with the ABC afterschool special "Just A Regular Kid: An AIDS Story" and "Who Will Love My Children." She has also appeared in theatrical productions of "A Little Night Music," "Happy Birthday and Other Humiliations," "Dames at Sea," "Wait Until Dark," "The Miracle Worker," "Finian's Rainbow," "The Music Man" and "Quiet on the Set."

She joined "All My Children" in 1989, and her work soon won her an Emmy and a *Soap Opera Digest* Award. In her spare time, McClain likes to tap dance and draw cartoon animals.

Dixie Cooney
"All My Children"

Dixie, the niece of Palmer Cortlandt, fell under the spell of Cortlandt's enemy, Adam Chandler. She conceived Adam, Jr., out of wedlock and eventually married Adam. However, he was only interested in obtaining custody of her son, and he tried to drive her crazy and have her committed. Tad rescued her and they married, then divorced. On the day they were to remarry, Tad fell off a bridge and was presumed dead. Dixie went on to marry Craig, then Brian. Tad's recent reappearance has thrown her into emotional chaos.

MARIE MASTERS

BORN: February 4

HEIGHT: 5'4"

EYES: Green

STATUS: Divorced

CHILDREN: Twins—Jenny and Jesse

OTHER SOAP ROLES:
Hester Ferris, "Love of Life"
Helen Murdoch, "Days of Our Lives"

As a child, Masters was interested in both acting and sculpture and she attended Marion College on an art scholarship. After her graduation, she moved to New York to study acting with Uta Hagen and Wynn Handman. She supported herself by working at the fashion trade publication *Women's Wear Daily* before making her stage debut in the off-Broadway play "The Sound of Silence."

Her daytime career began in 1966, when she played Hester Ferris on "Love of Life." She was a cast member of "As the World Turns" for eleven years before leaving to move to Los Angeles in 1979. While on the West Coast, she had a short role on "Days of Our Lives." She returned to New York and rejoined "As the World Turns" in 1986. In addition to her soap work, Masters has appeared in the films "Scream For Help" and "Slayground" and has guest-starred on "Kate and Allie," "Here's Boomer" and "King's Crossing."

Masters is the mother of twins, now in their twenties. Her daughter Jenny once played her young daughter Emily Stewart on "As the World Turns." Masters continues to appear on stage and work on her sculpture. She enjoys cooking, classical music and sports.

Dr. Susan Burke Stewart
"As the World Turns"

Masters was the sixth actress to portray Susan Burke, who had a tumultuous marriage to Dr. Dan Stewart. At one point, Dan took their child Emily and fled to England. Susan became a bitter alcoholic and was fired from her job at the hospital. Now Susan is a recovered alcoholic and is married to Larry McDermott. She and Larry are trying to have a child by in vitro fertilization, with Emily volunteering to supply an egg.

JOHN MCCOOK

BORN: June 20; California

STATUS: Married to Laurette Spang

CHILDREN: Seth, Jake, Bucky, Molly

OTHER SOAP ROLES: Lance Prentiss, "The Young and the Restless"

AWARDS: *Soap Opera Digest* Award, Favorite Male Newcomer, 1977

*M*cCook grew up in California and worked at Disneyland while attending Long Beach State College. His first professional job was singing and dancing in the chorus for musicals at the San Diego Circle Arts Theater. After moving up to feature roles in a number of musicals, McCook moved to New York, where he appeared in the City Center revival of "West Side Story." Scouts from Warner Brothers spotted him and signed him to a contract. He later worked at Universal Pictures until he was forced to join a new employer—the U.S. Army.

After two years playing the piano and conducting the Army's men's chorus, McCook returned to music theater on the West Coast. After several years performing in Los Angeles, Las Vegas and Sacramento, he got his first daytime role in

1975 as Lance Prentiss on "The Young and the Restless." He left that show in 1980 to resume his musical performances. He starred as the boss of three female secret agents in the short-lived NBC prime time series "Codename: Foxfire" and he appeared on such other series as "Too Close for Comfort," "Alice" and "Three's Company." In 1987, he joined "The Bold and the Beautiful" as tycoon Eric Forrester, head of Forrester Creations and patriarch of the Forrester family.

McCook married actress Laurette Spang in 1980. They have three children and McCook has an older son by a previous marriage. In his spare time, McCook enjoys scuba diving and playing with his kids.

Eric Forrester
"The Bold and the Beautiful"

Eric is the dominating head of Forrester Creations. He was married to Stephanie and he's the father of Ridge and Thorne. He and Brooke Logan had Eric, Jr. He recently married nurse Sheila Brown.

KELLEY MENIGHAN

BORN: February 15

HEIGHT: 5'6"

EYES: Blue

STATUS: Single

*M*enighan was the middle of three sisters born into a tightly-knit Catholic family. She was an adventurous child who always wanted to be an actress. After graduating from Southern Methodist University, she moved to Los Angeles, where she got a job with a production company owned by friends of her father. She had no success at acting jobs and she had just begun to circulate resumes seeking a production job at a major studio when she auditioned for "As the World Turns." Shortly afterwards, she signed a three year contract.

Memorizing the tremendous amount of dialogue necessary for her role consumes a lot of Menighan's time—she's dyslexic and memorization is a long process. In her spare time, she enjoys music.

Emily Stewart
"As the World Turns"

Emily Stewart, the daughter of Dan and Susan and the granddaughter of Ellen and David, had an extremely turbulent and unhappy childhood. She was at the center of vicious custody fights between her father, who eventually died of a blood disease, and her scheming, alcoholic mother. She grew up as a nymphet, working her way through a string of affairs with James, Craig, Tonio, Paul, Brock, Gavin, Marty and, currently, Royce. She also became a shrewd business woman who uses her sex appeal to get her way.

JAMES MITCHELL

BORN: February 29; Sacramento, California

HEIGHT: 5'10"

EYES: Brown

STATUS: Single

OTHER SOAP ROLES:
Captain Lloyd Griffin, "Edge of Night"
Julian Hathaway, "Where the Heart Is"

AWARDS: Emmy nomination, Outstanding Lead Actor, 1980, 1981-1985, 1989; *Soap Opera Digest* Award, Outstanding Villain, 1980

*M*itchell, who was born in California, spent the first part of his career as a dancer in many different stage musicals. On Broadway, he starred in "Mack and Mable," "Carnival," "Paint Your Wagon," "Brigadoon" and "Bloomer Girl" and he toured in "Funny Girl," "The Threepenny Opera" and "The King and I." His feature film roles include "That's Dancing," "The Turning Point," "The Bandwagon," "Oklahoma" and "Deep in My Heart." He has also danced with the Agnes DeMille Dance Theater and the American Ballet Theater.

His first daytime role was on "Edge of Night," and he then spent four years in the central role of Julian Hathaway on the half hour daytime serial, "Where the Heart Is," which ran from 1969 to 1973. He was hired by "All My Children" in 1979 and was such a success that he received six consecutive Emmy nominations.

Off camera, Mitchell has taught theater and dance at Yale, the Julliard School and Drake University. He enjoys movies and cooking.

Palmer Cortlandt
"All My Children"

Wealthy industrialist Palmer Cortlandt established himself as a villain to be reckoned with shortly after he moved to Pine Valley. He went to great lengths to break up his daughter Nina's relationship with Cliff and even shot himself in despair when his schemes didn't work. But he recovered to marry Daisy, Donna, Cynthia, Natalie and Opal. He continues to vie with Adam Chandler for the title of Pine Valley's wealthiest and most conniving resident.

RONN MOSS

BORN: March 4; Los Angeles, California

HEIGHT: 6'2"

EYES: Brown

STATUS: Married to Shari Shattuck

Ronn Moss was born into a show business family. His father was a record company executive, and music was his passion, too. He learned to play the drums at age eleven. By the time he was a teenager, he was playing in a number of bands that performed at weddings, bar mitzvahs, dances and nightclubs. In 1976, he formed the music group Player. Player recorded three albums, "Player," "Danger Zone" and "Room With a View" and toured with such famous artists as Boz Scaggs and Eric Clapton. In 1979, the band's single "Baby Come Back" spent three weeks as Billboard's Number One hit.

However in 1981 Moss decided to forego music and study

acting. After studying with several famous teachers, he appeared in the films "Hard Ticket to Hawaii," "Hot Child in the City" and the Italian film "Hearts and Amour." In 1987, he took his first daytime role in "The Young and the Restless."

Moss is married to actress Shari Shattuck, who he met on the set of "Hot Child in the City." In his spare time, he enjoys photography, painting, skiing, rollerskating, cycling and martial arts.

Ridge Forrester
"The Bold and the Beautiful"

The womanizing Ridge Forrester is the oldest child of Eric Forrester. He's the father of Brooke's baby, Bridget, but he's married to Dr. Taylor Hayes.

CHRISTINE TUDOR NEWMAN

BORN: June 22; Baltimore, Maryland

HEIGHT: 5'8"

EYES: Blue

STATUS: Married to Craig Newman

The youngest of five children, Newman was raised in Baltimore, Maryland. She began entertaining in junior high school and her vocal skills won her a scholarship to Baltimore's prestigious Peabody Conservatory of Music. She gradually became more interested in theater, so she transferred to the University of Florida at Gainesville where she studied set building, costume design, production and performance en route to a Bachelor of Fine Arts degree.

After college, she performed with several regional theater companies in such shows as "Cat On a Hot Tin Roof," "Pajama Game" and "Plaza Suite." In 1984, she won the role of Gwyneth Alden on "Loving." She left the show in 1989, but returned to the role in 1991. Newman has appeared in the films "The Final Mission" and "Deadly Games" as well as the made-for-TV movie "Having Babies, Part II."

She is married to Craig Newman, a sales executive for a medical supply company. In college, Newman did volunteer work with retarded teenagers. She later became a partner in "Youth at Risk," a program dealing with troubled teens, especially gang members and leaders. In 1986, she created the Celebrity Development Division of the Breakthrough Foundation, which was designed to inspire celebrity support of "Youth at Risk." In their rare spare time, Newman and her husband love to travel.

Gwyneth Alden
"Loving"

Gwyneth Alden is the ex-wife of Clay Alden, by whom she had Trisha and Curtis. A powerful businesswoman, she once had an affair with a TV producer who was also seeing Trisha. She has recently had relationships with Armand and Buck.

LISA PELUSO

BORN: July 29; Philadelphia, Pennsylvania

HEIGHT: 5'4"

EYES: Green

STATUS: Single

OTHER SOAP ROLES:
Wendy Wilkins, "Search for Tomorrow"
Billie Giordano, "One Life to Live"

*L*isa Peluso may have had the earliest start in show business of any soap star—at age four months, she was the Philadelphia Phillies' "caption baby" and her photo (complete with cute sayings in captions) appeared in team advertisements. At age five, she began working in commercials and at age nine she appeared on Broadway with Angela Lansbury in "Gypsy." At age twelve, she played John Travolta's little sister in the smash hit movie, "Saturday Night Fever."

Also at age twelve, she made her daytime drama debut as Wendy Wilkins on "Search for Tomorrow." She grew up on that show, maturing from a pre-teen to a stunning young woman of twenty-two. She left "Search for Tomorrow" in 1986 and, after a short run on "One Life to Live," joined "Loving" in 1988.

Peluso devotes a lot of her time to charities that include the Association for Retarded Citizens, Juvenile Diabetes, the Special Olympics and the Lifeway Program. She lists a variety of interests, including writing poetry, singing, horseback riding, skiing, ice skating, gardening and playing Nintendo.

Ava Rescott Alden Masters
"Loving"

Sexy, conniving Ava Rescott tricked Jack Forbes into marrying her by passing off her sister's baby as their own. She later married Curtis Alden and Alex Masters, who was masquerading as Clay Alden. She was engaged to Paul Slavinsky until he was paralyzed in an explosion.

MARK PINTER

BORN: March 7; Decorah, Iowa

HEIGHT: 6'1"

EYES: Hazel

HAIR: Brown

STATUS: Married to Colleen Zenk-Pinter

CHILDREN: Dylan, Georgia, Hannah, Kelsey, Morgan, Siki

OTHER SOAP ROLES:
Dr. Tom Crawford, "Love of Life"
Mark Evans, "Guiding Light"
Brian McColl, "As the World Turns"
Dan Hollister, "Loving"

The youngest of five children, Pinter decided in high school that he wanted to pursue a career as an actor. After graduating with a degree in theater arts from Iowa State University, he co-founded The Old Creamery Theater Company in Garrison, Iowa. His professional experience led to a graduate program in theater study at Wayne State University, from which he received a Master's degree.

Moving to Los Angeles, Pinter appeared in a number of plays, including "Who's Afraid of Virginia Wolf." He soon won his first daytime role in 1979 as Dr. Tom Crawford on the long-running soap, "Love of Life." He also guest-starred on prime time television shows such as "Charlie's Angels," "Hart to Hart," "The Love Boat" and "Hunter," and he appeared in the TV movies "Crash" and "Go West, Young Man." After leaving "Love of Life" in 1980, he moved to New York to take the role of the evil Mark Evans on "Guiding Light." That villain plummeted off a cliff to his death in 1983, and Pinter moved on to "As the World Turns" (1984-1987) and "Loving" (1988-1989). After a two year hiatus from daytime, he joined the cast of "Another World" in 1991.

Pinter met and fell in love with fellow cast member Colleen Zenk while both were appearing on "As the World Turns," and they married in 1987. They live in Connecticut with their two young children and their four older children from previous marriages. Pinter loves to play golf, and he also enjoys gardening and skiing.

Grant Harrison
"Another World"

Pinter took over the role of Grant Harrison when actor Dack Rambo resigned from the cast after testing positive for the HIV virus. Grant Harrison is a powerful U.S. Senator who's used to getting his own way. He's married to Vicky (Marley's twin), who is really in love with Grant's brother Ryan.

NATHAN PURDEE

BORN: August 6; Tampa, Florida

HEIGHT: 6'2"

EYES: Brown

STATUS: Married to Roberta (Robe) Morris

CHILDREN: Taylor

OTHER SOAP ROLES:
Dr. Karlan, "General Hospital"
Nathan Hastings, "The Young and the Restless"
Jed, "Santa Barbara"

*P*urdee has always been a hard-worker, even as a child. His family moved frequently and Purdee's jobs ranged from paperboy to cook. After high school, he won a scholarship to Oregon's Lindfield College, where he majored in criminology and minored in theater. He moved on to Metropolitan State College in Denver, earning a degree in mental health. Soon the acting bug bit him, but it took years of struggle (part of the time living out of his car) before he got a job as house manager for a Los Angeles production company. He worked his way up to executive producer of the play "Soul of Nat Turner."

His big break came with his daytime debut as Dr. Karlan on "General Hospital." That led to a two-day role as a mob enforcer on "The Young on the Restless"—two days that turned into a six year stint as Detective Nathan Hastings. In 1989, he took a break for a ten-week role in "Santa Barbara" as Jed, who was involved in an interracial romance. He also starred in the movie, "The Return of Superfly." Purdee left "The Young and the Restless" in 1991 and, the next year, moved to New York to join the cast of "One Life to Live."

Purdee and his second wife, Roberta Morris, had a son in January, 1992. He is an accomplished artist, and has recently begun to sell his work. He still uses his mental health training as a hospital emergency room volunteer.

Hank Gannon
"One Life to Live"

Hank Gannon is the town's District Attorney. He was married to Nora, by whom he had Rachel. He then fell in love with Sheila Price.

TRACEY BREGMAN-RECHT

BORN: May 29 Munich, Germany

HEIGHT: 5'3"

EYES: Hazel

STATUS: Married to Ron Recht

CHILDREN: Austin

OTHER SOAP ROLES:
Donna Temple Craig, "Days of Our Lives"

AWARDS: *Soap Opera Digest* Award, Most Exciting New
Actress, 1979; Emmy Award, Outstanding Ingenue, 1985

*B*orn in Germany, Bregman lived in London until
she was eleven. After her family moved to
California, she took acting classes at the famous
Lee Strasberg Theater Institute. While still in high school, she
was hired to play the role of Donna Temple on "Days of Our
Lives," for which she received a *Soap Opera Digest* Award.

After leaving "Days," she guest-starred on several television series, including "The Fall Guy," "The Love Boat,"
"Gavilan" and "Fame." She appeared in the television
movies "The Girl With E.S.P.," "Three On a Date," "Fair
Weather Friend" and "The Littlest Hobo," as well as the feature films "Happy Birthday to Me" and "The Funny Farm."
In 1984, she joined the cast of "The Young and the Restless"
as Lauren Fenmore. She received an Emmy Award the following year.

Bregman is married to real-estate developer Ron Recht,
and she had a daughter in March, 1991. She is a strict vege-
tarian and stays in shape by taking daily dance lessons. She
is an accomplished singer and songwriter (her great uncle is
Tony-Award-winning composer Jule Styne). She also devotes
considerable time to charitable activities.

Lauren Fenmore
"The Young and the Restless"

Lauren Fenmore is a talented businesswoman who runs
Fenmore Department Stores. She was married to Paul

Williams. She then married Dr. Scott Grainger, gave birth to Scotty, divorced Scott, then remarried him.

JOHN REILLY

BORN: November 11; Chicago, Illinois

HEIGHT: 6' 1"

EYES: Brown

HAIR: Brown

STATUS: Married

OTHER SOAP ROLES:
Dan Stewart, "As the World Turns"

*R*eilly, who was born and raised in Chicago, Illinois, had worked for more than ten years as a salesman before his first exposure to acting. The abrupt career change came when a casual business contact turned into an offer to take over a stage role from an actor who had been dismissed. The response to his performance was so encouraging that he continued to moonlight as an actor. Eventually he gave up sales and moved to New York. He made his Broadway debut in "Status Quo Vadis" with two other actors who would become television stars—Ted Danson and Bruce Boxleitner.

Reilly moved to California, where he landed a succession of recurring roles on the TV series "Dallas," "How the West Was Won," "Paper Dolls" and "The Hamptons." His big screen credits include "Deal of the Century, The Great Waldo Pepper, and The Main Event". He made his daytime debut on "As the World Turns," appearing on that show from 1974-1976. In 1984, producer Gloria Monty offered him the role of Sean Donely on "General Hospital," a role that has made him one of daytime's most prominent leading men.

Away from "General Hospital," Reilly can often be heard in commercials. In his spare time, he plays tennis and writes screenplays.

Sean Donely
"General Hospital"

Sean Donely first appeared on the show as the secret agent sidekick to Robert Scorpio. He has since become police commissioner of Port Charles. Donely is married to glamorous TV anchorwoman Tiffany Hill Donely.

CLINT RITCHIE

BORN: August 9;
Grafton, North Dakota

HEIGHT: 6'1"

EYES: Brown

STATUS: Single

*N*o actor could be more perfect for a role than Clint Ritchie is for Clint Buchanan. Ritchie was born and raised on a farm in North Dakota. He knew he wanted to be an actor, but he never tried out for school plays because he was always "too shy to do anything in school." But at age 16, he got up the courage to leave home for California. He supported himself with odd jobs while he studied acting.

In 1965, he made his television debut as a cavalry lieutenant in the pilot of the Robert Conrad series, "Wild, Wild West." His performance as McMurphy, the principal character in the stage production of "One Flew Over the Cuckoo's Nest," led to a contract at 20th Century Fox. He appeared in such movies as "Patton," "A Force of One," "The St. Valentine's Day Massacre" and "Bandolero!" He guest-starred on "Dallas" and appeared in the TV miniseries "The Centennial." In 1979, he joined the cast of "One Life to Live" as newspaper editor Clint Buchanan, son of Asa Buchanan.

Ritchie stays close to his roots by raising and training horses on his northern California ranch. He also enjoys competing in 50- to 100-mile horseback endurance races. He's most comfortable wearing western boots and a cowboy hat off camera and he's engaged to the owner of a neighboring ranch.

Clint Buchanan
"One Life to Live"

Clint Buchanan, the editor of the Llanview newspaper "The Banner," is the son of Texas oil millionaire Asa Buchanan. His long-term marriage to Viki was marked by stormy ups and downs, until it recently fell apart. He is the father of Jessica and stepfather to Kevin and Joey.

ANTONIO SABATO, JR.

BORN: February 29; Rome, Italy

STATUS: Divorced

*S*abato was born in Rome, Italy. His father, Antonio Sabato, Sr., is an actor who appeared in many Italian-made spaghetti westerns, while his mother, Yvonne, is in real estate. When he was twelve, his family moved to California so that he and his sister Simone could have a wider range of opportunity. After two difficult years learning English, Sabato began to feel like he fit in and he decided to follow in his father's footsteps.

He made his film debut in "Karate Rock" and he followed that by winning the male lead in the Janet Jackson music video, "Love Will Never Do." His big break came when he was hired by "General Hospital"—in just a few months, he became a star.

Sabato divorced 29-year-old Tully Jensen after just three months of marriage. In his spare time, he enjoys surfing and riding his motorcycle.

Jagger Cates
"General Hospital"

This lover-boy loner works at Ruby's diner and has been involved with Karen and Brenda.

STEPHEN SCHNETZER

BORN: June 11; Boston, Massachusetts

HEIGHT: 6'0"

EYES: Brown

STATUS: Married to Nancy Snyder

CHILDREN: Max, Ben

OTHER SOAP ROLES:
Steve Olsen, "Days of Our Lives"
Marcello Salta, "One Life to Live"

AWARDS: *Soap Opera Digest* Award, Outstanding Comic Actor, 1989

S chnetzer, born and raised in Boston, graduated from the University of Massachusetts with a degree in French. He went on to study drama at the Julliard School in New York and dance at Alvin Ailey's American Dance Theater. He made his Broadway debut in "A Talent for Murder" (with Claudette Colbert). He spent four seasons as a member of the repertory company of the American Conservatory Theater in San Francisco, as well as appearing in the national tour of "Shakespeare's People," in "Romeo and Juliet" and in the PBS presentation of "The Taming of the Shrew."

He made his daytime debut in 1978 when he took over the role of Steve Olsen, brother of Julie Olsen on "Days of Our Lives." In 1980, he moved to "One Life to Live" to play Marcello Salta. Schnetzer joined "Another World" in 1982 and, except for a brief hiatus in 1986, he's been one of daytime's most popular leading men ever since. He has balanced his regular work with guest appearances on such television shows as "Fantasy Island," "Love Boat" and "Hawaii Five-0."

Schnetzer met his wife, actress Nancy Snyder, when she was playing Katrina Karr on "One Life to Live." They have two sons. His passions outside of work are sports and the theater.

Cass Winthrop
"Another World"

Charming, handsome attorney Cass Winthrop has been a solid presence on this show for two decades. Recently, he ended his relationship with Kathleen to woo and marry private detective Frankie Frame.

MELODY THOMAS SCOTT

BORN: April 18;
Los Angeles, California

HEIGHT: 5'5"

EYES: Blue

STATUS: Married to Edward Scott

CHILDREN: Alexandra, Elizabeth

*S*cott was discovered at age three by Ethel Meglin, who was instrumental in the career of Shirley Temple. She performed in variety shows as a young child, then made her film debut at age eight as the title character in Alfred Hitchcock's thriller "Marnie." She also appeared in "The Beguiled" (with Clint Eastwood), "Dirty Harry" (also with Eastwood), "Posse," "The Shootist," "The Fury," "Studs Lonigan" and "Movieola." And she had a recurring role on "The Waltons" and appeared in the mini-series "Secrets."

In 1978, the young actress joined the cast of "The Young and the Restless" and has since become a star of that show. She is married to Edward Scott and their household includes their daughter Elizabeth, her daughter Alexandra from a previous marriage, and his daughter Jennifer from a previous marriage. She is extremely active in environmental causes, especially the Save the Earth Foundation.

Nikki Abbott
"The Young and the Restless"

Nikki Abbott, now married to Jack Abbott, was the sister of Dr. Casey Reed. A former stripper, she was married to Greg Foster, Kevin Bancroft and Victor Newman (by whom she had Vicky and Nicholas). She's had a host of problems, including accidently killing her own father and being stalked by a mad killer. Although she's married to Jack, she's still attracted to Victor and young Cole.

KIN SHRINER

BORN: December 6

HEIGHT: 5'11"

EYES: Blue

STATUS: Single

OTHER SOAP ROLES:
Jeb Hampton, "Texas"

AWARDS: Emmy award, Outstanding Supporting Actor, 1993; Emmy nomination, Outstanding Supporting Actor, 1990; *Soap Opera Digest* Award, Outstanding Villain, 1982, 1991

*S*hriner's father was the late Herb Shriner, a comedian who had his own variety shows and hosted a game show ("Two For the Money") in the 1950s. Kin has a twin brother, Wil, also a comedian who hosted a syndicated talk show. Both were named after friends of their father—Wil after Will Rogers and Kin after Kin Hubbard. Shriner began acting while attending college at UCLA. He has guest-starred on the prime time television shows "Rituals," "Full House," "The Six Million Dollar Man," "Baa Baa Black Sheep," "The Waltons" and "Eight Is Enough." He made his film debut in "MacArthur" and also appeared in "Manhunter," "Nowhere to Hide" and "Angel III." He had roles in the prime time epics "Rich Man, Poor Man, Book Two" and "War and Remem-brance."

His daytime career began on "General Hospital" in 1977. He left the show in 1979 to take a role on the new soap "Texas." After that soap was canceled, he returned. He left "General Hospital" again in 1982, then returned in 1987. His recent performance garnered him a coveted Emmy Award.

In his spare time, Shriner enjoys water skiing, scuba diving and motorcycle riding.

Scott Baldwin
"General Hospital"

Shriner was the sixth actor to play Scott Baldwin, son of nurse Meg Bentley, who married lawyer Lee Baldwin before she died. Scott Baldwin grew up to follow in his step-father's footsteps by becoming a lawyer. Scott had just married

Laura Vining Webber when Luke Spencer came on the scene and stole her away. His recent love affair with Dominique tragically ended with her death shortly after their marriage.

ERIKA SLEZAK

BORN: August 5; Hollywood, California

HEIGHT: 5'5"

EYES: Blue

STATUS: Married to Brian Davies

CHILDREN: Michael, Amanda

AWARDS: Emmy Award, Outstanding Leading Actress, 1984, 1986, 1992; Emmy nomination, Outstanding Leading Actress, 1983.

Slezak was born to a distinguished show business family. Her grandfather, Leo Slezak, was a world-renowned opera tenor who performed at leading opera houses in Europe as well as New York's Metropolitan Opera. Her father, the late Walter Slezak, was a Tony Award-winning theatrical actor who starred in many memorable film roles. Her mother, Johanna Van Rign, was also an opera singer. Slezak was raised in a bilingual (German and English) household and attended boarding schools. She always knew she wanted to be an actress and at age 17 she began her studies at the Royal Academy of Dramatic Arts in London. She is the only sibling to pursue a show business career—her sister is an attorney and her brother is a pilot.

After completing her course of study, she returned to the United States and joined the company of the Milwaukee Repertory Theater. After three years, she moved to the company of the Alley Theater in Houston. In March, 1971, she accepted the role of Victoria Lord on "One Life to Live." During the course of the last 22 years, she has become one of the most celebrated and popular actresses in daytime television, winning three Emmy Awards.

Slezak lives with her husband and two teenage children in a New York suburb. In her spare time, she enjoys reading, skiing, tennis, riding, cooking and needlepoint.

Victoria Lord Buchanan
"One Life to Live"

Viki is the daughter of the late, rich and powerful Victor Lord, founder of The Banner. Victor treated Viki like a son, grooming her to take over the paper. The pressure caused her to develop a split personality, Nicki Smith, who caused untold havoc over the years, including bearing a child Vicki didn't know she had. Viki had two children, Joey and Kevin, during her marriage to Joe Riley. After his death, she married Clint Buchanan and had a daughter, Jessica.

ROBIN STRASSER

BORN: May 7; New York, New York

HEIGHT: 5'4"

EYES: Brown

STATUS: Divorced

OTHER SOAP ROLES:
Rachel Davis, "Another World"
Christina Karras Martin, "All My Children"

AWARDS: Emmy Award, Outstanding Lead Actress, 1982; Emmy nomination, Outstanding Lead Actress, 1985.

Strasser was born in New York City; as a teenager, she apprenticed at the New York Shakespeare Festival and the Williamstown Summer Theater before winning a scholarship to the Yale Drama School. After Yale, she appeared in several theatrical productions and TV specials before winning the role of the conniving Rachel Davis Matthews Frame on "Another World." After almost five years, she moved on to the role of Dr. Christina Karras Martin on "All My Children."

In 1979, she joined "One Life to Live" as Dorian, one of

soap's most enduring villains. She says that she enjoys playing villains because, "To be a bad person, the troublemaker, you're always fomenting and that's exciting." Her skill won her a 1982 Emmy and a 1985 Emmy nomination. In 1987, she left "One Life to Live" to pursue a career in television and films. Among dozens of credits are her recurring roles on "Coach" and "Knots Landing." She has appeared in five Broadway plays, including Neil Simon's "Chapter II" and "The Shadow Box." In February, 1993, she came back to "One Life to Live" to resume the role of Dorian Lord. Strasser lives in Manhattan with her two sons.

Dorian Lord
"One Life to Live"

Dorian married tycoon Victor Lord shortly before his death; Lord's daughter Viki still believes that she married Victor for his money and may have even murdered him. She has been one of the foremost soap opera villains over the last two decades. Formerly married to Herb Callison, she is the mother of Cassie.

MICHAEL SWAN

BORN: June 11; San Jose, California

HEIGHT: 6'0"

EYES: Brown

STATUS: Divorced

*S*wan's mother is an actress, so he was introduced to performing while growing up in Palo Alto and San Francisco, California. For a while, he considered becoming a winemaker (his cousin, Joseph, is owner of the Joseph Swan Vineyards in Sonoma, California), but he eventually decided to return to acting, his first love. He appeared in student and regional productions while attending Foothill College.

He made his film debut in the 1970 feature "The Strawberry Statement." He went on to appear on almost 150 episodes of prime time series, including the famous last episode of "M*A*S*H*," "Murder, She Wrote," "Magnum,

P.I.," "The Rockford Files" and the pilot of "Falcon Crest." In 1986, he joined the cast of "As the World Turns."

A father of two, Swan writes short stories and poems and he is also an accomplished singer who occasionally performs in cabarets. He enjoys exercise, music and traveling.

Duncan McKechnie
"As the World Turns"

Duncan McKechnie is the co-owner of the newspaper The Argus, and he's married to Jessica. They recently became parents of a new baby.

LAUREN-MARIE TAYLOR

BORN: November 1; Bronx, New York

HEIGHT: 5'6"

EYES: Hazel

STATUS: Married to John Didrichsen

CHILDREN: Katie, Wesley, Olivia

*L*auren-Marie was born and raised in New York City. She was interested in acting at a very young age and she appeared in television commercials while attending private school. After graduating from high school, she attended classes at two New York universities and at the theater school of the prestigious Circle in the Square repertory company.

While taking classes, she pursued theater, television and film opportunities, the most notable of which was a featured role in the John Belushi film, "Neighbors." Then, at age 20, she auditioned for the producers of a new ABC soap, "Loving." She won the role of Stacy Donovan, daughter of Patrick Donovan, a retired policeman who is head of security at Alden University. Ten years later, she is the only original cast member still with the show.

Lauren-Marie married songwriter John Didrichsen in 1983 and she is the devoted mother of three young children. Her primary recreation in her scarce spare time is running. She runs four to seven miles a day and she's won several awards in long-distance running events. She also enjoys skiing, tennis and mountain climbing and her dream is to have the time to hike the entire length of the Appalachian Trail with her husband.

Stacey Donovan
"Loving"

An original character, Stacey fell in love with and married Jack Forbes, by whom she had Jack, Jr. She later became pregnant by the villainous Rick Steward and married him, but soon filed for divorce and remarried Jack. After Jack disappeared on a cruise and was presumed dead, Stacey married conniving Clay Alden, who covets her shares in Alden Enterprises. Estranged from Clay, she fell in love with Jeremy.

JEFF TRACHTA

BORN: October 6; Staten Island, New York

HEIGHT: 6'2"

EYES: Blue

STATUS: Single

OTHER SOAP ROLES:
Boyce McDonald, "One Life to Live"
Hunter Belden, "Loving"

Trachta grew up in New York City and received a degree in psychology from St. John's University. He was working with blind and retarded children when he was urged by some friends to take summer acting classes. He quickly got roles in such plays as "Prince in Cinderella," "Little Shop of Horrors," "Cabaret," "Africanus Instructus," "Grease," "Equus" and "Bleacher Bums."
After a very brief appearance on "One Life to Live," he was hired to play the evil drug dealer Hunter Belden on "Loving." Eight months later, his character was shot dead and Trachta was out of a job. He had a lean two years, eventually ending up as a Santa Claus at Macy's department store. But his luck changed when he landed the role that was being recast on "The Bold and the Beautiful."

Trachta loves to sing, a talent he demonstrates on his show. He enjoys skiing, tennis and working around the house.

Thorne Forrester
"The Bold and the Beautiful"

Thorne Forrester is involved in his family's business, Forrester Creations. His marriage to Macy was broken up by his relationship with Karen, but his continuing attraction to Macy turned the situation into a romantic triangle.

TAMARA TUNIE

BORN: March 14; Pittsburgh, Pennsylvania

HEIGHT: 5'9"
EYES: Brown

STATUS: Single

OTHER SOAP ROLES:
Dana, "As the World Turns"

Tunie loved to perform as a child, but in high school she worked hard in preparation for a career as a pediatrician. After she was enrolled in Carnegie Mellon University, she switched her plans to theater and received a bachelor of fine arts degree. She moved to New York and after making her professional debut in dinner theater, won roles in the stage productions "Lena Horne: The Lady and Her Music," "Basin Street," "The Storyville Musical," "To Whom It May Concern," "The Fantasticks," "The Sound of Music," "Sweet Charity," "Lost in the Stars," "Don't Bother Me, I Can't Cope" and "Bubblin' Brown Sugar." She has also appeared in the movies "Wall Street," "Sweet Loraine," "Ishtar," "Hannah and Her Sisters," "F/X" and "Desperately Seeking Susan."

Her first daytime role was a brief appearance on "As the World Turns" and she returned to that soap in 1987. In her time off, she sings and dances and she has appeared in several music videos.

Jessica Griffin McKechnie
"As the World Turns"

Jessica Griffin McKechnie is an attorney who recently married Duncan McKechnie, co-owner of The Argus. The two are proud new parents.

JERRY VERDORN

BORN: November 23; Sioux City, Iowa

HEIGHT: 5'11"

EYES: Blue

STATUS: Married to Beth verDorn

CHILDREN: Jake, Peter

AWARDS: Emmy nomination, Outstanding Supporting Actor, 1990, 1991, 1992

*V*erDorn's father was a salesman and his family moved frequently while he was growing up. He enrolled at Moorehead State University intending to follow the more stable profession of teaching English. But his career plans changed when he became involved with the theater department. After appearing in student productions and studying at the Studio of the Performing Arts in London, verDorn won a role in a production of the play "Black Elk Speaks," which brought him to the attention of a New York producer.

His performance in the play "Man and Superman" at the Circle in the Square Theater led to the offer of a role on "Guiding Light." He only intended to remain on the show for eighteen months, but that has now stretched to a decade and a half. During his breaks from daytime, verDorn continues to perform on stage and produce regional theater.

Married to his college sweetheart Beth, verDorn has two children. He is active in literacy programs and devotes his spare time to cycling, reading and his family.

Ross Marler
"Guiding Light"

Ross Marler is an attorney and a former district attorney. He has recently become involved with Blake Spaulding, daughter of Holly and Roger.

TONJA WALKER

BORN: September 19; Huntington, West Virginia

HEIGHT: 5'6"

EYES: Blue

STATUS: Single

OTHER SOAP ROLES:
Lizbeth Bachman, "Capitol"
Olivia Jerome, "General Hospital"

*W*alker always wanted to be in show business and her first public recognition came when she won the 1979 Miss Teen All American and the 1980 Miss Maryland (in the Miss USA Pageant) titles. An accomplished singer/songwriter, she also studied music at Baltimore's renowned Peabody Conservatory of Music.

At age 19, she moved to California. She soon found work in TV commercials, two TV pilots and the feature film "Liar's Moon." She also toured as a singer with country stars The Bellamy Brothers and Hoyt Axton. In 1982, she took her first soap role as the picture-perfect, sweet Lizbeth Bachman on "Capitol." In 1986, she moved to a very different role, the hated Olivia Jerome on "General Hospital." When the character was written out of the show, she auditioned for the role of Tina on "One Life to Live." That role went to Karen Witter, but soon after Walker was offered the part of Alex Olanov.

Walker enjoys working out, decorating and gardening and she's an avid football fan.

Alex Olanov Hesser
"One Life to Live"

The beautiful Alex Olanov was an ex-federal agent turned lawyer when she met and married crime boss Carlo Hesser. As his widow, she's turned to crime and is determined to avenge his death.

RUTH WARRICK

BORN: June 29

HEIGHT: 5'6"

STATUS: Widowed

CHILDREN: Karen, Jon Erik, Robert

OTHER SOAP ROLES:
Janet Johnson, "Guiding Light"
Edith Hughes, "As the World Turns"

AWARDS: Emmy award nomination, Outstanding Actress, 1975, 1977; *Soap Opera Digest* Award, Favorite Mature Actress, 1980, 1981

*W*arrick was raised in St. Joseph, Missouri and moved to Kansas City as a teenager. She was always interested in theater and music and appeared in college productions at the University of Kansas City. She eventually moved to New York, where she sang and acted on a number of radio programs. She performed at Orson Welles's Mercury Theater and, after she moved to Hollywood, made her film debut in his "Citizen Kane," which is widely proclaimed as the greatest motion picture of all time. Her many other films include "The Great Bank Robbery," "Perilous Holiday," "China Sky," "Let's Dance," "Guest in the House," "Daisy Kenyon," "The Corsican Brothers" and "Song of the South."

Her soap opera career began on "Guiding Light" in 1953. In 1956, she joined "As the World Turns" for five years. In 1964, she moved to the hit nighttime soap "Peyton Place" as Hannah Cord, a role that earned her a prime time Emmy nomination. She joined "All My Children" shortly before the soap premiered in 1970. She also penned a best-selling auto-biography, The Confessions of Phoebe Tyler.

Warrick is almost as well known for her humanitarian and charitable activities as she is for her acting. She has served on advisory boards on the subject of the arts in education under four presidents and she was the first recipient of the Arts in Education Award, an honor that has been renamed the Ruth Warrick Award. She has also been involved nation-ally and internationally in civil rights and environmental issues. She continues to devote a lot of her time to writing and the theater.

Phoebe Tyler Wallingford
"All My Children"

As Pine Valley's Grand Dame, Phoebe has made a career of involving herself in other people's business. Phoebe married Dr. Charles Tyler in 1974. After his death, she married con man Langley Wallingford, with whom she has had a stormy but enduring marriage. Phoebe is Brooke English's aunt.

WALT WILLEY

BORN: January 26; Ottowa, Illinois

HEIGHT: 6'3"

EYES: Blue

STATUS: Divorced

OTHER SOAP ROLES:
Jack Novak, "Ryan's Hope"
James LaRusso, "Another World"

*W*illey, whose father was an ex-minor league baseball pitcher, was born and raised in a small Illinois town. He was very interested in cartoon-ing and majored in art at Southern Illinois University.

Although he was also interested in the theater, he went into business and eventually became director of sales for a men's clothing company. On a whim, he auditioned for a play that was to be performed at Southern Illinois and he got the part. Shortly afterward, at age 30, he moved to New York to pursue an acting career.

Ironically, his first professional job was as an extra on "All My Children." After appearing in off-Broadway productions, he worked on "Ryan's Hope" and "Another World" before landing a major role on "All My Children." He has appeared in the plays "Frankenstein," "Cyrano de Bergerac," "Five Finger Exercise" and "Barefoot in the Park."

Away from daytime, Willey has developed a stand-up comedy act, which he performs at comedy clubs across the country. Also an Accomplished cartoonist, he sells tee shirts adorned with his work. He also enjoys scuba diving and snorkeling.

Jackson Montgomery
"All My Children"

Jackson Montgomery, an attorney, had a long and torrid love affair with Erica Kane while she was twice married to his brother, Travis. After that affair ended, he became involved with Laurel.

KAREN WITTER

BORN: December 13; Long Beach, California

HEIGHT: 5'6"

EYES: Blue

STATUS: Single

*W*itter is an independent, adventure-loving daughter of two California educators. At age 15, she spent a summer building a schoolhouse in Jaramillo, Mexico and later spent another summer on a ranch in Montana. She lived on a sailboat for two years while attending the University of Hawaii, then got a job as a stewardess on a hot air balloon to earn money for tuition at the University of California at Irvine. Between semesters, she went on safari in Africa.

After college, she worked as a model, then snared acting roles on TV series such as "Cheers," "Mike Hammer," "Hunter," "Matt Houston," "Trapper John, M.D." and "Hardcastle and McCormick." She appeared in the films

"Paramedics," "Dangerously Close," "Hero and the Terror," "The Perfect Match," "Midnight" and "The Vineyard." In 1990, she auditioned to replace Andrea Evans in the important role of Tina Lord Roberts on "One Life to Live" and won it.

In her spare time, Karen enjoys gymnastics, acrobatics, sailing and painting on ceramic tiles. She is fluent in sign language and is studying French. In 1992, she attended L'ecole de Trapeze, a trapeze school in Paris, and she continues to practice her trapeze skills in Paris and Montreal on her vacations.

Tina Lord Roberts
"One Life to Live"

Witter is the fourth actress to portray the trouble-prone Tina, half-sister of Viki Lord Buchanan. She has had two marriages interrupted at the altar, and once fell over a waterfall in Argentina while pregnant, then showed up with a baby she claimed was Cord Roberts' son (it wasn't) as he was standing at the altar to marry another woman. She married Cain, but has been involved in the long term Cain-Tina-Cord love triangle.

ROBERT S. WOODS

BORN: March 13; Maywood, California

HEIGHT: 5'11"

EYES: Blue

STATUS: Married to Loyita Chapel Woods

CHILDREN: Tanner

OTHER SOAP ROLES: Paul Steward, "Days of Our Lives"

AWARDS: Emmy Award, Outstanding Lead Actor, 1983; Emmy nomination, Outstanding Lead Actor, 1985, 1993

R aised in California as the youngest in a family of transplanted Texans, Woods had to postpone the pursuit of an acting career when he was drafted for fifteen months in Vietnam as a Green Beret. After his discharge, he majored in broadcasting at California State College at Long Beach, then studied at several actors' workshops. He played the recurring roles Dr. David Spencer on "The Waltons" and Lt. Bob King in "Project U.F.O.," and he guest-starred on "Family," "City of Angels" and "Newhart."

In 1979, Woods won the role of Bo Buchanan on "One Life to Live" and he moved to New York. After an Emmy Award and nomination, he left the show for a new role on "Days of Our Lives." Unhappy, he left that show and portrayed Commander Eugene Lindsey in the miniseries "War and Remembrance," starred in the TV movie "Carly's Web" and did two stage plays. In 1988, he returned to the role of Bo Buchanan on "One Life to Live."

Woods and Loyita Chapel married in 1973, divorced in 1981 and remarried in 1985. She gave birth to twin sons in February, 1990, but tragically one boy died a month later. Woods is active in the New York Vietnam Veterans Commission, which sponsors job training and employment programs. He spends the rest of his spare time with his wife and son Tanner.

Bo Buchanan
"One Life to Live"

Bo is the younger son of wealthy Asa Buchanan and he at one time married his father's ex-wife, Delilah. He has been involved with a number of women. He was married to Sarah Gordon, who died and left him a widower. He has been involved in a relationship with Nora, District Attorney Hank Gannon's ex-wife.

COLLEEN ZENK-PINTER

BORN: January 20; Barrington, Illinois

HEIGHT: 5'4"

EYES: Brown

HAIR: Brown

STATUS: Married to Mark Pinter

CHILDREN: Dylan, Georgia, Hannah, Kelsey, Morgan, Siki

Colleen Zenk-Pinter was born in the affluent Chicago suburb of Barrington, Illinois. As a child she studied ballet and jazz dancing, aiming for a career as a dancer. Unfortunately she suffered a serious knee injury as a teenager, and she had to change her career goal to acting. After appearing in high school productions, she enrolled in Catholic University in Washington, D.C. and four years later she received a degree in theater arts.

After graduation, she took a job with U.S. Army Special Services, touring as a performer throughout the United States and Europe. In 1978, she got her big break when she was hired to play the role of Barbara Ryan on "As the World Turns." In addition to her daytime work, Zenk-Pinter has appeared on Broadway in "Bring Back Birdie" and in the plays "They're Playing Our Song," "Can Can," "Barefoot in the Park" and "Where's Charley." She also had a role in the film version of "Annie."

She met and fell in love with Mark Pinter when he played her love interest on "As the World Turns." Both divorced their then-spouses and married in 1987. She volunteers her time to the March of Dimes and Cystic Fibrosis, and in her spare time enjoys golf, skiing, gardening and collecting antiques. She and Pinter live with their children in Connecticut.

Barbara Ryan Munson
"As the World Turns"

Shortly after her character appeared on the show, Barbara found herself mired in a horrible marriage to soap arch-villain James Stenbeck. She was rescued from that marriage by James' heroic brother Gunner, who became the great love of her life. She later married police chief Hal Munson, from whom she is now divorced.

Appendix

Soap Opera Digest Awards

W hen the only soap awards voted on by viewers originated in 1977, they were called the "Soapies." In 1984, the name was changed to the *Soap Opera Digest* Awards by their sponsor, the largest circulation soap opera weekly.

The editors of the magazine meet annually to determine the categories and make seven nominations in each one. The winners, who are determined by popular vote, receive their awards in a nationally televised prime time special.

1977

Favorite Soap Opera: "Days of Our Lives"
Outstanding Actress: Susan Seaforth Hayes (Julie Williams, "Days of Our Lives")
Outstanding Actor: Bill Hayes (Doug Williams, "Days of Our Lives")
Favorite Heroine: Susan Seaforth Hayes (Julie Williams, "Days of Our Lives")
Favorite Hero: Donald May (Adam Drake, "Edge of Night")
Most Exciting New Actress: Candice Earley (Donna Beck, "All My Children")
Most Exciting New Actor: John McCook (Lance Prentiss, "The Young and the Restless")
Favorite Villainess: Beverlee McKinsey (Iris Carrington, "Another World")
Favorite Villain: John Fitzpatrick (Willis Frame, "Another World")
Favorite Juvenile Actress: Suzanne Davidson (Betsy Stewart, "As the World Turns")
Favorite Juvenile Actor: Christopher Lowe (Eric Heywood, "Search for Tomorrow")

Jed Allan won the Soap Opera Digest *Outstanding Actor Award in both 1978 and 1979 for his role as Don Craig on "Days of Our Lives."*

1978

Favorite Soap Opera: "Days of Our Lives"
Outstanding Actress: Victoria Wyndham (Rachel Cory, "Another World")
Outstanding Actor: Jed Allan (Don Craig, "Days of Our Lives")
Most Exciting New Actress: Andrea Hall-Lovell (Samantha Evans, "Days of Our Lives")
Most Exciting New Actor: Josh Taylor (Chris Kositchek, "Days of Our Lives")
Favorite Villainess: Beverlee McKinsey (Iris Carrington, "Another World")
Favorite Villain: Roberts Blossom (Sven Peterson, "Another World")
Favorite Actress/Mature Role: Frances Reid (Alice Horton, "Days of Our Lives")
Favorite Actor/Mature Role: Macdonald Carey (Tom Horton, "Days of Our Lives")
Favorite Juvenile Actress: Brandi Tucker (Karen Becker, "The Young and the Restless")
Favorite Juvenile Actor: John E. Dunn (Tad Gardner, "All My Children")

1979

Favorite Soap Opera: "Days of Our Lives"
Outstanding Actress: Judith Light (Karen Wolek, "One Life to Live")
Outstanding Actor: Jed Allan (Don Craig, "Days of Our Lives")
Most Exciting New Actress: Tracey Bregman (Donna Temple, "Days of Our Lives")
Most Exciting New Actor: Rod Arrants (Travis Sentell, "Search for Tomorrow")
Favorite Villainess: Jackie Zeman (Bobbie Spencer, "General Hospital")
Favorite Villain: Gerald Anthony (Marco Dane/Mario Corelli, "One Life to Live")
Favorite Actress/Mature Role: Frances Reid (Alice Horton, "Days of Our Lives")
Favorite Actor/Mature Role: Macdonald Carey (Tom Horton, "Days of Our Lives")
Favorite Juvenile Actress: Dawn Marie Boyle (Dottie Thorton, "All My Children")
Favorite Juvenile Actor: Brian Lima (Charlie Tyler, "All My Children")

1980

Favorite Soap Opera: "General Hospital"
Outstanding Actress: Judith Light (Karen Wolek, "One Life to Live")
Outstanding Actor: Tony Geary (Luke Spencer, "General Hospital")
Most Exciting New Actress: Taylor Miller (Nina Cortlandt, "All My Children")
Most Exciting New Actor: Peter Bergman (Cliff Warner, "All My Children")
Favorite Villainess: Jane Elliot (Tracy Quartermaine, "General Hospital")
Favorite Villain: James Mitchell (Palmer Cortlandt, "All My Children")
Favorite Actress/Mature Role: Ruth Warrick (Phoebe Wallingford, "All My Children")
Favorite Actor/Mature Role: David Lewis (Edward Quartermaine, "General Hospital")

Favorite Juvenile Actress: Dawn Marie Boyle (Dottie Thorton, "All My Children")
Favorite Juvenile Actor: Philip Tanzini (Jeremy Hewitt, "General Hospital")

1981

Favorite Soap Opera: "General Hospital"
Outstanding Actress: Genie Francis (Laura Baldwin, "General Hospital")
Outstanding Actor: Tony Geary (Luke Spencer, "General Hospital")
Most Exciting New Actress: Renee Anderson (Alexandria Quartermaine, "General Hospital")
Most Exciting New Actor: Tristan Rogers (Robert Scorpio, "General Hospital")
Favorite Villainess: Robin Mattson (Heather Webber, "General Hospital")
Favorite Villain: Andre Landzaat (Tony Cassadine, "General Hospital")
Favorite Actress/Mature Role: Ruth Warrick (Phoebe Wallingford, "All My Children")
Favorite Actor/Mature Role: David Lewis (Edward Quartermaine, "General Hospital")
Favorite Juvenile Actress: Daniela Francesca Serra (Bonnie McFadden, "All My Children")
Favorite Juvenile Actor: Philip Tanzini (Jeremy Hewitt, "General Hospital")

1982

Favorite Soap Opera: "General Hospital"
Outstanding Actress: Deidre Hall (Marlena Evans, "Days of Our Lives")
Outstanding Actor: Tony Geary (Luke Spencer, "General Hospital")
Most Exciting New Actress: Kim Delaney (Jenny Gardner, "All My Children")
Most Exciting New Actor: John Stamos (Blackie Parrish, "General Hospital")
Favorite Villainess: Robin Mattson (Heather Webber, "General Hospital")

Favorite Villain: Kin Shriner (Scotty Baldwin, "General Hospital")

Favorite Actress/Mature Role: Anna Lee (Lila Quartermaine, "General Hospital")

Favorite Actor/Mature Role: David Lewis (Edward Quartermaine, "General Hospital")

1983

Favorite Soap Opera: "General Hospital"

Outstanding Actress: Deidre Hall (Marlena Evans, "Days of Our Lives")

Outstanding Actor: Tristan Rogers (Robert Scorpio, "General Hospital")

Favorite Actress/Supporting Role: Sharon Wyatt (Tiffany Hill, "General Hospital")

Favorite Actor/Supporting Role: John Stamos (Blackie Parrish, "General Hospital")

Most Exciting New Actress: Sharilyn Wolter (Celia Quartermaine, "General Hospital")

Most Exciting New Actor: Steve Bond (Jimmy Lee Holt, "General Hospital")

Favorite Villainess: Robin Mattson (Heather Webber, "General Hospital")

Favorite Villain: Quinn Redeker (Alex Marshall, "Days of Our Lives")

Favorite Actress/Mature Role: Anna Lee (Lila Quartermaine, "General Hospital")

Favorite Actor/Mature Role: David Lewis (Edward Quartermaine, "General Hospital")

1984

Favorite Soap Opera: "Days of Our Lives"

Outstanding Actress: Deidre Hall (Marlena Evans, "Days of Our Lives")

Outstanding Actor: Peter Reckell (Bo Brady, "Days of Our Lives")

Outstanding Supporting Actress: Lisa Trusel (Melissa Anderson, "Days of Our Lives")

Outstanding Supporting Actor: John de Lancie (Eugene Bradford, "Days of Our Lives")

Outstanding Female Newcomer: Kristian Alfonso (Hope

Williams, "Days of Our Lives")
Outstanding Male Newcomer: Michael Leon (Pete
Jennings, "Days of Our Lives")
Outstanding Villainess: Nancy Frangione (Cecile de
Poulignac, "Another World")
Outstanding Villain: Joseph Mascolo (Stefano DiMera,
"Days of Our Lives")
Outstanding Actress/Mature Role: Frances Reid (Alice
Horton, "Days of Our Lives")
Outstanding Actor/Mature Role: Macdonald Carey (Tom
Horton, "Days of Our Lives")
Outstanding Youth Actress: Andrea Barber (Carrie Brady,
"Days of Our Lives")
Outstanding Youth Actor: David Mendenhall (Mike
Webber, "General Hospital")

1985

Outstanding Show: "Days of Our Lives"
Outstanding Actress: Deidre Hall (Marlena Evans, "Days of
Our Lives")
Outstanding Actor: Peter Reckell (Bo Brady, "Days of Our
Lives")
Outstanding Supporting Actress: Arleen Sorkin (Calliope
Jones, "Days of Our Lives")
Outstanding Supporting Actor: John de Lancie (Eugene
Bradford, "Days of Our Lives")
Outstanding Female Newcomer: Arleen Sorkin (Calliope
Jones, "Days of Our Lives")
Outstanding Male Newcomer: Charlie Shaughnessy (Shane
Donovan, "Days of Our Lives")
Outstanding Villainess: Cheryl-Ann Wilson (Megan
Hathaway, "Days of Our Lives")
Outstanding Villain: Joseph Mascolo (Stefano DiMera,
"Days of Our Lives")
Outstanding Actress/Mature Role: Frances Reid (Alice
Horton, "Days of Our Lives")
Outstanding Actor/Mature Role: Macdonald Carey (Tom
Horton, "Days of Our Lives")
Outstanding Youth Actress: Andrea Barber (Carrie Brady,
"Days of Our Lives")
Outstanding Youth Actor: Brian Autenrieth (Zach Parker,
"Days of Our Lives")

1986

Outstanding Show: "Days of Our Lives"
Outstanding Actress: Patsy Pease (Kim Brady, "Days of Our Lives")
Outstanding Actor: John Aniston (Victor Kiriakis, "Days of Our Lives")
Outstanding Supporting Actress: Harley Kozak (Mary Duvall, "Santa Barbara")
Outstanding Supporting Actor: Stephen Nichols (Steve Johnson, "Days of Our Lives")
Outstanding Younger Leading Actress: Ellen Wheeler (Marley Love, "Another World")
Outstanding Younger Leading Actor: Peter Reckell (Bo Brady, "Days of Our Lives")
Outstanding Villainess: Linda Gibboney (Gina Capwell, "Santa Barbara")
Outstanding Villain: John Aniston (Victor Kiriakis, "Days of Our Lives")
Outstanding Comic Performer: Arleen Sorkin (Calliope Jones, "Days of Our Lives")
Outstanding Youth Actor/Actress: Kimberly McCullough (Robin, "General Hospital")
Favorite Super Couple: Charles Shaughnessy/Patsy Pease (Shane and Kim, "Days of Our Lives")

1987

No awards: annual event moved from late in each year to early in each year.

1988

Outstanding Show: "Days of Our Lives"
Outstanding Actress: Kim Zimmer (Reva Shayne, "Guiding Light")
Outstanding Actor: Stephen Nichols (Steve Johnson, "Days of Our Lives")
Outstanding Supporting Actress: Anna Lee (Lila Quartermaine, "General Hospital")
Outstanding Supporting Actor: Nicolas Coster (Lionel Lockridge, "Santa Barbara")
Outstanding Heroine: Robin Wright (Kelly Capwell, "Santa Barbara")

Outstanding Hero: A Martinez (Cruz Castillo, "Santa Barbara")

Outstanding Villainess: Brenda Dickson (Jill Abbott, "The Young and the Restless")

Outstanding Villain: Justin Deas (Keith Timmons, "Santa Barbara")

Outstanding Comic Actress: Arleen Sorkin (Calliope Jones, "Days of Our Lives")

Outstanding Comic Actor: Michael Weiss (Mike Horton, "Days of Our Lives")

Outstanding Newcomer: Ian Buchanan (Duke Lavery, "General Hospital")

Favorite Super Couple: Charles Shaughnessy/Patsy Pease (Shane and Kim, "Days of Our Lives")

1989

Outstanding Show: "Days of Our Lives"

Outstanding Actress: Jeanne Cooper (Kay Chancellor, "The Young and the Restless")

Outstanding Actor: Eric Braeden (Victor Newman, "The Young and the Restless")

Outstanding Supporting Actress: Joy Garrett (Jo Johnson, "Days of Our Lives")

Outstanding Supporting Actor: Quinn Redeker (Rex Sterling, "The Young and the Restless")

Outstanding Heroine: Marcy Walker (Eden Castillo, "Santa Barbara")

Outstanding Hero: Stephen Nichols (Steve Johnson, "Days of Our Lives")

Outstanding Female Newcomer: Anne Heche (Marley Love, "Another World")

Outstanding Male Newcomer: Scott Thompson Baker (Colton Shore, "General Hospital")

Outstanding Villainess: Lynn Herring (Lucy Jones, "General Hospital")

Outstanding Villain: Matthew Ashford (Jack Deveraux, "Days of Our Lives")

Outstanding Comic Actress: Robin Mattson (Gina Timmons, "Santa Barbara")

Outstanding Comic Actor: Stephen Schnetzer (Cass Winthrop, "Another World")

Favorite Super Couple: Stephen Nichols/Mary Beth Evans (Steve and Kayla, "Days of Our Lives")

1990

Outstanding Show: "Santa Barbara"
Outstanding Actress: Marcy Walker (Eden Castillo, "Santa Barbara")
Outstanding Actor: A Martinez (Cruz Castillo, "Santa Barbara")
Outstanding Supporting Actress: Jane Rogers (Heather Donnelly, "Santa Barbara")
Outstanding Supporting Actor: Robert Gentry (Ross Chandler, "All My Children")
Outstanding Heroine: Finola Hughes (Anna Devane, "General Hospital")
Outstanding Hero: Doug Davidson (Paul Williams, "The Young and the Restless")
Outstanding Female Newcomer: Jean Carol (Nadine Cooper, "Guiding Light")
Outstanding Male Newcomer: Kurt Robin McKinney (Ned Ashton, "General Hospital")
Outstanding Villainess: Jane Elliot (Anjelica Curtis, "Days of Our Lives")
Outstanding Villain: David Canary (Adam Chandler, "All My Children")
Outstanding Comic Actress: Robin Mattson (Gina Timmons, "Santa Barbara")
Outstanding Comic Actor: Joe Marinelli (Bunny Tagliatti, "Santa Barbara")
Outstanding Storyline: Eden's rape ("Santa Barbara")
Outstanding Super Couple: A Martinez/Marcy Walker (Cruz and Eden, "Santa Barbara")

1991

Outstanding Show: "Days of Our Lives"
Outstanding Actress: Finola Hughes (Anna Devane, "General Hospital")
Outstanding Actor: A Martinez (Cruz Castillo, "Santa Barbara")
Outstanding Supporting Actress: Julia Barr (Brooke English, "All My Children")
Outstanding Supporting Actor: Jordan Clarke (Billy Lewis, "Guiding Light")
Outstanding Heroine: Cady McClain (Dixie Cooney, "All My Children")

Outstanding Hero: Doug Davidson (Paul Williams, "The Young and the Restless")
Outstanding Female Newcomer: Kimberley Simms (Mindy Lewis, "Guiding Light")
Outstanding Male Newcomer: Michael Watson (Decker Moss, "General Hospital")
Outstanding Villainess: Lynn Herring (Lucy Jones, "General Hospital")
Outstanding Villain: Kin Shriner (Scott Baldwin, "General Hospital")
Outstanding Storyline: Robin, Anna and The Alien, "General Hospital")
Outstanding Limited Run: Gerald Anthony (Marco Dane, "One Life to Live")
Outstanding Super Couple: Matthew Ashford/Melissa Reeves (Jack and Jennifer, "Days of Our Lives")

1992

Outstanding Show: "Days of Our Lives"
Outstanding Actress: Anne Heche (Marley Love/Vicky Hudson, "Another World")
Outstanding Actor: David Canary (Adam/Stuart Chandler, "All My Children")
Outstanding Supporting Actress: Jane Elliot (Tracy Quartermaine, "General Hospital")
Outstanding Supporting Actor: Doug Davidson (Paul Williams, "The Young and the Restless")
Outstanding Younger Leading Actress: Tricia Cast (Nina Webster, "The Young and the Restless")
Outstanding Younger Leading Actor: Ricky Paull Goldin (Dean Frame, "Another World")
Outstanding Female Newcomer: Alla Korot (Jenna Norris, "Another World")
Outstanding Male Newcomer: Paul Michael Valley (Ryan Harrison, "Another World")
Outstanding Villainess: Lynn Herring (Lucy Jones, "General Hospital")
Outstanding Villain: Michael Zaslow (Roger Thorpe, "Guiding Light")
Outstanding Comic Performer: Robert Mailhouse (Brian Scofield, "Days of Our Lives")
Best Wedding: Matthew Ashford/Melissa Reeves (Jack and Jennifer, "Days of Our Lives")

Best Death Scene: Marcy Walker (Eden Castillo, "Santa Barbara")

1993

Favorite Show: "Days of Our Lives"

Outstanding Actress: Susan Lucci (Erica, "All My Children")

Outstanding Actor: Peter Bergman (Jack, "The Young and the Restless")

Outstanding Supporting Actress: Ellan Dolan (Margo, "As the World Turns")

Outstanding Supporting Actor: Richard Biggs (Marcus, "Days of Our Lives")

Outstanding Younger Leading Actress: Alicia Coppola (Lorna, "Another World")

Outstanding Younger Leading Actor: Matt Borlenghi (Brian, "All My Children")

Outstanding Female Newcomer: Yvonne Perry (Rosanna, "As the World Turns")

Outstanding Male Newcomer: Monti Sharp (David, "Guiding Light")

Outstanding Villain/Villainess: Kimberlin Brown (Sheila, "The Young and the Restless," "The Bold and the Beautiful")

Outstanding Comic Performer: Matthew Ashford (Jack "Days of Our Lives")

Outstanding Child Actor: Kimberly McCullough (Robin, "General Hospital")

Outstanding Social Issue Storyline: Margo's Rape ("As the World Turns")

Favorite Song: "One Dream" ("Days of Our Lives")

Hottest Male Star: Mark Derwin (Mallet, "Guiding Light")

Hottest Female Star: Crystal Chappell (Carly, "Days of Our Lives")

Daytime Emmy Awards

Although the Emmy Awards originated in 1948, it wasn't until the 1971-1972 season that the awards program acknowledged daytime serials by establishing a special awards category, Outstanding Achievement in Daytime Drama. Just two years later, interest in daytime awards had increased so much that NBC gave them their own awards show, broadcast in front of Rockefeller Center in New York. A dispute between NBC and the National Academy of Television Arts and Sciences kept the awards off the air in 1982-1983 and 1983-1984, but the broadcast resumed in 1984-1985. The awards show moved to prime time for the 1990-1991 TV season and garnered the second highest rating for the broadcast week.

1971-1972
Outstanding Achievement in Daytime Drama: "The Doctors"

1972-1973
Outstanding Achievement in Daytime Drama: "The Edge of Night"
Outstanding Achievement as Individual In Daytime Drama: Mary Fickett (Ruth Brent, "All My Children")

1973-1974
Outstanding Daytime Drama Series: "The Doctors"
Best Actor in Daytime Drama: Macdonald Carey (Dr. Thomas Horton, "Days of Our Lives")
Best Actress in Daytime Drama: Elizabeth Hubbard (Dr. Althea Davis, "The Doctors")
Best Individual Director for a Daytime Series: H. Wesley (Kenny, "Days of Our Lives")
Best Writing for a Daytime Drama: "The Edge of Night"

1974-1975

Outstanding Daytime Drama Series: "The Young and the Restless"

Outstanding Actor in Daytime Drama: Macdonald Carey (Dr. Thomas Horton, "Days of Our Lives")

Outstanding Actress in Daytime Drama: Susan Flannery (Dr. Laura Spencer, "Days of Our Lives")

Outstanding Individual Director for a Daytime Series: Richard Dunlap, "The Young and the Restless"

Outstanding Writing for a Daytime Drama: "Another World"

1975-1976

Outstanding Daytime Drama Series: "Another World"

Outstanding Actor in Daytime Drama: Larry Haines (Stu Bergman, "Search for Tomorrow")

Outstanding Actress in Daytime Drama: Helen Gallagher (Maeve Ryan, "Ryan's Hope")

Outstanding Individual Director for a Daytime Series: David Pressman, "One Life to Live"

Outstanding Writing for a Daytime Drama: "Days of Our Lives"

1976-1977

Outstanding Daytime Drama Series: "Ryan's Hope"

Outstanding Actor in Daytime Drama: Val Dufour (John Wyatt, "Search for Tommorrow")

Outstanding Actress in Daytime Drama: Helen Gallagher (Maeve Ryan, "Ryan's Hope")

Outstanding Individual Director for a Daytime Series: Lila Swift, "Ryan's Hope"

Outstanding Writing for a Daytime Drama: "Ryan's Hope"

1977-1978

Outstanding Daytime Drama Series: "Days of Our Lives"

Outstanding Actor in Daytime Drama: James Pritchett (Dr. Matt Powers, "The Doctors")

Outstanding Actress in Daytime Drama: Laurie Heinemann (Sharlene Matthews, "Another World")

Outstanding Individual Director for a Daytime Series: Richard Dunlop, "The Young and the Restless"

Outstanding Writing for a Daytime Drama: "Ryan's Hope"

1978-1979

Outstanding Daytime Drama Series: "Ryan's Hope"

Outstanding Actor in Daytime Drama: Al Freeman, Jr. (Lt. Ed Hall, "One Life to Live")

Outstanding Actress in Daytime Drama: Irene Dailey (Liz Matthews, "Another World")

Outstanding Supporting Actor in a Daytime Drama: Peter Hansen (Lee Baldwin, "General Hospital")

Outstanding Supporting Actress in a Daytime Drama: Suzanne Rogers (Maggie Horton, "Days of Our Lives")

Outstanding Individual Director for a Daytime Series: Jerry Evans, Lela Swift, "Ryan's Hope"

Outstanding Writing for a Daytime Drama: "Ryan's Hope"

1979-1980

Outstanding Daytime Drama Series: "Guiding Light"

Outstanding Actor in Daytime Drama: Douglas Watson (Mackenzie Cory, "Another World")

Outstanding Actress in Daytime Drama: Judith Light (Karen Wolek, "One Life to Live")

Outstanding Supporting Actor in a Daytime Drama: Warren Burton (Eddie Dorrance, "All My Children")

Outstanding Supporting Actress in a Daytime Drama: Francesca James (Kitty Shea, "All My Children")

Outstanding Individual Director for a Daytime Series: Jerry Evans, Lela Swift, "Ryan's Hope"

Outstanding Writing for a Daytime Drama: "Ryan's Hope"

1980-1981

Outstanding Daytime Drama Series: "General Hospital"

Outstanding Actor in Daytime Drama: Douglas Watson (Mackenzie Cory, "Another World")

Outstanding Actress in Daytime Drama: Judith Light (Karen Wolek, "One Life to Live")

Outstanding Supporting Actor in a Daytime Drama: Larry Haines (Stu Bergman, "Search for Tomorrow")

Outstanding Supporting Actress in a Daytime Drama: Jane Elliot (Tracy Quartermaine, "General Hospital")

Outstanding Individual Director for a Daytime Series:

Marlena Laird, Alan Pultz, Philip Sogard, "General Hospital"
Outstanding Writing for a Daytime Drama: "Guiding Light"

1981-1982

Outstanding Daytime Drama Series: "Guiding Light"
Outstanding Actor in Daytime Drama: Anthony Geary (Luke Spencer, "General Hospital")
Outstanding Actress in Daytime Drama: Robin Strasser (Dorian Lord, "One Life to Live")
Outstanding Supporting Actor in a Daytime Drama: David Lewis (Edward Quartermaine, "General Hospital")
Outstanding Supporting Actress in a Daytime Drama: Dorothy Lyman (Opal Gardner, "All My Children")
Outstanding Individual Director for a Daytime Series: Marlena Laird, Alan Pultz, Philip Sogard, "General Hospital"
Outstanding Writing for a Daytime Drama: "Guiding Light"

1982-1983

Outstanding Daytime Drama Series: "The Young and the Restless"
Outstanding Actor in Daytime Drama: Robert S. Woods (Bo Buchanan, "One Life to Live")
Outstanding Actress in Daytime Drama: Dorothy Lyman (Opal Gardner, "All My Children")
Outstanding Supporting Actor in a Daytime Drama: Darnell Williams (Jesse Hubbard, "All My Children")
Outstanding Supporting Actress in a Daytime Drama: Louise Shaffer (Rae Woodard, "Ryan's Hope")
Outstanding Individual Director for a Daytime Series: Allen Fristoe, Norman Hall, Peter Miner, David Pressman, "One Life to Live"
Outstanding Writing for a Daytime Drama: "Ryan's Hope"

1983-1984

Outstanding Daytime Drama Series: "General Hospital"
Outstanding Actor in Daytime Drama: Larry Bryggman (John Dixon, "As the World Turns")

Outstanding Actress in Daytime Drama: Erika Slezak (Viki Lord Buchanan, "One Life to Live")
Outstanding Supporting Actor in a Daytime Drama: Justin Deas (Tom Hughes, "As the World Turns")
Outstanding Supporting Actress in a Daytime Drama: Judi Evans (Beth Raines, "Guiding Light")
Outstanding Individual Director for a Daytime Series: Larry Auerback, George Keathley, Peter Miner, David Pressman, "One Life to Live"
Outstanding Writing for a Daytime Drama: "Ryan's Hope"

1984-1985

Outstanding Daytime Drama Series: "The Young and the Restless"
Outstanding Actor in Daytime Drama: Darnell Williams (Jesse Hubbard, "All My Children")
Outstanding Actress in Daytime Drama: Kim Zimmer (Reva Lewis, "Guiding Light")
Outstanding Supporting Actor in a Daytime Drama: Larry Gates (H.B. Lewis, "Guiding Light")
Outstanding Supporting Actress in a Daytime Drama: Beth Maitland (Tracy Abbott, "The Young and the Restless")
Outstanding Juvenile/Young Man in a Daytime Drama: Brian Bloom (Dustin Donovan, "All My Children")
Outstanding Ingenue in a Daytime Drama: Tracey Bregman (Lauren Fenmore Williams, "The Young and the Restless")
Outstanding Individual Director for a Daytime Series: John Whitesell II, Bruce Barry, Matthew Diamond, Irene M. Pace, "Guiding Light"
Outstanding Writing for a Daytime Drama: "All My Children"

1985-1986

Outstanding Daytime Drama Series: "The Young and the Restless"
Outstanding Actor in Daytime Drama: David Canary (Adam/Stuart Chandler, "All My Children")
Outstanding Actress in Daytime Drama: Erika Slezak (Viki Lord Buchanan, "One Life to Live")
Outstanding Supporting Actor in a Daytime Drama: John Wesley Shipp (Doug Cummings, "As the World Turns")

Outstanding Supporting Actress in a Daytime Drama:
Leann Hunley (Anna Brady DiMera, "Days of Our Lives")
Outstanding Younger Leading Man in a Daytime Drama:
Michael Knight (Tad Martin, "All My Children")
Outstanding Ingenue in a Daytime Drama: Ellen Wheeler
(Victoria Love/Marley McKinnon, "Another World")
Outstanding Individual Director for a Daytime Series:
Dennis Steinmetz, Rudy Vejar, Frank Pacelli, "The Young
and the Restless"
Outstanding Writing for a Daytime Drama: "Guiding
Light"

1986-1987

Outstanding Daytime Drama Series: "As the World
Turns"
Outstanding Actor in Daytime Drama: Larry Bryggman
(John Dixon, "As the World Turns")
Outstanding Actress in Daytime Drama: Kim Zimmer
(Reva Lewis, "Guiding Light")
Outstanding Supporting Actor in a Daytime Drama:
Gregg Mars (Tom Hughes, "As the World Turns")
Outstanding Supporting Actress in a Daytime Drama:
Kathleen Noone (Ellen Shepherd, "All My Children")
Outstanding Younger Leading Man in a Daytime Drama:
Michael Knight (Tad Martin, "All My Children")
Outstanding Ingenue in a Daytime Drama: Martha Byrne
(Lilly Walsh, "As the World Turns")
Outstanding Guest Performer in a Daytime Drama: John
Wesley Shipp ("Santa Barbara")
Outstanding Individual Director for a Daytime Series:
Rudy Vejar, Frank Pacelli, "The Young and the Restless"
Outstanding Writing for a Daytime Drama: "One Life to
Live"

1987-1988

Outstanding Daytime Drama Series: "Santa Barbara"
Outstanding Actor in Daytime Drama: David Canary
(Adam/Stuart Chandler, "All My Children")
Outstanding Actress in Daytime Drama: Helen Gallagher
(Maeve Ryan, "Ryan's Hope")
Outstanding Supporting Actor in a Daytime Drama:
Justin Deas (Keith Timmons, "Santa Barbara")
Outstanding Supporting Actress in a Daytime Drama:

Ellen Wheeler (Cindy Parker, "All My Children")
Outstanding Younger Leading Man in a Daytime Drama:
Billy Warlock (Frankie Brady, "Days of Our Lives")
Outstanding Ingenue in a Daytime Drama: Julienne
Moore (Frannie and Sabrina Hughes, "As the World Turns")
Outstanding Individual Director for a Daytime Series:
Rudy Vejar, Frank Pacelli, Heather Hill, "The Young and the
Restless"
Outstanding Writing for a Daytime Drama: "All My
Children"

1988-1989

Outstanding Daytime Drama Series: "Santa Barbara"
Outstanding Actor in Daytime Drama: David Canary
(Adam/Stuart Chandler, "All My Children")
Outstanding Actress in Daytime Drama: Marcy Walker
(Eden Castillo, "Santa Barbara")
Outstanding Supporting Actor in a Daytime Drama:
Justin Deas (Keith Timmons, "Santa Barbara")
Outstanding Supporting Actress in a Daytime Drama:
Debbie Morgan (Angie Baxter, "All My Children") & Nancy
Lee Grahn (Julia Wainwright, "Santa Barbara")
Outstanding Juvenile Male in a Daytime Drama: Justin
Gocke (Brandon Capwell, "Santa Barbara")
Outstanding Juvenile Female in a Daytime Drama:
Kimberly McCullough (Robin Scorpio, "General Hospital")
Outstanding Individual Director for a Daytime Series:
Rudy Vejar, Frank Pacelli, Heather Hill, Randy Robbins,
"The Young and the Restless"
Outstanding Writing for a Daytime Drama: "Santa
Barbara"

1989-1990

Outstanding Daytime Drama Series: "Santa Barbara"
Outstanding Actor in Daytime Drama: A Martinez (Cruz
Castillo, "Santa Barbara")
Outstanding Actress in Daytime Drama: Kim Zimmer
(Reva Lewis, "Guiding Light")
Outstanding Supporting Actor in a Daytime Drama:
Henry Darrow (Rafael Castillo, Santa Barbara")
Outstanding Supporting Actress in a Daytime Drama:
Julia Barr (Brooke English, "All My Children")
Outstanding Juvenile Male in a Daytime Drama: Andrew

Kavovit (Paul Stenbeck, "Another World")
Outstanding Juvenile Female in a Daytime Drama: Cady McClain (Dixie Cooney, "All My Children")
Outstanding Individual Director for a Daytime Series: Michael Gliona, Rick Bennewitz, Robert Schiller, "Santa Barbara"
Outstanding Writing for a Daytime Drama: "Guiding Light"

1990-1991

Outstanding Daytime Drama Series: "As the World Turns"
Outstanding Actor in Daytime Drama: Peter Bergman (Jack Abbott, "The Young and the Restless")
Outstanding Actress in Daytime Drama: Finola Hughes (Anna Devane, "General Hospital")
Outstanding Supporting Actor in a Daytime Drama: Bernie Barrow (Louie Slavinsky, "Loving")
Outstanding Supporting Actress in a Daytime Drama: Jess Walton (Jill Foster, "The Young and the Restless")
Outstanding Younger Actor in a Daytime Drama: Rick Hearst (Alan-Michael Spaulding, "Guiding Light")
Outstanding Younger Actress in a Daytime Drama: Anne Heche (Victoria Love/Marley McKinnon, "Another World")
Outstanding Individual Director for a Daytime Series: Michael Gliona, Rick Bennewitz, Robert Schiller, Peter Brinckerhoff, "Santa Barbara"
Outstanding Writing for a Daytime Drama: "Santa Barbara"

Index

"Somerset" 5, 18, 42
Sorel, Louise 30, 63, 69, 106
Sorkin, Arleen 263, 264, 265
Stabb, Leonard 33, 103
Stamos, John 100, 261, 262
Steele, Alexander and Britton 35
Stephens, Perry 29
Sternhagen, Frances 100
Stewart, Paul Anthony 34
St. John, Kristoff 38, 62, 76, 92
Storm, Jim 30, 63, 71, 85, 86, 131
Storm, Michael 63, 86
Strasser, Robin 36, 52, 126, 145, 243, 244,
  272
Stuart, Anna 27, 66
Stuart, Mary Ellen 64, 68
Swan, Michael 28, 60, 70, 244, 245
Sward, Anne 28, 66, 75, 85, 90
Sweeney, Alison 30, 64, 91

Tanzini, Philip 261
Taylor, Elizabeth 99, 100
Taylor, Josh 93, 259
Taylor, Lauren-Marie 35, 66, 76, 83, 90, 245,
  246
Templeton, Christopher 58, 86, 90
Thinnes, Roy 35
Thomas, Richard 100, 125
Thorson, Linda 62, 79
Todd, Russell 59, 76, 124
Tom, Heather 37, 66, 71, 91
Tomei, Marisa 100
Torpey, Erin 35
Torrez, Christiaan 93
Tovatt, Patrick 29, 66, 70
Trachta, Jeff 29, 64, 75, 105, 246, 247
Travanti, Daniel J. 100
Trusel, Lisa 262
Tucci, Christine 27
Tuck, Jessica 116
Tucker, Branki 259
Tudor-Newman, Christine 34, 62, 73, 230,
  231
Tunie, Tamara 28, 59, 77, 247, 248
Turner, Janine 100
Tyler, Robert 35, 60, 70, 88, 107, 111
Tylo, Hunter 29, 62, 78, 93, 102, 106
Tylo, Michael 37, 73, 93, 115, 131
Tyson, Cicely 7, 100

Underwood, Blair 100

Valley, Paul Michael 27, 64, 70, 93, 267
Van Devere, Trish 100
Van Doren, Mamie 100
Van Patten, Joyce 100
verDorn, Jerry 34, 66, 78, 248, 249
von Detten, Erik 30
Voorhies, Lark 30

Wagner, Helen 28, 43, 63, 78, 88
Wagner, Jack 82, 83
Walker, Marcy 265, 266, 268, 275
Walker, Paul 37, 63
Walker, Tonja 36, 73, 82, 85, 145, 249, 250

Wallace, David 66, 71
Walton, Jess 36, 54, 58, 73, 126, 146, 276
Warlock, Billy 275
Warrick, Ruth 26, 41, 62, 74, 89, 250, 251,
  260, 261
Watkins, Greg 28, 64, 78
Watson, Douglas 271
Watson, Michael 267
Wayne, John 92
Weatherly, Michael 34, 85, 91
Weaver, Patty 37, 64, 79, 85
Weaver, Sigourney 100
Weiss, Michael 125, 265
Wheeler, Ellen 133, 197, 264, 274, 275
Whitfield, Dondre 26, 60, 75, 91
Widdoes, Kathleen 29, 59, 70, 95, 131
Wiggin, Tom 28, 62, 75
Willey, Walt 26, 58, 88, 251, 252
Williams, Billy Dee 8, 100
Williams, Darnell 272, 273
Williams, JoBeth 100
Williams, Stephanie 58, 74, 86
Williams, Tonya Lee 37, 79
Williams, Vince 34, 62, 72, 83, 85
Wilson, Cheryl-Ann 263
Windom, William 101
Winsor, Roy 3, 10
Winstein, Josh Philip 36
Wintersole, William 71
Witter, Karen 36, 66, 69, 86, 88, 107, 252,
  253
Wolter, Sharilyn 262
Woods, Robert S. 35, 59, 69, 90, 103, 135,
  137, 253, 254, 272
Wright, Robin 101, 264
Wyatt, Jane 11
Wyatt, Sharon 31, 58, 78, 90, 107, 262
Wyndham, Victoria 27, 60, 71, 86, 89, 259

York, John J. 33, 66, 71, 107
"Young and the Restless, The" 4, 8, 9, 21, 23,
  24, 53, 55

Zaslow, Michael 34, 50, 66, 69, 89, 137, 145,
  152, 267
Zeman, Jackie 31, 59, 74, 86, 90, 142, 144,
  260
Zenk-Pinter, Colleen 128, 58, 72, 93, 254,
  255
Zimbalist, Efrem Jr. 11, 101
Zimmer, Kim 264, 273, 274, 275